I0868019

PLOTINUS

ENNEAD VI.8

THE *ENNEADS* OF PLOTINUS

With Philosophical Commentaries

Series Editors: John M. Dillon, Trinity College, Dublin and Andrew Smith, University College, Dublin

Also Available in the Series:

I.6: *On Beauty* by Andrew Smith

II.5: *On What Is Potentially and What Actually* by Cinzia Arruzza

II.9: *Against the Gnostics* by Sebastian Ramon Philipp Gertz

IV.3–4.29: *Problems Concerning the Soul* by John M. Dillon & H. J. Blumenthal

IV.4.30–45 & IV.5: *Problems Concerning the Soul* by Gary Gurtler

IV.7: *On the Immortality of the Soul* by Barrie Fleet

IV.8: *On the Descent of the Soul Into Bodies* by Barrie Fleet

V.1: *On the Three Primary Levels of Reality* by Eric D. Perl

V.5: *That the Intelligibles are not External to Intellect, and on the Good* by Lloyd P. Gerson

VI.4 & VI.5: *On the Presence of Being, One and the Same, Everywhere as a Whole* by Eyjólfur Emilsson & Steven Strange

Forthcoming Titles in the Series include:

I.1: *What Is the Living Thing? What Is Man?* by Gerard O'Daly

I.2: *On Virtues* by Suzanne Stern-Gillet

I.3: *On Dialectic* by Pauliina Remes

I.4: *On Well-Being* by Kieran McGroarty

I.5: *On Whether Well Being Increases With Time* by Danielle A. Layne

I.8: *On the Nature and Source of Evil* by Anne Sheppard

II.4: *On Matter* by Anthony A. Long

II.7: *On Complete Blending* by Robert Goulding

II.8: *On Sight* by Robert Goulding

III.4: *On Our Allotted Guardian Spirit* by Wiebke-Marie Stock

III.5: *On Love* by Sara Magrin

III.6: *On Impassibility* by Eleni Perdikouri

III.7: *On Eternity and Time* by László Bene

III.8: *On Nature and Contemplation* by George Karamanolis

IV.6: *On Sense-Perception and Memory* by Peter Lautner

V.2, **V.4**, and **V.6**: *On the One and Intellect* by Eleni Perdikouri

V.3: *On the Knowing Hypostases* by Marie-Élise Zovko

V.8: *On Intelligible Beauty* by Andrew Smith

V.9: *On Intellect, Ideas, and Being* by Matthias Vorwerk

VI.1–2: *On the Genera of Being (I+II)* by Damien Caluori & Regina Füchslin

VI.3: *On the Genera of Being (III)* by Riccardo Chiaradonna

VI.7: *The Forms and the Good* by Nicholas Banner

VI.9: *On the Good or the One* by Stephen R. L. Clark

PLOTINUS
ENNEAD VI.8

On the Voluntary
and
on the Free Will of the One

Translation with an Introduction
and Commentary

KEVIN CORRIGAN
AND
JOHN D. TURNER

PARMENIDES
PUBLISHING

Las Vegas | Zurich | Athens

PARMENIDES PUBLISHING
Las Vegas | Zurich | Athens

© 2017 Parmenides Publishing. All rights reserved.

This edition published in 2017 by Parmenides Publishing
in the United States of America

ISBN soft cover: 978-1-930972-39-1
ISBN e-Book: 978-1-930972-40-7

Library of Congress Cataloging-in-Publication Data

Names: Plotinus, author. | Corrigan, Kevin, translator, commentator. | Turner, John Douglas, translator, commentator.
Title: Ennead VI.8 : on the voluntary and on the free will of the one / Plotinus ; translation with an introduction and commentary, Kevin Corrigan and John D. Turner.
Other titles: Ennead. VI, 8. English | On the voluntary and on the free will of the one
Description: First edition. | Las Vegas : Parmenides Publishing, 2017. | Series: The Enneads of Plotinus with philosophical commentaries | Includes bibliographical references and index.
Identifiers: LCCN 2017023284 (print) | LCCN 2017035972 (ebook) | ISBN 9781930972407 (ebook) | ISBN 9781930972391 (pbk. : alk. paper)
Subjects: LCSH: Plotinus. Ennead. VI, 8. | Free will and determinism--Early works to 1800.
Classification: LCC B693.E52 (ebook) | LCC B693.E52 E5 2017b (print) | DDC 186/.4--dc23
LC record available at https://lccn.loc.gov/2017023284

Author photo of Kevin Corrigan by Arielle Doneson. Author photo of John Turner by Gregory Nathan. All rights reserved.

Typeset in Warnock and Futura by Parmenides Publishing
Printed digitally by Edwards Brothers Malloy, Chicago, IL
www.edwardsbrothersmalloy.com

www.parmenides.com

The authors dedicate this volume
to the memory of our dear friend,
colleague, former doctoral student,
and brilliant scholar of Plotinus,
Alexander J. "Zeke" Mazur,
who unexpectedly passed away
during the night of August 7, 2016.

Contents

Introduction to the Series With a Brief Outline of the Life and Thought of Plotinus (205–270 CE)

Plotinus was born in 205 CE in Egypt of Greek-speaking parents. He attended the philosophical schools in Alexandria where he would have studied Plato (427–347 BCE), Aristotle (384–322 BCE), the Stoics and Epicureans as well as other Greek philosophical traditions. He began his serious philosophical education, however, relatively late in life, at the age of twenty-seven and was deeply impressed by the Platonist Ammonius Saccas about whom we, unfortunately, know very little, but with whom Plotinus studied for some eleven years. Even our knowledge of Plotinus' life is limited to what we can glean from Porphyry's introduction to his edition of his philosophical treatises, an account colored by Porphyry's own concerns. After completing his studies in Alexandria Plotinus attempted, by joining a military expedition of the Roman emperor Gordian III, to make contact with the

Brahmins in order to learn something of Indian thought. Unfortunately Gordian was defeated and killed (244). Plotinus somehow managed to extract himself and we next hear of him in Rome where he was able to set up a school of philosophy in the house of a high-ranking Roman lady by the name of Gemina. It is, perhaps, surprising that he had no formal contacts with the Platonic Academy in Athens, which was headed at the time by Longinus, but Longinus was familiar with his work, partly at least through Porphyry who had studied in Athens. The fact that it was Rome where Plotinus set up his school may be due to the originality of his philosophical activity and to his patrons. He clearly had some influential contacts, not least with the philhellenic emperor Gallienus (253–268), who may also have encouraged his later failed attempt to set up a civic community based on Platonic principles in a ruined city in Campania.

Plotinus' school was, like most ancient schools of philosophy, relatively small in scale, but did attract distinguished students from abroad and from the Roman upper classes. It included not only philosophers but also politicians and members of the medical profession who wished to lead the philosophical life. His most famous student was Porphyry (233–305) who, as a relative latecomer to the school, persuaded him to put into writing the results of his seminars. It is almost certain that we possess most, if not all, of his written output, which represents his mature thought, since he didn't commence writing until the age of forty-eight. The school seemingly had inner and outer circles, and Plotinus himself was clearly an inspiring and sympathetic teacher who took a deep interest in the philosophical and spiritual progress of his students. Porphyry tells us that when he was suffering from severe depression Plotinus straight away visited him in his lodgings to help him. His concern for others is also illustrated by the fact that he was entrusted with the personal education of many orphans and the care of their property and careers. The reconciliation of this worldly involvement with the encouragement to lead a life of contemplation is encapsulated in Porphyry's comment that "he was present to himself and others at the same time."

The *Enneads* of Plotinus is the edition of his treatises arranged by his pupil Porphyry who tried to put shape to the collection he had inherited by organizing it into six sets of nine treatises (hence the name *"Enneads")* that led the reader through the levels of Plotinus' universe, from the physical world to Soul, Intellect and, finally, to the highest principle, the One. Although Plotinus undoubtedly had a clearly structured metaphysical system by the time he began committing himself to expressing his thought in written form, the treatises themselves are not systematic expositions, but rather explorations of particular themes and issues raised in interpreting Plato and other philosophical texts read in the School. In fact, to achieve his neat arrangement Porphyry was sometimes driven even to dividing certain treatises (e.g., III.2–3; IV.3–5, and VI.4–5).

Although Plotinus' writings are not transcripts of his seminars, but are directed to the reader, they do, nevertheless, convey the sort of lively debate that he encouraged in his school. Frequently he takes for granted that a particular set of ideas is already familiar as having been treated in an earlier seminar that may or may not be found in the written text. For this reason it is useful for the reader to have some idea of the main philosophical principles of his system as they can be extracted from the *Enneads* as a whole.

Plotinus regarded himself as a faithful interpreter of Plato whose thought lies at the core of his entire project. But Plato's thought, whilst definitive, does according to Plotinus require careful exposition and clarification, often in the light of other thinkers such as Aristotle and the Stoics. It is because of this creative application of different traditions of ancient thought to the interpretation of Plato that Plotinus' version of Platonism became, partly through the medium of later Platonists such as Porphyry, Iamblichus (245–325), and Proclus (412–485), an influential source and way of reading both Plato and Aristotle in the Middle Ages, the Renaissance, and up to the early 19th century, when scholars first began to differentiate Plato and "Neoplatonism." His thought, too, provided early Christian theologians of the Latin and particularly of the Byzantine tradition, with a rich variety of metaphysical concepts with which to explore and express difficult doctrinal ideas. His fashioning of Plato's ideas into a consistent metaphysical structure, though no longer accepted as a uniquely valid way of approaching Plato, was influential in promoting the notion of metaphysical systems in early modern philosophy. More recently increasing interest has centered on his exploration of the self, levels of consciousness, and his expansion of discourse beyond the levels of normal ontology to the examination of what lies both above and beneath being. His thought continues to challenge us when confronted with the issue of man's nature and role in the universe and of the extent and limitations of human knowledge.

Whilst much of Plotinus' metaphysical structure is recognizably an interpretation of Plato it is an interpretation that is not always immediately obvious just because it is filtered through several centuries of developing Platonic thought, itself already overlaid with important concepts drawn from other schools. It is, nevertheless, useful as a starting point to see how Plotinus attempts to bring coherence to what he believed to be a comprehensive worldview expressed in the Platonic dialogues. The Platonic Forms are central. They become for him an intelligible universe that is the source and model of the physical universe. But aware of Aristotle's criticism of the Platonic Forms as lifeless causes he takes on board Aristotle's concept of god as a self-thinker to enable him to identify this intelligible universe as a divine Intellect that thinks itself as the Forms or Intelligibles. The doctrine of the Forms as the thoughts of god had already entered Platonism, but not as the rigorously argued identity that Plotinus proposed. Moreover the Intelligibles, since they are identical with Intellect, are themselves actively intellectual; they are intellects. Thus Plato's world of Forms has become a complex and dynamic intelligible universe in which unity and plurality, stability, and activity are reconciled.

Now although the divine Intellect is one it also embraces plurality, both because its thoughts, the Intelligibles, are many and because it may itself be analyzed into thinker and thought. Its unity demands a further principle, which is the cause of its unity. This principle, which is the cause of all unity and being but does not possess unity or being in itself, he calls the One, an interpretation of the Idea of the Good in Plato's *Republic* that is "beyond being" and that may be seen as the simple (hence "one") source of all reality. We thus have the first two of what subsequently became known as the three Hypostases, the One, Intellect, and Soul, the last of which acts as an intermediary between the intelligible and physical universes. This last Hypostasis takes on all the functions of transmitting form and life that may be found in Plato, although Plato himself does not always make such a clear distinction between soul and intellect. Thus the One is the ultimate source of all, including this universe, which is then prefigured in Intellect and transmitted through Soul to become manifest as our physical universe. Matter, which receives imperfectly this expression, is conceived not as an independently existing counter-principle, a dangerously dualist notion, but is in a sense itself a product of the One, a kind of non-being that, while being nothing specific in itself, nevertheless is not simply not there.

But this procession from an ultimate principle is balanced by a return movement at each level of reality that fully constitutes itself only when it turns back in contemplation of its producer. And so the whole of reality is a dynamic movement of procession and return, except for matter, which has no life of its own to make this return; it is inert. This movement of return, which may be traced back to the force of "love" in Plato or Aristotle's final cause, is characterized by Plotinus as a cognitive activity, a form of contemplation, weaker at each successive level, from Intellect through discursive reasoning to the merest image of rational order as expressed in the objects of the physical universe.

The human individual mirrors this structure to which we are all related at each level. For each of us has a body and soul, an intellect, and even something within us that relates to the One. While it is the nature of soul to give life to body, the higher aspect of our soul also has aspirations toward intellect, the true self, and even beyond. This urge to return corresponds to the cosmic movement of return. But the tension between soul's natural duty to body and its origins in the intelligible can be, for the individual, a source of fracture and alienation in which the soul becomes over-involved and overwhelmed by the body and so estranged from its true self. Plotinus encourages us to make the return or ascent, but at the same time attempts to resolve the conflict of duties by reconciling the two-fold nature of soul as life-giving and contemplative.

This is the general framework within which important traditional philosophical issues are encountered, discussed and resolved, but always in a spirit of inquiry and ongoing debate. Issues are frequently encountered in several different contexts, each angle providing a different insight. The nature of the soul and its relationship to the body is examined at length (IV) using the Aristotelian distinctions of levels of soul (vegetative, growth, sensitive, rational) whilst maintaining the immortal nature of the transcendent soul in Platonic terms. The active nature of the soul in sense-perception is maintained to preserve the principle that incorporeals cannot be affected by corporeal reality. A vigorous discussion (VI.4 and 5) on the general nature of the relationship of incorporeals to body explores in every detail and in great depth the way in which incorporeals act on body. A universe that is the product of design is reconciled with the freedom of the individual. And, not least, the time-bound nature of the physical universe and human reason is grounded in the life of Intellect, which subsists in eternity. Sometimes, however, Plotinus seems to break outside the framework of traditional metaphysics: the nature of matter and the One, each as non-being, though in a different sense, strains the terminology and structure of traditional ontology; and the attempt to reconcile the role of the individual soul within the traditional Platonic distinction of transcendent and immanent reality leads to a novel exploration of the nature of the self, the "I."

It is this restless urge for exploration and inquiry that lends to the treatises of Plotinus their philosophical vitality. Whilst presenting us with a rich and complexly coherent system, he constantly engages us in philosophical inquiry. In this way each treatise presents us with new ideas and fresh challenges. And, for Plotinus, every philosophical engagement is not just a mental exercise but also contributes to the rediscovery of the self and our reintegration with the source of all being, the Platonic aim of "becoming like god."

While Plotinus, like Plato, always wishes to engage his audience to reflect for themselves, his treatises are not easy reading, partly no doubt because his own audience was already familiar with many of his basic ideas and, more importantly, had been exposed in his seminars to critical readings of philosophical texts that have not survived to our day. Another problem is that the treatises do not lay out his thought in a systematic way but take up specific issues, although always the whole system may be discerned in the background. Sometimes, too, the exact flow of thought is difficult to follow because of an often condensed mode of expression.

Because we are convinced that Plotinus has something to say to us today, we have launched this series of translations and commentaries as a means of opening up the text to readers with an interest in grappling with the philosophical issues revealed by an encounter with Plotinus' own words and arguments. Each volume will contain a new translation, careful summaries of the arguments and structure of the treatise, and a philosophical commentary that will aim to throw light on the philosophical meaning and import of the text.

John M. Dillon
Andrew Smith

Abbreviations

Armstrong Armstrong, A. H. 1966–1982. *Plotinus.* Greek Text with English Translation and Introductions. Cambridge, MA: Loeb.

Bonitz Bonitz, H. 1955. Index Aristotelicus. Graz: Akademische Druck- u. Verlagsantstalt.

Bréhier Bréhier, Emile. 1924–1938. Plotin, *Ennéades.* Greek Text and French Translation with Introductions and Notes. Paris: Les Belles Lettres.

Cilento Cilento, Vincenzo. 1947–1949. *Plotino, Enneadi.* Italian Translation and Commentary. Bari: Laterza.

Creuzer Creuzer, Georg Friedrich. 1835. *Plotini Enneades.* Greek Text, with Marsilio Ficino's Latin Translation and Commentary. Oxford: E Typographeo Academico.

EE	Aristotle, *Eudemian Ethics.*
EN	Aristotle, *Nicomachean Ethics.*
BHT	Harder, Richard, Rudolf Beutler, and Willy Theiler. 1956–1970. *Plotins Schriften* I–VI. Hamburg: Felix Meiner.
HS_1	Henry, Paul and Hans-Rudolph Schwyzer. 1951–1973. *Plotini Opera I–III* (*editio maior*). Paris: Desclée de Brouwer et Cie.
HS_2	Henry, Paul and Hans-Rudolph Schwyzer. 1964–1982. *Plotini Opera I–III* (*editio minor,* with revised text). Oxford: Clarendon Press.
Kirchhoff	Kirchhoff, Adolph. 1856. *Plotini Opera.* Leipzig: Teubner.
LS	Long, Anthony A. and David N. Sedley. 1987. *The Hellenistic Philosophers, Volume 1: Translation of the Principal Sources, with Philosophical Commentary.* Cambridge: Cambridge University Press.
LSJ	Liddell, H. G. and R. Scott. *A Greek-English Lexicon,* revised and augmented by H. G. Jones, R. McKenzie, P. G. W. Glare, and A. A. Thompson. 1996. Oxford: Oxford University Press.

MM Aristotle, *Magna Moralia.*

NHC Nag Hammadi Corpus.

PGL Lampe, G. W. H. 1961. *A Patristic Greek Lexicon.* Oxford: Oxford University Press.

SP Sleeman, J. H. and Gilbert Pollet. 1980. *Lexicon Plotinianum.* Leiden: Brill / Louvain: Louvain University Press.

SVF Von Arnim, Hans, ed. 1905. *Stoicorum Veterum Fragmenta.* Leipzig: Teubner.

TLG Thesaurus Linguae Greacae.

Acknowledgments

THE AUTHORS WOULD LIKE TO THANK the editors, John Dillon and Andrew Smith, for their invitation to prepare this volume and for their advice and support. We have also benefited from the help and encouragement of Lloyd Gerson, who very generously gave us some of his own materials as guides for the completion of the volume.

Every work depends upon collaboration, and we have profited at every point from the texts, translations and commentaries of all those before us, but especially the more recent works of Georges Leroux and Laurent Lavaud. To them and to many others we owe a debt of gratitude.

Finally, we are grateful for the enthusiastic support and patience of Gale Carr, Sara Hermann, Eliza Tutellier, and all at Parmenides Press.

Introduction to the Treatise

The Title

Ennead VI.8 is 39th in the chronological order in which Plotinus' 54 treatises were written, according to Porphyry in his *Life of Plotinus*. We translate its title, not in its accustomed form ("On free will and on the free will of the One"), but as "On the Voluntary and on the Free Will of the One."

This is a literal translation of Porphyry's title that may appear puzzling (Plotinus did not himself supply titles to his works). The "voluntary" only plays a role in the early chapters in relation to Plotinus' enquiry into what is "in our power" (*to eph' hemin*) and in what sense we, as human beings, can be said to be free (*eleutheroi*) and self-determining (*autexousioi*) (Chapters 1–6). By contrast, the majority of the chapters (Chapters 7–21) examine what it could mean to say that Intellect and, especially, the One or Good is purely free. However, one might argue that this is just as good a title in several respects as the one that has become customary, since it emphasizes in a down-to-earth way a real continuity between free human and divine willing. And, in fact, Plotinus makes this connection prominently himself between human and divine *voluntary* activity, and, by implication, shows its primary applicability to the Good's free will in Chapter 13.

On the other hand, Porphyry appears to get the other side of the title wrong, that is, "on the free will of the One," since it is striking in VI.8 that Plotinus refers exclusively to the free will of the Good, only once referring in the dative to "that One" in Chapter 18. Why he does so has escaped the notice of all readers, as far as we can see, from Porphyry to the present day, but we may suggest that he refers almost exclusively to the Good, perhaps because he stresses the culmination of all derivative goods in the Supreme Good, and perhaps because he wants to emphasize the Platonic Good that appears rarely in Gnostic and other contemporary texts by contrast with the One that is more frequently referenced therein. We follow Plotinus' preferred usage throughout our commentary.

The Importance of VI.8

Why is VI.8 an important work and how are we to assess its importance in the history of thought generally and in the chronological course of Plotinus' writings?

First, VI.8 gives us inner access to the living mind of a long dead sage as he tries to answer some of the most fundamental questions we in the modern world continue to ask: are we really free when most of the time we are overwhelmed by compulsions, addictions, and necessities, and how can we know that we are free? Can we trace this freedom through our own agency to the gods, to the Soul, Intellect, and the Good? How do we know that the world is meaningful and not simply the result of chance or randomness? If the intelligible and sensible universes emerge out of a "singularity," namely, the uniqueness of the Good or One, how do we know that this singularity did not just "happen to be" by chance or randomness and that all our concepts are not just failures to grasp the awful truth that there is no truth?

Second, VI.8 provides a new understanding of the importance and nature of free human agency. This notion, developed in Chapter 6, has been variously misunderstood as either a purely inner freedom outside of action or as a kind of Stoic autonomous self-will. But Plotinus articulates, in fact, a much more balanced and dynamic notion of human agency that brings together primarily Platonic and Aristotelian elements and that situates the primacy of will in the double activity of *both* inner self-determination and outer action, a notion that makes human agency real and concrete (Chapter 6).

Third, and even perhaps more important, VI.8 develops an entirely new way of thinking about God—Plotinus is the first to argue, in the precise way he does, that will comes before intellect and to posit the Good as pure freedom and as self-establishing cause of Itself (Chapters 7–21). What prompts him to do this we shall try to explain (see Introduction, Sections 4 and 5 and Commentary to Chapter 7).

Fourth, VI.8 articulates a creative idea of agency and radical freedom by showing how such terms as desire, will, self-dependence, and freedom in the human ethical sphere can be genuinely applied to Intellect and the Good in such a way that nevertheless preserves the radical inability of all metaphysical language to express anything about God or gods. But in order to do this, Plotinus admits that he must speak of the Good in an "incorrect" way that appears to introduce multiplicity into what should be the purest Unity.

Finally, and as a result of this, Plotinus provides for subsequent thinkers, however unwittingly, an implicit trinitarian model of the purest Divine Unity—or an implicit triad of concurrent moments in pure Unity—together with an important definition of the Good or One as "cause of itself" and "love of itself" that will be important for later theological thinking (from Marius Victorinus to Spinoza). In VI.8, Chapter 20, for instance, Plotinus argues that although we use such terms incorrectly of the Good, the (1) activity, (2) substance, and (3) perfection of (1) its making, (2) selfhood, and (3) eternal generation must be identical and "concurrent" in the Good.

If one puts this and other passages from VI.8 alongside claims by the later Neoplatonist Iamblichus and the Christian Bishop Eunomius that *Agennetos* or "ungenerated" is a more appropriate term for God than "cause of itself," then we are in an intellectual climate close to the emergence of Cappadocian Trinitarian theology in which there is a causal relation among the Persons of the Trinity and yet these different causal moments are "concurrent"; indeed, the word "concurrent" (*sundromon*) from VI.8, Chapter 20, 26 above (see also Chapter 13, 29–30) is used of the Trinity in Gregory of Nyssa.

The Broader Context

How then should we characterize this unusual and groundbreaking work more generally and can we point more clearly to what issues prompted Plotinus to write it as the 39th treatise of his 54 treatises overall? Does the work establish a new "voluntarist" tradition or does it remain within an "intellectualist" framework—two views that have been advanced? Does it create a new positive theology that contradicts Plotinus' usual thought according to which nothing can be affirmed of the One? And is it something entirely new in the history of thought? Let us first situate VI.8 in the broader context of the history of thought and of the sequence of the *Enneads* that lead up to it before presenting an overall evaluation of its character.

Plato and Aristotle

Let us start with Plato and Aristotle. In the account of the making of the World's body and soul in Plato's *Timaeus* (and also in the myth of the *Statesman*), God, the Demiurge (together with the lesser gods) is represented as doing or making many things: the Demiurge looks to the paradigm of the Eternal Living Creature (thought to contain the ideal prototypes of all things), deliberates, plans, desires, frames (*Timaeus* 28a–37d; *Statesman* 271d–274e), and so on, not unlike the God of the Bible. This is why Plato can seem to the later tradition none other than "Moses speaking Greek" (Numenius, fr. 8, Petty). And in that tradition, the demiurgic function comes sometimes to be divided, as in the *Chaldaean Oracles* (frs. 5, 33, 35, 37 [Majercik] or Numenius (fr. 16, Petty) between purely contemplative activity and a proactive doing or making aspect that can even acquire an evil function, like the irrational World Soul in Atticus and Plutarch of Chaeronea (*apud* Proclus, *In Timaeum* I.381, 26ff.), or become simply ignorant and blundering like the Valentinian Demiurge or downright maleficent, like the chief Archon of the Sethian *Apocryphon of John*—for example *Tripartite*

Tractate NHC I 104, 25ff. and the *Apocryphon of John* NHC II 9, 25–25, 16; 27, 31–30, 11. But throughout the Platonic tradition a divine or semi-divine force does or makes many things. In other words, God makes, moves, intervenes, withdraws—whether for good or ill.

By contrast, in Aristotle's *Metaphysics* and elsewhere, God or *Nous* moves, not by doing or making, but by being unmoved, that is, as a final cause or "as being loved" (*Metaphysics* 12, 7, 1072b3). For Aristotle, God's thought is the originative source of motion only as the object of desire, real or apparent; and this divine "thinking of thinking" is activity or energy in the purest sense (*Metaphysics* 12, 9 1075b34), that is, contemplation or pure consciousness (as Lloyd, 1990, 83 wants to translate the word *theōria*), a life that we sometimes participate in, but rarely and fleetingly (*Met.* 12, 7). God moves, but does or makes nothing. On the side of divine activity, one may think that the Unmoved Mover is hard to associate with any positive creativity, love or desire: and on the side of human reality, the contemplative life, which is the highest life for Aristotle, seems solitary and hard to associate with the ideal of the practical life, in which the human being enjoys community intrinsically and needs good friends for his or her best self-development (see Joachim, 1970, 241–243, and compare 284–297; Lear, 1988, 309320; Irwin, 1988, 347–372).

Moreover, this apparent lack of connection between contemplation, on the one hand, and action, doing or making, on the other, is exacerbated by several other features of late ancient thought. First, there is the Peripatetic view (of Alexander of Aphrodisias) that divine providence only extends as far as the movements of the heavenly bodies and the maintenance of sublunary *species*, but not as far as sublunary *individuals* (Sharples, 1982, 198–211). God's creative and sustaining activity, therefore, does not reach or touch our individual lives at all. In addition, the immediate context of VI.8 can be seen in its opening lines (*Ar' esti kai epi theōn ei ti estin ep' autois zētein*, etc,), namely, Alexander of Aphrodisias' denial that the notion of "what is in our power" (*to eph' hēmin*) can be applied to the gods since their being what they are is necessary and, therefore, cannot be said to be in their power: "In the case of the gods, being such [as they are] will no longer depend on them because being like this is present in their nature, and none of the things that are present in this way depends on oneself (*ep' autoi*)" (*On Fate* 204, 12–15; trans. Sharples). There therefore appears to be no divine guarantee of human freedom and certainly no connection between the divine and the human. If then the gods are powerless, is human freedom anything more than an illusion?

Jewish, Christian, and Gnostic Approaches

Second, Jewish and Christian writings (and many Gnostic texts that will figure prominently in this work) describe a God who acts, gets angry, forgives and loves. In short, this is a God who does many real things, who intervenes in human history. In addition, according to many Gnostic texts, all sorts of contemplation or revelations are possible—but only for the Gnostic enlightened few (cf. II.9 [33] 18, 36) and only with what appear to be properly registered guides. Furthermore, demiurgic activity tends to occur fairly low down the spiritual hierarchy and it is generally represented by anthropomorphic figures full of flaws and passions, if they are not outright evil themselves (e.g., *Tripartite Tractate* 74, 19–84, 37).

By contrast, the Neoplatonic hypostases—Soul, Intellect, and the One or the Good—do not *do* anything. Action or *praxis* is specifically denied of them. What they make or produce is not at all like human production or making either, but is achieved only by the power of contemplation (as we see in treatise 30 [III.8]). So the question emerges with some force: are the Neoplatonic spiritual principles really agents at all and in what sense could they be agents in any meaningful way that would successfully compete with the Bible's view of a God who directly intervenes in the historical process?

Middle Platonic Thinkers

Third, even major Middle Platonic thinkers, such as Numenius, seem to have no clear idea of what divine activity might be. For instance, Numenius says in one fragment that the "first God" is "idle of all works," while the demiurgic God rules "as he goes through the heavens" (Numenius, fr. 12, 12–14, Petty). The Demiurge "directs," "steers," and "takes judgment from contemplation [of the First], but is impelled by desire" (fr. 18, 110–114, Petty); and in another striking fragment, contemplation seems to alternate with demiurgic activity: "for the second, being double, self-makes his own idea as well as the cosmos—being Demiurge—[and is] then wholly contemplative" (fr. 16, 10–12, Petty). In other words, in one of the principal pre-Plotinian figures, whom Plotinus was accused of plagiarizing (Porphyry, *Life of Plotinus*, 17, 1–7), there is no coherent account of divine activity or agency. Does the demiurge deliberate after contemplation and draw motive power or impulse from desire? And after making both himself and the cosmos, does he return to contemplation? In such a scenario, there seems no intrinsic or internal relation between desire, making, and contemplation. Platonic and Aristotelian elements seem thrown at random into the mixing bowl. And if we put this into the context of Peripatetic thought (which appears to reject divine agency in the lives of individuals) and of Gnostic thought (which tends to present an externalized view of contemplation in privileged visions presented as interpretations of ancient texts such as the Bible, Plato, Aristotle, etc., access to which is open only to the few in contrast to the oblivion of the mass of ordinary humans), then we can see with some clarity the pressing issues of divine and human agency with which Plotinus had to wrestle. For Sethian Gnosticism generally, see Turner, 2001.

An independent treatment of the question of providence will have to wait until later in Plotinus' writing career, namely, III.2 and III.3 (treatises 47 and 48 in the chronological order), but in the works leading up to our treatise, VI.8, Plotinus develops three new models of causality that are surely relevant to the context of our work: first, a revolutionary new understanding of the relation between contemplation and making in III.8 (treatise 30); second, a profound critique of anthropocentric rationality as the paradigm for thinking about demiurgic activity in V.8 (treatise 31) and VI.7 (treatise 39); and, third, he then gradually comes to tackle the deeper problem of divine and human free agency in VI.8. The scenario we sketch here, then, includes some key features of these works, III.8, V.8, VI.7 and VI.8, contrasting in each case divine and human activity with questions of agency, in order to provide a chronological and topical context for our treatise.

The Chronological Context Leading Up to VI.8: Three New Models of Causality (III.8 [30]; V.8 [31]; VI.7 [38])

Causality as Creative Contemplation (III.8 and V.8)

Ennead III.8 [30] argues for the view that contemplation or philosophic wisdom, far from being private or external to the world, as the Gnostics appear to hold (Cf. II.9 [33] 18, 35–36), is the fundamental form of all natural making and, indeed, of all life. Everything—even plant life—is either contemplation (so that even nature's life, which Plotinus quaintly represents as a silent contemplation constantly giving rise to bodily forms [III.8.4, 3–10]), is a form of living intelligibility or thought (*noēsis*), no matter how lowly; and forms of living thought (plant life, making, action, sensation, imagination, and intellectual activity itself) become more unified the more they "hasten" to the intimate unity-in-duality of intellect, where thinking and object of thought are one (cf. III.8.8, 1–8). So, as Plotinus concludes the first part of his argument, everything is either contemplation (in the sense that it contains its intelligibility within itself, as does intellect) or a product or consequence of contemplation (in the sense that if you unpacked the intelligibility in anything whatsoever, it would lead you to everything else in the universe or to a more comprehensive view of reality as a whole); or, finally, a substitute for contemplation (in the sense that action and production are ways of coming to see or understand a reality that is at first too densely compacted for us to grasp it altogether)—see generally III.8 [30] 7–8 and VI.7 [38] 1–7. Contemplation or insight, therefore, is the primary creative force in both the spiritual and physical worlds.

Plotinus is aware of the paradoxical, even revolutionary nature of his project, as he attempts to uncover the contemplative reality of everything from plants to the divine. In contrast to the Gnostic elitist relation between a hierophant and favored initiate, Plotinus' method is dialogically more inclusive and radically democratic, starting in fact from the principle of all-inclusive play as Socrates advocates in *Republic* 7 537a–c: "Well, as this arises among ourselves (*pros hēmas*) there will be no risk of playing with our own things. Are we now contemplating as we play? Yes, *we and all who play* (*hēmeis kai pantes hosoi paizousi*) are doing this or at any rate this is what they desire as they play" (III.8 [30] 1, 8–12). This democratic emphasis also runs through the next two works of the *Großschrift*, V.8 [31] and V.5 [32]. In V.8.1, the central question posed is how can *anyone* contemplate intelligible beauty and its cause from the here and now of historical existence; in other words, the goal of the inquiry is not to privilege names, individuals or groups but to show the Beautiful and the Good to *anyone*, and this is a motif that reaches its culmination in the next treatise V.5 [32] 12, 34–35:

"The Good is gentle and kindly and gracious and present to *anyone* when *anyone* wants."

At the same time, Plotinus interprets Aristotle's heritage in a new way. Divine contemplation or thought is the fullest reality that extends to, and moves, everything not simply as a final cause, but as an internal formal cause. A. H. Armstrong has observed that, in III.8 [38] 7, Plotinus goes far beyond Aristotle, establishing a new universal sense of *theōria* (contemplation) that takes its starting point from *EN* K 6 and 7, but ends up abolishing "Aristotle's distinction between *praktike* and *theoretike episteme* or *dianoia* (*EN* 1, 1095a5; 6, 1139a21–b4; 10, 1179a35ff.) and [making] the whole life, not only of man but of the universe, philosophy in Aristotle's sense" (Armstrong, Loeb III 382–383n1). In our view, however, Plotinus does not really abolish Aristotle's distinction between *praktikē* and *theōretikē epistēmē*; nor does he create, as John Deck has suggested with some plausibility, a new form of formal-efficient causality in developing the notion that *theōria* is productive (Deck, 1967, 107–108). I suggest that he is aware of another line of thinking in Aristotle, since Aristotle does say that the right functioning of the two rational parts of the human being is contemplative in both directions—in that of particular variable things and in that of things that cannot be otherwise (*EN* 1139a5–6). It is also true that while *sophia* and *nous,* as contemplative in the highest sense, do not literally "make" anything (*EN* 10

8, 1178b20–21), Aristotle says a little later in *EN* Book 6 that they make or produce happiness in a different way, not externally but "as health makes health," that is, not as an efficient or motive cause, but rather as a formal cause. This is, in fact, integral to Plotinus' argument from the outset, namely, that desire or final causality operates as a formal cause throughout all of nature internally; and this is why he cites Aristotle at the conclusion of the first part of his argument: "For all other things (apart from the first principle) desire this if the goal for them all is their originative principle." In other words, he emphasizes Aristotle's own dictum that *nous* is both *archē* and *telos* (compare III.8 [30] 7, 1–15 with *EN* 6, 1143b10).

As Lloyd, 1991, 99 (also Rutten, 1956, 100–106) has shown, Plotinus adapts Aristotle's model of physical causation to non-physical causation; but Plotinus here also adapts this model to the internal workings of physical causation in so far as these are activities (and not simply qualities, for instance)—for the distinction, see II.6 [17]. Just as teaching and learning involve two different subjects, but constitute a single activity (*energeia*) from different perspectives (Aristotle, *Physics* 8, 255a33–b5; 3, 202a13–21), so also what is an action or an external production from one viewpoint is a manifestation of the real, and from another an *energeia* or activity of living insight. They are not two activities separated from one another (*Physics* 202b7–8) but a single activity seen from two different points of view. And since the real is not a patchwork of pieces, but a whole expression or participation in the life of God, my making of something can be "mine" from one viewpoint, and from another a window into reality or divine thought; in moral action, for instance, to the degree that I get something "right," that action embodies contemplation or insight. Energy or contemplation, therefore, is a formal activity that internally makes my action or production possible. Plotinus puts this succinctly in treatise 39, VI.8.6, 19–22: ". . . in practical actions, self-determination and what depends on us are not referred to practice or outward activity, but to the inner activity which is the thought and contemplation proper to its best functioning." Contemplation, as creation or co-creation, then, is what really *makes* at the heart of all forms of action and production. The inner activity of action is its thought and contemplation.

So, Plotinus appears to hold the view that nothing in the universe is entirely private, or unconnected with anything else, and that this is because all desires—even apparently blind reproductive impulses—reflect, however dimly or unconsciously, a developmental desire to manifest the living, totality-in-one of intellect. As life, this contemplation is already unrestricted; "Contemplation and vision have no limits," Plotinus states at III.8.5, 29–30: "and that's why they are everywhere." And in the case of intellect desiring the One, Plotinus applies his theory of creative contemplation to the whole of reality in a striking formulation: intellect "is always desiring and always attaining" (III.8.11, 22–24: *kai ephiemenos aei kai aei tynchanōn*). Intellect, too, therefore cannot be conceived as a static, fixed essence; its real nature is dynamic—to be drawn out of itself incessantly into itself and the Good. This is one source, we suggest, of Gregory of Nyssa's doctrine of *epektasis*, according to which the soul is continually drawn out of herself into God (see Daniélou, 1944, 309–326).

Is there, then, any place for individual agents in Plotinus' dynamic model of contemplative creation? Agency, at first sight, seems to disappear into desire and contemplation. Yes, we, the readers and interlocutors, actively trace the lines of creation internally through ourselves and other physical things into the intensifying unity of subject and object in intellect (III.8 [30] 1–7). Implicitly, the deepening range of unity as we ascend is where organizing subjectivity may appear, and so Plotinus traces a series of the "ones" of everything ("the one of the plant . . . the one of the animal . . . of the soul . . . of the all . . . of the things that exist in truth") back to the One itself (Ch. 10). But though the One is "fountainhead," and "root" of a mighty tree, "why would it have to see or be active at all?" (III.8 [30] 11, 9). Plotinus' answer is effectively that the One is "the power for all things," a power that has "given a trace of itself upon intellect for intellect to have by seeing" (*To men oun ep' autou ichnos autou tōi nōi horōnti edōken echein*, III.8.11, 22–23). Subject-agency, then, in III.8 [30] is undiminished giving at its fullest, the highest form of unrestricted vision that is productive contemplation for all things. But it is not clear how or where precisely in creative contemplation qualities such as freedom, will or choice fit into such a picture.

Non-deliberative Demiurgic Causality (VI.7)

In *Ennead* VI.7 [38] Plotinus develops another new model of divine causality (one already prefigured in V.8 [32] 4–7), according to which the making of the cosmos occurs neither in time nor by deliberative thought, but spontaneously and intelligibly in such a way that a single enfolded totality becomes unfolded in time and space so that what is, in reality, all together can, when unfolded, be experienced sequentially as a "this after this" (VI.7 [38]1, 54–58). For Plotinus, one major problem bequeathed from Plato is the need to overcome the apparent necessity for deliberation or planning valorized by the (mythical or narratized) representation of the Demiurge deliberating or taking thought. A second problem is the apparent absurdity of including wild animals in the intelligible paradigm of the *Timaeus*. What then does divine demiurgic agency entail?

To counter the first problem, Plotinus argues that Plato cannot mean that the Demiurge actually reasons or deliberates because such a representation of rationality in any form of creation is a *defect*, not an achievement. Reason is necessary to work things out after the fact; but understanding grasps reality all at once without the need for deliberation. If divine activity cannot be in any sense defective or incomplete (that is, demiurgic creation cannot be an Aristotelian incomplete motion, as Numenius, fr. 12 [Petty] had appeared to claim), then it must be "whole and entire" and "in anything of those things that belong to the divine everything must inhere" so that we can unfold it later in temporal succession as a "this after this" (VI.7.1, 45–55). The total "all-togetherness" of intellect means that it contains its cause in itself (VI.7.1, 57–58) as the implicate or enfolded interconnectedness of everything. Even in the unfolded or explicate physical world, Plotinus argues, we can sometimes see this interconnectedness in the simultaneous unity of cause and fact in knowledge and perception (as in Aristotle's example of an eclipse, where cause and fact are identical, *Posterior Analytics* 93a 14–b20; *Metaphysics* 8 1044b9–15). A similar dynamic grasp of cause and fact can also be glimpsed in the parts of natural organisms, Plotinus argues; the eye of a living being, for example, is organically related to all the other parts so that the causal interrelation of the parts makes each a cause in respect of all the rest (VI.7 [38] 2, 18; cf. VI.8 [39] 14, 18–29).

In other words, the all-togetherness of divine activity and its outpouring in the making of the world without deliberation or rationality are an integral part of our present experience of ordinary things and events in the physical world. And Plotinus then goes on to extend this analysis to all living creatures in order to counter the second problem—how can *nous* embrace the goods of all things?—and this results in a highly sophisticated, new view of intelligence:

"But someone will say, 'I grant the valuable living animals, but . . . how could the cheap and irrational ones [be there in the Complete Living Creature]?' . . . Now, there . . . intelligence (*to noein*) is different in man and in the other living creatures, and reasoning (*to logizesthai*) is also different, for there are present somehow also in the other living creatures many works of deliberate thought (*polla dianoias erga*). Why then are they not equally rational? And why are human beings not equally so in comparison to each other? But one must consider that the many lives, which are like movements, and the many thoughts [are] different . . . in brilliance and clarity . . . . For just as any particular life does not cease to be life, so neither does an intellect of a particular kind cease to be intellect . . . since the intellect appropriate to any particular living being does not on the other hand cease to be the intellect of all, of man also, for instance, granted that each part, whichever one you take, is actually all things, but perhaps in different ways. For it is actually one thing, but has the power to be all; but we apprehend in each what it actually is; and what it actually is, is the last, so that the last of this particular intellect is horse . . . as the powers unfold they always leave something behind . . . and as they go out they lose something . . . and in losing different things different ones find and add on something else because of the need of the living being . . . nails . . . claws and fangs" (VI.7.9, 1–43, trans. A. H. Armstrong, adapted).

Here intelligence, far from being a single paradigm of rationality as it tends to be in the modern world, is more like a variegated continuum of different intensities of organized life that allows for a sort of natural selectivity, of which we see only the last manifestation. There is a kind of geological depth to each species that prevents us from recognizing that each is, in fact, a holographic representation of a much larger intelligible organism which manifests design or purpose without a designer or deliberative agent. All animals have reason or implicit rationality in such different ways that the barriers are porous. Even human beings are not all equally rational. In fact, we are more "life-kinds" than separated rigidly into different human and other-animal species (as Clark, 2011, 52 has observed: "Evolutionary change is no great surprise for either Platonists or Aristotelians"). And Plotinus in subsequent chapters extends this holistic, demiurgic understanding even to the elements that possess different relations to soul and intellect (VI.7 [38] 10–11). In other words, Plotinus eliminates deliberation, planning, deliberate design and divided movement from divine production, and instead provides a reasonable case for seeing specific times and spaces as single strands or separated viewpoints of what is ultimately the complete activity of a divine being eternally creating and sustaining the world.

The Problem of Agency and VI.8

But what does this mean for agency? There is a paradoxical result to Plotinus' arguments in VI.7.1–13. Plotinus starts VI.7 by getting rid of the only agent readily available—Plato's Demiurge—and instead works toward a larger contextual model in which will and freedom do not really appear at all. Certainly, if one reads carefully, one may discern in Chapters 4–5 a view of what the human active subject, as a complex compound, may be: Plotinus asks what it is that "*makes* this human being, a *logos* not separate, but indwelling in the compound" (4, 28–30). And in the next chapter he defines "the human being here" as a complex compound that requires substantial agency derived from the presence of soul: "Soul in a specific kind of logos," he replies, "the logos being a specific kind of activity" (that is, an organic body), "and the activity being unable to exist without the acting subject" (VI.7 [38] 5, 2–5). So Plotinus wants to define the agent-subject that makes, transforms and also emerges from the complex unity that is the human being. Or again, later in VI.7 [38] 7, he sees the confluence of different forces of agency, as individual souls articulate the outline-traces made for them by the World Soul and as they become those particular traces in shaping themselves (VI.7 [38] 7, 8–17). Or still later in Chapter 15, there is a remarkable subject-agent picture of intellect as "an all-face thing shining with luminous faces" (VI.7 [38] 15, 26). And, finally, the question of the Good's present agency is posed with some urgency: granted that the Good has made all things, what does the Good *make now,* Plotinus asks at the end of VI.7 [38] 23: "Now as well it is keeping those things in being and making the thinking things think and the living things live, inspiring thought, inspiring life and, if something cannot live, existence." Certainly, the idea of agency seems to be coming more to the forefront as this treatise progresses—and, arguably, treatise 38 is Plotinus' greatest work.

However, it is not too difficult (according to the scenario we are sketching out here) to imagine Christians or Jews (perhaps a Gnostic known to have frequented Plotinus' school, or simply a visitor) asking him the following questions with increasing urgency: "Yes, your One is good, but surely It cannot do anything other than make by spontaneous reflex, indistinguishable from necessity or blind chance? In addition, if the One does not need anything, it must be indifferent, as the Epicureans suppose? In fact, it is neither a believable subject nor a meaningful agent. By contrast, the Biblical God is a real creative agent, intervening and caring for His people and, in the New Testament, sending his only Son to die on His people's behalf. Your One and your Demiurge cannot even compete. Besides, even if we grant that God does not deliberate, how can we have a God who doesn't even *will anything*? A will-less God will be a chance event, completely incompatible with a Biblical, Gnostic or Peripatetic notion, and, in fact, even with Plato's notion of the primacy of freedom ("virtue is without a master"). How do you answer?"

VI.8, Chapter 7: "the rash argument . . . from a different viewpoint"

Something like this is how we interpret the "rash argument . . . from a different viewpoint" or simply "from the other side of the question" that Plotinus mentions in VI.8 [39] 7, and then goes on to attack in subsequent chapters, an argument to the effect that the Good acts by chance, being neither master nor cause of itself, and therefore has no freedom or self-determination. Six major candidates for this rash argument have been proposed: a materialist, perhaps an Epicurean; a Gnostic (Bréhier, Cilento); a pure thought-experiment [*Gedankenexperiment*] initiated by Plotinus himself (Harder, Theiler, Leroux); a

Christian (Armstrong); or a Peripatetic [Aristotelian school] (Lavaud); or simply Plotinus in dialectical argument with himself (O'Meara). Any "visitor" might, in fact, have proposed this; no special adherence to any one school is necessary to lodge such an objection. And, at the same time, it does emerge dialectically through Plotinus taking up the other side of the question. For references see commentary on 7, 11–15.

We suggest then that several of the views above can be plausibly linked. VI.8 argues from the beginning against the position of Alexander that "what is in our power" cannot be granted paradigmatically to the gods. Since the principal proposition here in Chapter 7 is that the Good has neither freedom nor "what is in its power," then it is reasonable to suppose that Plotinus has Alexander in mind. Since, too, Aristotle had argued in *Metaphysics* 12, 1072b10–11 (cf. Szlezák, *Nuslehre,* 162), that the Prime Mover is a "necessary" being and since this necessity in divine natures is the reason Alexander argues against giving them anything "in their power," then clearly Plotinus wants to overcome this side of Peripatetic thought perhaps by finding a different way through it, or by an interpretation of other aspects of Peripatetic thought.

At the same time, Plotinus' response to the objection in the fourteen following chapters is much more far-reaching than this, since what is at stake is not simply Peripatetic thought, but the intelligibility of a universe founded upon an ultimate principle, the Good, that is itself no longer intelligible. Plotinus therefore does need to overcome other claims such as the primacy of chance or, again, material-like determinism. The question of chance and randomness that Plotinus argues against in later chapters shows that generally Epicurean or any cognate views are included in his broad focus. And the question of what notion the objector has in mind is clearly intended to counter a Stoic materialist and determinist viewpoint (see Chapter 7, 22–30) that holds that our notions are matter-dependent, however "immaterial," and derived from sense-perception. For Plotinus, reality-based notions are neither matter-dependent nor perception-derived; to be real, they must come through soul from the substantial being in Intellect. In other words, our notions cannot be simply self-generating or self-referential. They require a world of real reference. The Stoics, therefore, have to be included.

However, the scenario we are sketching here is broader still, since it is not too difficult to imagine Christians or Jews (perhaps a Gnostic known to have frequented Plotinus' school or simply a visitor) criticizing Plotinus' own thought in precisely these terms, by contrast with their own fully volitional view of God, and asking Plotinus, over the course of the eight works leading up to VI.8 (from the "anti-Gnostic" works, treatises 30–33 through treatise 38 [VI.7]), with increasing urgency the questions we have outlined above and thereby challenging him to demonstrate how *their* views about a God who wills and acts could ever be included and then better explained within Plotinus' *own* philosophy.

Ennead VI.8, we believe, is Plotinus' answer to such critical questions both from himself and, perhaps, from some person or persons external to the School, but familiar with Platonic, Peripatetic, Epicurean, Stoic, Jewish, Christian or Gnostic thought (if we can separate out "Gnostic" thought in this way). His answer is of major importance for the reasons we have indicated above: first, it develops an entirely new way of thinking about God—Plotinus is the first to argue, in the precise way he does it, that will comes before intellect and to posit the One as pure freedom, a self-establishing cause of Itself—and, second, it articulates a creative idea of agency and radical freedom by showing how such terms as "desire," "will," "self-dependence" and "freedom" in the human ethical sphere can be genuinely applied to Intellect and the One in a unambiguous manner that nevertheless preserves the radical inability of all metaphysical language to express anything about God or gods. For two other approaches to this question, by contrast with Leroux's view of a new positive theology in Plotinus (1990, 13; 38–39; 104–105), compare Lavaud, 189–194 and O'Meara, 1992, 343–349.

VI.8, Chapters 1–5

VI.8 [39], then, examines the nature and source of real agency in human beings, Intellect and, ultimately, the Good. Its immediate and larger context is Alexander of Aphrodisias' denial that the notion of "what depends on us" (*to eph' hēmin*) cannot be applied to the gods since their being what they are is necessary and, therefore, cannot be said to be in their power (*De Fato*, Ch. 32, 204, 12–15, 22–5, Bruns). For terminology, see commentary on 1, 15–16, "Excursus on important terms: Aristotle, Alexander, and the Stoics." To determine whether the notion of "what depends on us" can be applied to the gods and, above all, to the One, we first have to determine "whether anything happens to depend on us" (1, 15–16). In ordinary life, Plotinus notes, we find ourselves besieged by opposing compulsions and passions, and we think that we as subjects are nothing. We hope that if we could escape from these compulsions, what we wish might be free (1, 22–33). In other words, we hope with Aristotle that an action depends on us if it originates in the agent. And certainly, what is "voluntary" is what we do without compulsion and with knowledge; and "what depends on us" is what we are masters of, or competent in, doing. However, unlike Aristotle, Plotinus argues, we need more than knowledge of the circumstances, but a "general" knowledge—otherwise, like Oedipus, we will kill Laius in supposed freedom but in ignorance of the real circumstances or of what we ought to do. To act without knowing what we should know cannot be truly voluntary (1, 33–44). To what, then, should we attribute "what depends on us"—to desire, passion, lust, or rational calculus with correct desire, or imagination? But if we are "led by" any one of these, how can this be self-determining? We must then trace freedom to "will" residing in correct reasoning with knowledge (*epistēmē*), since correct opinion on its own is not necessarily self-determining. Nor can we put self-determination in perception or knowledge (*gnosis*) since each simply perceives or knows: "something else leads to action," Plotinus argues (VI.8 [39] 2, 30). But if we attribute freedom simply to intellect, this will not be freedom "in action," since everything involving action is mixed and, here, self-determination is not pure (2, 35–37). So Plotinus argues that we do not have to go as far as Intellect proper, since we can realistically trace self-determination to "intellectual activity" and grant that "the premises derived from there are truly free and that the desires awakened from thinking are not involuntary" (3, 22–26), for desire of the Good does not lead either Intellect or us outside of ourselves, but rather makes us enter our proper nature; and this is true for soul too, he argues "when it is active according to intellect and does things according to virtue."

Should we then grant self-determination to the agent, but not to the accomplishment of the action, Plotinus asks (5, 1–8); however, if we do this, we risk putting freedom outside of action, whereas what we actually experience is the transforming, dynamic power of virtue actually *doing* things; and this gives us freedom, so that virtue is a question of decision, that is, of will and choice: being good is in our power "if we will and choose it" (5, 30–32).

VI.8, Chapter 6, and the Definition of Human Free Agency

So Plotinus concludes the first part of his argument about human free will in Chapter 6 as follows: " . . . so that both self-determination in practical actions and what is in our power is referred neither to practical action nor to the external activity, but to the inner activity, namely, the thinking and contemplation of virtue itself. . . . So it is clearer that what is free is that which is immaterial, and that it is this to which being in our power is to be referred, namely, the will itself that is master and self-dependent, even if something directs it to what is outside because of necessity. Everything therefore that comes from and because of this will is in our power—both everything external and everything self-dependent; what it wills and actualizes without hindrance, this too is primarily in our power" (6, 19–30).

It may seem that the above passage refers only to acts of will that have nothing to do with action. But this is not so. Plotinus specifies that he means *practical actions* and that we refer *everything* self-dependent and in our power, *both external and internal,* to free will rooted in the immaterial. What is real in action is the inner activity, *noēsis* and *theoria,* as we saw in III.8 [30] above. And only the free subject truly acts or makes in the physical world, since his or her *praxis* manifests externally the inner energy that forms one reality with it; and the inner activity is the action's formal and final cause, *"the thought and contemplation of its healthy functioning."* Free agency, therefore, is a fully real, historical fact, grounded in each subject's firm orientation to Intellect and the Good through which it wills, orders, and makes the world to be good.

VI.8, Chapter 6 and Following: Intellect and Freedom

The contemplative Intellect, "the primary one," that Plotinus goes on to mention immediately, possesses a still higher degree of freedom, in that "its work depends not at all on another, but is entirely turned to itself and its work is itself and it lies in the Good, without need, fulfilled, and living, as it were, according to its will" (6, 32–36; cf. Aristotle, *De Anima* III 9, 432b27–9; cf. Lavaud, 264–5n95). Intellect is not bound by the necessity of its own nature, then, but is identical with its nature, has its cause in itself, and is "causative substance" (14, 37) beyond chance and randomness (cf. 14, 31–42), a free complete substance that without deliberation "gives the why and the being together as a whole" to soul and physical things (14, 32–33). Intellect, like soul, is grounded in the Good, but its freedom—like that of the Good—is the pure spontaneous creativity of its will that makes and sustains the world in itself and through us. Only of Intellect in VI.8 does Plotinus use *proairesis*: "each thing in the universe and this universe are as the maker's choice willed it" (17, 2–4). The significance of this is, perhaps, that while his notion of freedom is not decisionist—namely freedom as a choice between alternatives— Plotinus does not eliminate the meaning of *proairesis* in our choosing of the Good. The Demiurge does not deliberate, as Plotinus had argued in VI 7, but it establishes the paradigm of what deliberative free choice should be.

Overall Evaluation of VI.8 and Chapters 7–21

In the case of the One's freedom, Ernst Benz in 1932 saw Plotinus as the precursor of later voluntarism, and the first to overcome the tradition of Greek intellectualism (Benz, 1932, 301). Horn, 2007, 153–178 has argued, to the contrary, that Plotinus' account is intellectualist in the broad sense "that the divine will is strictly dependent on God's insight," that it never "transgresses the Corpus Platonicum," but that it does develop a new dynamic, spontaneous view of Divine Free Will. The terms of this debate are anachronistic and, therefore, misleading; in addition, Plotinus emphasizes the primacy of will in a way that does not make it "dependent on God's insight."

Moreover, while Plotinus' thought about this founding freedom of the One is groundbreaking (for the phrase see Collette-Dučić, 2014, 421–436), it does not produce a new positive theology that contradicts or stands uneasily beside Plotinus' usual thought. Plotinus emphasizes in 13, 1–5 that he is compelled "for the sake of persuasion" to speak "incorrectly." Finally, when we come to evaluate the "originality" of this work, we have to remember that Plotinus himself is against "innovation" either because of his own wish to adhere to Plato as faithfully as possible or even in any sense that may resemble modern notions of "individual" originality. Plotinus does not wish to be "original" as we might wish this for ourselves, but of course he is thoroughly original in a different sense—insofar as we can see him thinking through problems in a highly creative and open-ended way.

From this overall perspective, Plotinus is almost certainly prompted by the need to respond to Jewish, Christian and Gnostic perspectives according to which God wills creation and intervenes in the created world in many ways. Certainly, Plotinus builds into his treatment of the Good's freedom some striking features of Gnostic thought, such as the characterization of the Good as love and the self-production of the First Principle, as in the Valentinian *Tripartite Tractate* and other texts, as well as earlier Platonism. For example, we can compare the aloneness of the Good—*Ennead* VI.8, Chapter 7, 38–39; 9, 10–13 with the *Tripartite Tractate* (NHC I) 51 74; the image of root and tree—VI.8, Chapter 15, 33–36; *Trip. Tract.* 51, 17–19 and 74, 10–13; the characterization of the One as love (VI.8.16, 34; 19, 13; *Trip. Tract.* 55.22); the all-important self-production of the First principle—VI.8, Chapter 13, 54; 21, 17; *Trip. Tract.* 56, 1–4 and for Gnostic and Hermetic self-generation see *Tripartite Tractate*, NHC 1.5, 56, 1–6; *Gospel of the Egyptians*, NHC IV 2, 79, 5–6; *Three Steles of Seth*, NHC VII 5, 124, 25–29; 126, 1–7; *Zostrianos*, NHC VIII 1, 20, 4–14; 74, 20–24; NHC VII 1, 124, 17–19; *Allogenes*, NHC XI 3, 56, 10–15; 65, 22–27; *Corpus Hermeticum*, IV 10, 17; *Eugnostos the Blessed*, NHC III 3, 75, 2–8. In the case of earlier Platonism, we can compare Numenius, fr. 16, for example, or Alcinous, *Didaskalikos*, 10, 3, 15–18: The good "by his own will . . . has filled all things with himself, rousing up the soul of the world," or the *Chaldean Oracles*, 37, 2, 4; 81, 4; 107, 4.

Despite these striking parallels, Plotinus' emphasis on the dynamic primacy of Divine Will from different perspectives in Chapters 13–21 is striking for its daring quality (even given Plotinus' caveat at VI.8 [39] 13, 4–5). And even though he notes at many points that he is not speaking properly, he does not reduce the One's agency to that of either a divine theatrical character or an anthropomorphic subject.

What is remarkable too is the extent to which Plotinus, after denying things of the Good in Chapters 7–12, is prepared for the sake of "persuasion" to develop modes of expression in Chapters 13–21 that appear to contradict his entire metaphysics: The Good makes itself (7, 53; 13, 55); it is exactly what it wishes to be (9, 44–45); the Good is ruler of himself (7, 13; 35; 9, 44, etc.); it didn't "happen to be" by chance or randomness; it is not by necessity the sort of thing it is, but because being what it is is the best (10, 25–26); its will is identical with its existence (13, 55–56); it is cause of itself, exists by itself, and for itself (14, 41–42); it brought itself into being (16, 15); it is as it woke itself up to be (16, 33); it is entire will (21, 14).

In these later chapters, then, Plotinus weaves together several perspectives on the Good's free will, some of which are worth sketching briefly here: First, the Divine will is "choosable:" "the nature of the Good is more worthy of choice for itself" (13, 15–20)—clearly this does not involve a decision between alternatives, but such a will constitutes the paradigm for all affirmative *decisive* power (cf. Aristotle, *Metaphysics* 12, 1072a26; 1072a35; and compare Alexander (against the Stoics), *De Fato* 196, 25 Bruns). Second, Divine will is pure agency and the source of subjectivity in everything else: "So if it is by this that each thing makes itself something, it doubtlessly becomes clear that it (the Good) is primarily what it is by itself and is that by which other things exist by their own selves" (13, 24–27). Third, Divine will is desirable and desire, not only the goal of all appetition, but love and self-loving: "And he himself is loveable and love and self-love" (15, 1). An active love brings the Good into new focus against the background of Christian thought, in particular, but it also poses the question for later (Neoplatonic) thought how all created things and their deepest aspirations can be meaningfully included in that love (see, for example, Iamblichus, *De Mysteriis* V 26, 237, 6–239, 10). Fourth, Divine will is everywhere and nowhere, bringing itself into subsistence and "he gives existence to the others neighboring him" (16, 1–16). Here existence is prior to essence, in the most eminent mode possible, and providentially present to all individual beings, against the Peripatetic view that providence does not extend to sublunary individuals.

Consequently, the Divine will is supremely causal: "he is <Father> of formative principle and <cause> and causative being" (14, 37–38); it is also self-creative, as the Gnostics and others (e.g., Numenius) had supposed: "he would as it were make himself, not as he chanced to be, but as he wills" (16, 21–22). In other words, the Good constitutes causality, not by transferring chance or randomness into himself, but—with Aristotle—by rendering chance or spontaneity as transparent as they can be in the light of regular causality in the world (cf. *Physics* 198a9–10). Divine will is therefore also a self-related and a structuring power: "that such an inclination of himself to himself—being as it were his activity and his remaining in himself—makes his being what he is" (16, 24–6); "the 'having made' is concurrent with his own self" (20, 26–27); "his awakening is <beyond being> and Intellect and <intelligent life>, . . . these are from him and not from another" (16, 33–37). Finally, the Divine will is autonomous, unique and primordially spontaneous as expressing the Good's purest independence. It is reliant purely on itself.

Here, then, is a Divine Will that is eminently choosable, desirable, self-productive, supremely causative, a self-related, structuring agency, operative everywhere and present to anything, no matter how lowly. This is a Will that goes beyond anything in the earlier tradition. The Divine Will is, in fact, not dependent on insight or intellect, but "*primarily* will" (21, 16). And it is not solitary or detached: "And his containing himself is to be understood, if one were to express it rightly, such that all else that exists is contained by him" (21, 19–21). The will of the Good is the comprehensive *connectivity* of everything (*Metaphysics* 12, 1074b2–3) and it is a radically simple, universal experience, "something like waking up" (16, 32; *Metaphysics* 12, 1072b17; 9, 1048b1–5). It is striking in the last sentence of VI.8 [39], then, that Plotinus should return to the democratic viewpoint that connects subjects in their upward connective movement: "for *even you can touch upon something* about which it is no longer possible to speak or apprehend; rather only this that is truly free lies far above, this alone truly free, because it is not enslaved to itself, but is only itself and really itself, while everything else is itself and something else." The phrase "for it is possible for even you to touch upon something" is a *Symposium*-montage, first, of Diotima's words to Socrates at the beginning of the "greater mysteries" ("pay attention and even you can learn," *Symposium* 209e5–210a4) and, second, of her final words about "touching upon the beautiful" at the end of those mysteries, the ladder of ascent to the Beautiful (ibid. 212a2–5). The last sentence of VI.8, then, is addressed to *anyone who can touch*, in following the transformed identity of Socrates, the Good as ultimate guarantor of agency. In addition, the "something" (*tinos*) that lies above is ineffable, but also remarkably positive and concrete, a reflexive memory, perhaps, of V.5 [32] 12:

"The Good is gentle, kindly and gracious, and accessible to anyone whenever anyone wishes." The *free will* of the Good—"only itself"—is open to the *free wish* of anyone—"itself and something else"—by virtue of that which wills or wishes in each subject.

In sum, while there is a complex tradition about the freedom of the virtuous will from Plato onwards (on this see Romano, 1999, 151–191), and while Gnostic models of Divine willed self-production predate Plotinus, the three models we have outlined here—models of creative contemplation, non-deliberative demiurgic production and, finally, agency and divine self-causality—provide entirely new ways of thinking about the spontaneous non-rational causality of both divine and physical subjects and ultimately show how divine activity and human action can cooperate and yet retain their independence in a single activity. In VI.8 [39], finally, Plotinus first determines the reference and function of human agency and then applies this daringly to Intellect and the Good, weaving together several convergent perspectives of the Good's free will that lead to the positing of a radical Divine free will prior to being and intellect, a will that is the ground of all subjectivity, from the Divine Intellect to the most ordinary subject. Despite his repeated warnings that he is not speaking properly about the Good (in VI.8 [39] 13–21), it is striking that Plotinus should finish the treatise without a full retraction of his positive statements, and this perhaps intimates his concern to show dialectically (VI.8 [39], Chapters 7–12 and 13–21) how Gnostic and other views might be incorporated into his own thought by an examination of the meaning of agency without reducing the Divine to a "sound and light" action sequence. We have also seen throughout how the interpretation and development of Aristotle in relation to fundamental Platonic problems figure prominently at every point of Plotinus' argument.

Whether or not this is the beginning of a new voluntarist tradition (and we suggest that it is not), it is certainly a groundbreaking development in the history of thought, whose consequences are profound, as can be seen in Werner Beierwaltes' claim that Plotinus is the predecessor of Spinoza's later concept of God as *Causa sui* (Cause of itself) as well as the founder of the modern idea of radical freedom (Beierwaltes, 2001, 123–159; cf. Hadot, 1971, Bd. I. 976–977; Narbonne, 1993, 177–195). These consequences are already to be found in Marius Victorinus (*Adv. Arium* I, 55, 19–21; cf. I, 52, 28–30) and also, as we have suggested above, in later Christian Trinitarian thought. In subsequent Neoplatonism, Iamblichus (ca. 245–325 CE) rejects Plotinus' model of the Good's self-causation; only the term "Unbegotten" can appropriately be applied to the Godhead. Iamblichus' view was transmitted to Eunomius, Bishop of Cyzicus (died ca. 393 CE), who argued that God is only "Unbegotten," an absolutely simple Being into whose nature no act of generation can be introduced without blasphemous duality. Against Eunomius, the great Cappadocian Fathers—Basil of Caesarea, Gregory Nazianzus, and Gregory of Nyssa—developed their own Trinitarian thought, and we can find in Gregory of Nyssa a hidden "Trinitarian" model already articulated by Plotinus (Corrigan, 2008, 114–134). Whatever may be the case, the later chapters of VI.8 [39] provide for subsequent thinkers a trinitarian model of the purest Divine Unity. In Chapter 20, for instance, Plotinus argues that although we use such terms incorrectly of the Good, the (1) activity, (2) substance, and (3) perfection of (1) making, (2) selfhood, and (3) eternal generation must be identical in the Good:

"Indeed an activity not enslaved to substantial being is purely free, and thus he is himself from himself. For if he were kept in being by another, he wouldn't be first from himself, and if he is rightly said to contain himself, he is himself, even the one who introduces himself forward, since what he contains by nature is what from the beginning he has made to exist. So then, if there were a time when he began to be, the phrase 'he has made' would be most properly said; but now, if he were what he is before eternity was, let this phrase 'he has made himself' be understood to mean the concurrence of the 'having made' with his own self, for the being is one with the making and is as it were an eternal generation" (VI.8 [39] 20, 17–27).

If one puts this passage alongside Iamblichus' and Eunomius' claim that *Agennetos* is a more appropriate term for God, then we are in an intellectual climate, as we have suggested, very close to the emergence of Cappadocian Trinitarian theology and, indeed, the word "concurrent" (*sundromon*; 13, 29; 20, 26) from the passage above is used of the Trinity in Gregory of Nyssa (see *Apologia in Hexaemeron* 6, 9, 1; *Oratio Catachetica* 2, 33; 8, 150; *Contra Eunomium* 1, 1, 396, 2; 440, 3; 662, 7; 2, 1, 227, 3; 3, 7, 22, 9. For later Fathers, Lampe, *PL*, s.v.).

Finally, Werner Beierwaltes' view that through VI.8 [39] Plotinus is the founder of the modern idea of radical freedom finds strong confirmation in the great American Neoplatonic thinker, Ralph Waldo Emerson. Plotinus' view of radical free will in the Good as self-production and self-reliance, and as *the* model for understanding all freedom, together with Plato's description of virtue as "without a master"—this view is at the root of Emerson's notion of self-reliance, as in the following passage that clearly derives from VI.8 [39]: "This is the ultimate fact which we so quickly reach on this, as on every topic, the resolution of all into the ever-blessed ONE. *Self-existence is the attribute of the Supreme Cause,* and it constitutes the measure of good by the degree in which it enters into all lower forms. All things real are so by so much *virtue* as they contain." (Emerson, *Self-Reliance, The Collected Works,* Volume 2, 1979, 40). Self-existence/Self-reliance is the birth of freedom in the One that extends to all subsequent forms of existence—and this self-reliance has come, strangely enough, to characterize the birth and continuing legacy of a New World.

Note on the Greek Text

Line numbers in the translation are approximate and do not always match the original Greek text. Since the commentary follows the sequence of the English translation, there may sometimes be a slight discrepancy in the ordering.

The Greek text adopted is that of the Oxford edition, that is, the *editio minor* (for comparison between readings in HS_1 and HS_2 see vol. 3, xiii–xiv). Deviations from the text are noted in the commentary.

Each *Ennead* is referred to by Roman numerals, followed by the number of the treatise, the chapter of the treatise, and, finally, separated by a comma, the line number or numbers, for example, VI.8.8, 24–27, that is, *Ennead* VI, treatise number 8, Chapter 8, lines 24–27.

It is customary to add the chronological number given by Porphyry in his *Life of Plotinus* (*Vita Plotini*), so that, for example, VI.8 is designated VI.8 [39], that is, *Ennead* VI.8 is 39th in the chronological order. So we adopt the convention as follows: either VI.8.8, 1–5 (where the chronological number is not given) or VI.8 [39] 8, 1–5 (where it is given).

In this series the chronological number is given only in the Introduction and in other places where it may be of significance for understanding the chronological presentation of Plotinus' philosophical stance. The following chart indicates the chronological order.

Chronological Order of the *Enneads*

Enn.		*Enn.*		*Enn.*		*Enn.*		*Enn.*		*Enn.*	
I.1	**53**	II.1	**40**	III.1	**3**	IV.1	**21**	V.1	**10**	VI.1	**42**
I.2	**19**	II.2	**14**	III.2	**47**	IV.2	**4**	V.2	**11**	VI.2	**43**
I.3	**20**	II.3	**52**	III.3	**48**	IV.3	**27**	V.3	**49**	VI.3	**44**
I.4	**46**	II.4	**12**	III.4	**15**	IV.4	**28**	V.4	**7**	VI.4	**22**
I.5	**36**	II.5	**25**	III.5	**50**	IV.5	**29**	V.5	**32**	VI.5	**23**
I.6	**1**	II.6	**17**	III.6	**26**	IV.6	**41**	V.6	**24**	VI.6	**34**
I.7	**54**	II.7	**37**	III.7	**45**	IV.7	**2**	V.7	**18**	VI.7	**38**
I.8	**51**	II.8	**35**	III.8	**30**	IV.8	**6**	V.8	**31**	VI.8	**39**
I.9	**16**	II.9	**33**	III.9	**13**	IV.9	**8**	V.9	**5**	VI.9	**9**

	Enn.		*Enn.*		*Enn.*		*Enn.*		*Enn.*		*Enn.*
1	I.6	**10**	V.1	**19**	I.2	**28**	IV.4	**37**	II.7	**46**	I.4
2	IV.7	**11**	V.2	**20**	I.3	**29**	IV.5	**38**	VI.7	**47**	III.2
3	III.1	**12**	II.4	**21**	IV.1	**30**	III.8	**39**	VI.8	**48**	III.3
4	IV.2	**13**	III.9	**22**	VI.4	**31**	V.8	**40**	II.1	**49**	V.3
5	V.9	**14**	II.2	**23**	VI.5	**32**	V.5	**41**	IV.6	**50**	III.5
6	IV.8	**15**	III.4	**24**	V.6	**33**	II.9	**42**	VI.1	**51**	I.8
7	V.4	**16**	I.9	**25**	II.5	**34**	VI.6	**43**	VI.2	**52**	II.3
8	IV.9	**17**	II.6	**26**	III.6	**35**	II.8	**44**	VI.3	**53**	I.1
9	VI.9	**18**	V.7	**27**	IV.3	**36**	I.5	**45**	III.7	54	I.7

Note on Translations

THE TRANSLATION OF VI.8 is by the authors. Unless otherwise stated, all translations of passages from the rest of the *Enneads* are by A. H. Armstrong, *Plotinus,* volumes 1–7 (Loeb Classical Library, Cambridge, MA and London: Harvard University Press, 1966–1988). For works of Aristotle, we use R. McKeon's *The Basic Works of Aristotle* (New York: Random House, 1966), and for works of Plato we use Edith Hamilton and Huntington Cairns, *The Collected Dialogues of Plato Including the Letters* (Princeton: Princeton University Press, 1989). For Alexander of Aphrodisias, *On Fate,* we use R. Sharples (London: Duckworth, 1983) and *Alexander of Aphrodisias, Supplement to On the Soul* (London/New York: Bloomsbury, 2004). For Hellenistic writers generally, we use LS (see abbreviations). For the Nag Hammadi treatises, we use the translations in *The Nag Hammadi Scriptures* (M. Meyer, ed. New York: HarperCollins, 2007) in conjunction with the critical editions of these texts in the "Bibliothèque copte de Nag Hammadi" series (Louvain: Peeters and Quebec: Presses de l' Université Laval, 1975–present). All other translations are our own.

Synopsis

Ennead VI.8 can be divided into three parts:

The first part, Chapters 1–7, investigates the nature of freedom at the levels of embodied existence, soul, and intellect/ Intellect.

The second part, Chapters 8–12 (after the pivotal presentation of the "rash discourse . . . from a different viewpoint" in Chapter 7), examines the freedom of the Good from the negative perspective that if we can strictly attribute nothing to the Good, we cannot, therefore, speak about it being free.

The third part, Chapters 13–21, examines what it means to talk positively about the freedom of the Good, even if we speak incorrectly and more positively about it.

Part 1, Chapters 1–7: Working toward definitions of freedom at the levels of agency in the human compound, soul and intellect, and at the level of Intellect in relation to the Good.

Chapter 1: Can we apply our notions of something being "in our power" or of omnipotence to the gods and can we even apply it to ourselves when we find ourselves overwhelmed by external compulsions and addictions?

1–13. Setting out of the goal and scope of the work; what does it mean to say that something "has power?"

13–30. What does the expression "what is in our power" mean in relation to human experience?

30–44. The distinction between "what is voluntary" and "what is in our power."

Chapter 2: To which faculty or power of soul should we trace "what is in our power?"

1–12. Should we trace it to desire, high spirit or anger, or to a combination of desire and reason?

12–35. An examination of different possible relations between desire and reason.

35–37. Preliminary Conclusion: nothing related to action can be completely in our power.

Chapter 3: From soul to intellect—if we trace "self-determination" [a new term introduced here] and "what is in our power" back through intellect rather than through imagination and other powers, we may be able to link them to the gods.

1–20. Can what is in our power be related to opinion or to imagination?

21–26. Free self-determination must be traced primarily through our intellect to Intellect itself, for the premises derived from Intellect and the desires that Intellect awakes in us are not involuntary.

Chapter 4: Objections: how can desire be compatible with freedom? How can intellect/Intellect be free if it acts out of necessity? How can intelligible things be free if they have no practical action?

1–4. How can desire that needs something outside itself be compatible with freedom?

4–11. How can intellects be free if they must follow the necessity of their natures (as according to Alexander of Aphrodisias)?

11–32. Reply to the objections: For intelligible things, if being and acting are not separate, and if their nature and necessity are identical, then one cannot be enslaved to the other.

32–40. To be in one's own power is to be in the Good and, therefore, to be more free.

Chapter 5: Self-determination and being in one's power are not only in intellect/Intellect but also in soul. How then are freedom and virtue related?

1–27. Is the virtue of soul that governs action really free? If virtue is compelled and only the inner determination is free, then freedom will be outside action.

27–37. But if virtue organizes practical life, has no master, and establishes freedom, perhaps this makes it "another intellect" and a "habit" that organizes the soul—and then still this is outside of action in the restful quiet of intellect.

Chapter 6: Resolution of the impasse between inner freedom and external action, and the definition of human freedom as including both. Soul through virtue, and intellect even more so, is self-dependent. So we refer what is in our power and self-determination in actions not to action as such but to the inner activity, thought or contemplation that makes the outer activity in that focus free.

1–26. Only virtue, identified with the inner activity of thought, and contemplation are free.

26–29. What is free and self-dependent is the immaterial and to this we make ultimate reference in us.

29–32. But everything that comes from and because of our will is in our power—both everything external and everything self-dependent. What it wills and actualizes without hindrance is primarily in our power.

32–40. Transition from the (implicit) practical intellect (under discussion), through the contemplative intellect, to Intellect in the full sense, and the will of the Good.

Chapter 7: Transition: presentation of the rash argument from a different viewpoint.

1–6. There are different degrees of freedom in the soul, Intellect, and the Good.

6–11. But surely we cannot apply the expression "in its power" to the Good?

11–15. The rash argument: the Good is not free since it "happens to be" and is not master of its own nature.

16–30. Reply: not to give freedom to the Good destroys the possibility of free agency and the meaning of "what is in our power"; moreover, this rash argument thinks on the level of nonexistent things making up notions that have no basis in the realities: soul, intellect, or the Good.

31–46. A further series of replies: do we seek another "Good" apart from the Good? How can it be by chance, if chance applies only to things in the physical world? If it is as it is, is this because it has not come to be (unlike everything else)? But this uniqueness or singularity of its nature does not mean that it is hindered by anything, but that it is uniquely self-determining.

46–54. If its being and its activity, so to speak, are even more one than in Intellect, how can it be other than eternally self-making self-dependence?

Part 2, Chapters 8–12: How can we speak about the Good as free, if we cannot predicate anything of it? The negative path toward the Good.

Chapter 8: The inadequacy of all language in relation to the Good.

1–3. The Good is not subject to the attribution of properties, but if we remove the power for contraries that characterizes lesser things [the power for good and bad, for instance], we can see that the Good must be pure self-related self-determination: "itself to itself."

4–23. We remove every characteristic or relation including self-determination and "in its power."

23–27. And the same is true for chance, spontaneity, and "it happened to be"—all these designations are later than the Good.

Chapter 9: What does the objector think he means? Continued refutation of applying chance and "it happened to be" to the Good.

1–5. But when our interlocutor says that the Good just chanced or happened to be, what is he or she actually thinking? He means that though it has a nature, this just happened or chanced to be the case.

5–17: But this is to make it in some sense deficient, whereas it is unique and, though necessary, it is not bound by necessity; instead, it constitutes necessity for others. It is "what must be" not "what happened to be."

17–23. And not even is it what "must be" but as the King appears to his followers, not following the lead of anything, but really "what he is."

23–35. And "happened to be" cannot even apply to Intellect, for chance is later than Intellect; and therefore it applies even less to the Good.

36–49. To characterize it as happening "in this way" is to determine it, when it is above even "willing."

Chapter 10: How could the objector either refute or confirm the "happened to be" hypothesis? Continued refutation of applying chance and "it happened to be" to the Good, partly through an examination of the nature of causality.

1–3. How could our interlocutor evaluate his own position, for he has no principle by which either to refute or to introduce his "happened to be?"

4–6. If he does introduce "a nature" will he then rule out "happened to be" or remove "happened to be" because of chance, and where will he put this nature or "what doesn't happen by chance?"

5–21. How can that which is cause of Intellect, formative principle, and order exist by chance? Order cannot be a function of chance, but rather the other way round. A chance event is possible only to the extent that it might have happened for a reason or purpose, but actually didn't [so our interlocutor is not really thinking anything at all].

21–25. Even if it were not master of its own substantial self-generation, but had an instrumental relation to itself, it would still necessarily be itself and not otherwise.

25–38. No, it is not constrained by necessity but is necessity and law for the others, being brought into existence by the agency neither of another nor of itself.

Chapter 11: How do we think, represent or speak about the Good? The problem of thinking about something that did not come into existence prevents any scientific enquiry and provokes us to imagine falsely that it is somehow thrown into a pre-existing empty space, when in fact it is prior to all space, and neither quantity nor quality nor relation nor accidental happening can be attributed to the Good.

1–13. The problem of something that did not come into existence reduces us to silence, since every enquiry stops at an originative principle and cannot go any further. The same is true with all the other questions we pose (the "what" something is, "what kind" it is, "why" it is, "if" it is); we cannot attach anything to it.

13–28. Our thinking about the Good must be purified of all spatial representation.

28–38. Neither quantity nor quality nor relation nor accidental happening can be attributed to the Good.

Chapter 12: But we remain un-persuaded in soul, because our freedom is derivative and removed from full substantial being, yet still real, nonetheless; and precisely because it is derived, through Intellect's substantial being, from the Good, we cannot logically deny freedom of the ultimate "freemaker." But the doubleness implied in the term self-mastery is incorrect, since the Good is one.

1–3. But the soul remains un-persuaded and at a loss: isn't he master of what he is or of his being beyond being?

3–17. As bodily beings, we are far from substantial being in the full sense, but we are individual substantial beings; we participate in such being on the level of soul, have experience of freedom ourselves, and so can understand the greater self-identical freedom of Intellect itself.

17–31. How then can we deny freedom of the originative principle that makes Intellect and us free?

31–37. The term self-mastery is misleading because it implies two items, as if the essential self and the activity were separate, but in the case of the Good they are not "two as one," but simply "one."

Part 3, Chapters 13–21: Positive discourse about the freedom of the Good.

Chapter 13: Beginning of the positive discourse about the Good.

1–5. The need to persuade demands a certain deviation from proper thought.

5–11. The Good is as he wills, and is therefore master of himself.

12–33. Everyone desires the Good and, once one has it, it becomes both one's will and one's voluntary substantial being. One is what one wills, just as the Good is what he wills.

33–46. Since the Good is singular/unique, there is no good other than himself that he would want to choose, so to choose himself is to will himself.

47–50. Although normal discourse doesn't permit the use of such terms as "choosing," "willing," "wanting," etc. in reference to the Good, we use them only for illustrative purposes, always prefaced by an "as it were."

51–59. Since the Good wills itself and its being is from itself, the Good didn't just happen to be, but made itself to be what he willed.

Chapter 14: Just as there is no contingency in the intelligible realm, there is no contingency in the Good who transcends Intellect; as self-determined, he is "cause of himself.

1–16. One must distinguish the realm of true being, the things that are what they are in themselves, such as humanity, from the individuals of the sensible realm, such as individual humans who merely participate in ideal humanity; since the latter rank below the things that are in themselves, things that cannot be random, the reality that is above them also cannot be due to chance, if it has given itself existence.

16–35. A single source lies behind all causation and accounts for every "why?"

35–42. The Good is not only Father of cause, causative principle, and causative being, but also cause of himself.

Chapter 15: The Good is self-desire or self-love, cause of beings, cause of himself, and Father of every formative principle and cause.

1–10. For the Good who desires himself, the desiring agent and the object loved are one and the same and constitute his very being.

10–21. The experience of seeing in ourselves a nature that seems completely independent of ourselves and our everyday experience is not just an accident, but is due to illumination from the omnipresent Good whose own existence is not by chance but from himself.

21–36. Our souls' freedom allows us to reascend to the Good, certainly not by chance, and not even by reasoning or formative principle (logos), but because of the transcendent beauty of the Good, who is the tree from whose root all formative principles derive.

Chapter 16: The Good is everywhere and nowhere.

1–8. The everywhere and nowhere pervaded by the Good is actually the Good himself.

8–15. The self-determination of the Good includes self-directed love, activity, vision, inclination, and awakening.

16–23. The self-directed activity of the Good stems not from chance but from his own self-directed will.

24–30. The Good is omnipresent, supreme, immobile, and eternally active; indeed the Good's power is his act.

30–39. The self-awakening of the Good is not a conscious act, but an eternal state of wakefulness, an act beyond any sort of intelligizing, let alone any sort of happenstance.

Chapter 17: Providence assures that neither intelligibles nor sensibles exist by accident.

1–11. The Good as turned toward itself and interior to itself.

11–18. Since Intellect is an ordered "one-in-many," it cannot be subject to irrational chance.

18–27. The Good is a single originative principle unrelated to anything but itself alone.

Chapter 18: Seek the Good from its interior as container and measure of all things.

1–2. Seek nothing after the Good outside him, but only what is within him.

2–31. The Good is like the center and radii of a circle whose circumference is tangent to Intellect.

32–43. Intellect is a plurality of formative principles that are the dispersed image of the Good—the cause of causes—and thus not a mere happenstance.

43–51. Platonic Metaphors: The Good is "that which needed to be" "in a timely fashion."

52–53. One is unable to speak of the Good as one would wish.

Chapter 19: Contemplation of the Good is superior to all speech about him.

1–12. All these questions about the Good will only be resolved, not by rational argument, but by ascending to him and seeing him directly by the eyes of the soul.

12–20. The Good is "beyond substantial being."

Chapter 20: If the Good is self-produced, does he then precede himself?

1–9. In the self-making of the Good, there can be no distinction, logical or temporal, between the maker and the product made.

9–27. Since the Good's self-making is an eternal activity or process and not caused by some substantial reality other than himself, there can be no "before" or "after" in his self-making.

28–39. "Ruling himself" cannot entail any distinction between ruler and ruled; the Good is entirely self-determined.

Chapter 21: The Good cannot produce himself as other than he is.

8–19. A perfect identity between the will and reality of the good.

19–25. The meaning of containing himself.

25–33. To attain to the good, one must abandon all things.

Translation of Plotinus Ennead *VI.8 [39]*

On the Voluntary and on the Free Will of the One

1. Is it possible to inquire, even about the gods, whether there is anything in their power, or would such an inquiry be proper only in the case of human inabilities and debatable powers, while one is required to ascribe omnipotence to the gods, such that not just | something, but everything is in their power? Or is it that we should ascribe omnipotence and having everything in its power only to one (god), but with the other gods some things are this way and some that way, and to which gods should we ascribe each of these cases? We must indeed inquire about these matters and dare to inquire about even the first things and that | which is above all, how being in one's power applies even if one grants omnipotence. And we must also investigate what is meant by this phrase "to have

power," lest we claim that sometimes it means potency or sometimes actuality, even a future actuality.

But for the time being, we must | postpone these issues and first inquire as we usually do whether there is anything that happens to be in *our* power. First, we must ask, what "being in our power" should mean, that is, what is the notion of such a thing, for in this way it might be known whether it is appropriate to transfer it—or not—to the gods, or, still more, to God. Or if we should | transfer it, we must inquire how being in one's power applies both to the other gods and to the first things.

What then are we thinking when we say "what is in our power" and why are we investigating it? I myself think that when we are moved by opposing chances and compulsions and violent onslaughts of passions possessing our soul, we accept all | these things as our masters, and, enslaved to them and carried wherever they lead us, we are at a loss whether we are not nothing and whether there is anything in our power—as if what would be in our power is that which we will to do and do, when we are not enslaved by chance, compulsion or strong passions, with nothing opposing our wills. | But if so, our notion of what is in our power would be enslaved to our will and would or would not happen to the extent we willed it. For everything that is voluntary is done knowingly and without violent force and what is in our power is that of whose doing we are masters; and both may often coincide,

| even if their definitions are different. For example, if one were master of killing, it wouldn't be a voluntary act if one did so not knowing that the victim was his father. But perhaps that (ignorance) would be inconsistent with having something in one's power; then certainly the | knowledge in a voluntary act mustn't be based only on the particular circumstances, but also on the whole picture. For why, if one doesn't know that someone is a relative, is it involuntary, but not involuntary if one doesn't know he mustn't do it? Perhaps because he ought to have learned? Not knowing that he ought to have learned is not voluntary, nor is what leads one away from learning.

2. But we must investigate the following: This (function) that is certainly referred to us as "being in our power"—to what should we assign it? Do we assign it to impulse and some kind of desire—for example, what is done or not done out of high spirit or desire or out of rational calculation about what is advantageous together with desire? | But if we assign it to high spirit and desire, we will grant that something is in the power of children and beasts and mad persons and those beside themselves and addicted to drugs and those assailed by imaginations of which they are not masters. But if we assign it to rational calculation together with desire, is this so if rational calculation is erroneous? Or should we assign it to correct calculation and | correct desire? And yet even here one might inquire whether the

calculation moved the desire or the desire the calculation. For even if the desires are according to nature, if they belong to a living being, that is, the compound being, the soul has followed the necessity of nature, but if we assign it to the soul alone, | many of the things now said to be in our power would be outside this. Then again, what bare calculation precedes the passions? Or when imagination compels and desire drags us to whatever object it may lead, how does this make us masters in such cases?

And how generally can we be masters where we are led? | For what is in need and what desires fulfillment out of necessity has no mastery over that to which it is merely led. And how generally can something be from itself which is dependent on something else and whose origin is attributed to something else from which it has come to be what it is? For it lives just as it has been fashioned by that, or | in the same way inanimate things too will be able to grasp something in their power; for even fire acts as it has come to be. But if it is because the living being, and the soul, knows what it does by sense-perception, what help is that for what is in their power? For sense-perception doesn't make one master of the work just by seeing. But if by knowledge—knowledge of what is being done, here | too it only knows, but something else leads to action. But if reason or knowledge counteracts and controls desire, we must inquire what this refers to and generally where this occurs. And if reason itself makes yet another desire, then how must we understand this? But if reason stops desire and stands still, and here is what is in our power, this will not be in action, but this will stand still in intellect, since everything in action—even if reason controls it—is mixed and cannot have the "being in our power" in a pure state.

3. That is why we must investigate these matters, for already again we are also getting close to our discourse about the gods. Having now traced what is in our power back to will, and then situated this in reason and then in correct reason—and perhaps we must add the qualification that "correct" | reason belongs to science, for if someone had correct opinion and acted upon it, he wouldn't equally have the unambiguous power of self-determination if he acted without knowing why he is correct, but was led to what he ought to do by chance or some imagination. Since if we say that imagination is also not in our power, how could we rank those who act in accordance with imagination in the class of | self-determining subjects? But we do say this about imagination in the proper sense, namely, that which is aroused by the bodily passions (for being empty or again full of food and drink somehow shapes imaginations, and so too one who is full of semen has different imaginations according to each quality of the fluids in a body); we will not classify those | who act

in accordance with such imaginations under a principle of self-determination.

That is also why we will not grant to bad people, who do many things in accordance with these imaginations, either the capacity of having something in their power or voluntary action, but we do grant self-determination to those free of the bodily passions who act through the activities of intellect—| tracing what is in our power to a most beautiful originative principle, namely, the activity of intellect, we will also grant that the premises derived from here are truly free, and we shall grant that the desires aroused from thinking are not involuntary, | and we will say that this power is present in the gods who live in this way [as many as live by Intellect and by desire in accord with Intellect].

4. And yet one may also inquire how that which comes about in accord with desire will ever be self-determined when desire leads to what is outside oneself and experiences neediness, for that which desires is led, even if it is led to the good. And then too we must be at a loss | about intellect itself, if, when it actualizes what is in its nature and acts according to its nature, it might be said to have freedom and what is in its power when it does not have it in its power *not* to act; and then, in general, whether "in their power" can strictly be said of those things for whom there is no practical action.

But even for those things that engage in practical action | necessity is from outside, for they will not act without purpose. But then how is there freedom if these too are slaves to their own natures? Yet if there is no compulsion to follow another, how can one speak of slavery? How could something carried to the good be compelled, when its desire is voluntary, if it knows that it is good and knows that it goes to a good. For the involuntary is a departure from the good toward what is compelled if/when something is carried toward what is not good for it; and that is enslaved which is not master of coming to the good, but because something else that is stronger stands over it, it is enslaved to that and led away from its own goods. For that is why slavery is also | censured, not when one has no power to go to the bad, but when one has no power to advance to one's own good but is led away to the good of another.

Now to speak of slavery to one's own nature makes two things, one that is enslaved and another that to which it is enslaved. But how could a simple nature and a single activity—| when one part is potential and one part actual—not be free? For it could not be said to be active by nature, as if its substance were one thing and its activity another, if being and acting there are the same thing. If then the activity is neither because of another nor in the power of another, how is it not free? And if "being in its own power" is inapplicable, but | is in this case something greater than being in its power, it is still in its own power because it is not in the power of another nor is another the master of its activity, nor even master of its substance, if it is an originative principle. And if intellect has another originative principle, it is not outside it, but it is *in* the Good. And if it is | in accordance with that Good, it is much more in its own power and free, since one seeks freedom and being in one's own power for the sake of the Good. So if it acts in accordance with the Good, it would be even more in its own power; for it already has in itself too the object of its vision toward which it is directed and from which it has come, which is better for it to be in it, | if indeed it is directed to it [the Good].

5. Are then self-determination and being in one's own power in intellect alone when it thinks and in an intellect that is pure, or is it also in soul when it acts in accordance with intellect and engages in practical action in accordance with virtue? Now if we grant this to the soul in its practical action, first we need not | grant it to the accomplishment of the action, for we are not masters of the outcome. But if this refers to doing well and doing everything from oneself, perhaps one might rightly claim this.

But how is that in our power, if, for example, we were brave because of war? I mean, how is the activity then in our power, when—if no war occurs—this activity wouldn't | be carried out? But it's the same way with all the other actions in accordance with virtue, since when faced with contingencies, virtue is always being compelled to do this or that. For if one gave virtue itself a choice whether, in order to be active, it would prefer that there be wars so as to be brave, and that there should be injustice so as to | define what is just and set things in order, and poverty so as to show liberality, or, if all were well, to lead a life of restful quiet, it would choose to rest quietly from its deeds since nothing needed its curative service, as if a physician like Hippocrates were to wish that no one | needed his skill.

If then, when it is active in practical deeds, virtue is compelled to be helpful, how would things be purely in its power? Would we then say that its actions are compelled, while the will and reason that precede the actions are not compelled? But if so, when we place these only in what comes | before that which is done, we will put self-determination and what depends on virtue itself outside the action.

And what of virtue itself which operates in accordance with habit and disposition? Will we say that when the soul is in a bad state, it comes into order by bringing its passions and desires | into measured balance? In what way do we say that being good is in our power and "virtue has no master"? Yes indeed, this is so for those who will it and choose it! Or that when (virtue) comes to be, it establishes freedom and being in our own power and no longer allows us to be slaves to that to which we were previously enslaved?

If therefore virtue is | another intellect, as it were, and a habit that so to speak makes the soul become intellectualized, then again, being in our power is not in the realm of action, but rather in an intellect quietly at rest from actions.

6. So how did we previously refer this to will when we said “what would happen to the extent that it was willed”? There it was also said “or would not happen.” So if what was just now said is correct, and what was said before agrees with this, we shall say | that virtue and intellect have mastery, and one must refer being in one’s power and freedom to them; and since these things are without a master, it (intellect) is self-dependent, and virtue wills to be self-dependent, overseeing the soul to make it good and—up to this point—to be free | and render the soul free. But when compulsive passions and actions assail it, although the soul has not *willed* these things to happen, nevertheless even in these cases, the soul maintains its self-dependence by referring back to itself even here. For it will not follow the lead of the circumstances—for | example, rescuing one in danger—but if it seems good to the soul, it will abandon this particular person and command him to give up his life and property and children and even his country, having as its goal its own beauty

but not the existence of what is subject to it. So that both self-determination in practical actions and what is in | our power is referred neither to practical action nor to the external activity, but to the inner activity, namely, the thinking and contemplation of virtue itself. But we must say that this virtue is a certain intellect not counted along with the passions that are enslaved or measured by reason, for these he (Plato) says, "cleave | to the body," regulated "by custom and practice."

So it is clearer that what is free is that which is immaterial, and that it is this to which being in our power is to be referred, namely, the will itself that is master and self-dependent, even if something directs it to what is outside because of necessity. Everything therefore that comes from and | because of this will is in our power—both everything external and everything self-dependent; what it wills and actualizes without hindrance, *this too is primarily in* our power.

Now it is the contemplative, primary *intellect* that is thus in its own power, since its work depends not at all on another, but is entirely turned to itself and its work is itself and it lies in the | Good, without need, fulfilled, and living, as it were, according to its will. And its will is thinking, but it was called "will," because it was so-minded (in accord with intellect), for what is called will imitates what accords with its mind (intellect). For will *wants* the Good, but thinking is truly *in* the Good. So that intellect has

| what its will wants, and when it attains this, it becomes thinking. So if we ascribe being in our power to the will of the Good, who is already established in what its will wishes to be, how does it not have what is in its power? Or we must suppose it to be greater, if one is unwilling to refer being in its power | to this.

7. Soul then becomes free when it hastens unhindered to the Good through intellect, and what it does because of this is in its power. But intellect does this through itself, and the nature of the Good is itself the object of its desire and is that through which the others have what is in | their power, when the one is able to attain it without hindrance and the other to have it.

As for the very master of all the worthy things that come after it—the one that occupies the first seat, toward which the others wish to ascend and depend upon and have their powers from it so they can have what is in their power—how could one reduce it to what is in | your and my power, to which even intellect was only just dragged, albeit by violence?

Unless some rash account originating from a different viewpoint would claim that: "since (the Good) happens to be as it is and since it is not master of what it is and does not have its being what it is from itself, it would not have freedom, nor would its doing or not doing | what it is compelled to do or not do be in its power."

This argument is contrary to our own view and would lead to an impasse and would altogether destroy the nature of free will and self-determination and the notion of what is in our power, so that to say these things is *empty* and just sounds about non-existent things. | For to make a sound like this not only means nothing is in anyone's power, but for one to talk like this is necessarily neither to think nor to understand. But if he did admit that he understood it, he would already be easily refuted, since the notion of what is in our power is fitted to things that he said do not fit. For the notion does not busy itself with the substantial beings nor in addition | does it grasp the substance—for it is impossible for something to make itself and bring itself into reality—but reflection wants to contemplate what, among real things that actually exist, is slave to others, and what has self-determination and what is not subject to another, but is itself master of its activity, which purely pertains to eternal beings insofar as they are | eternal and to the beings pursuing or having the good without hindrance.

Since the Good itself is indeed beyond all these, it is absurd to seek some other kind of good apart from it. Then it is also incorrect to say that it exists by chance, for chance applies to things later than it and to multiplicities. But we would say that the | First is neither by chance nor is not master of its own coming to be, because it hasn't come to be.

And the claim that it does "as it is" is absurd if one claims that it is free whenever it does something or acts against its nature. Nor indeed does its uniqueness take away its freedom if it has this uniqueness, not by being hindered by something | else, but by being this itself and so to speak pleased with itself and not having anything else greater than itself, or else one will in this way take away self-determination from what attains the good. And if this is absurd, it would be even more absurd to deprive the Good itself of self-determination just because it is good and remains self-dependent with no | need of moving toward something else, since the others move toward it while it needs nothing. But when its so-to-speak "reality" is its so-to-speak "activity"—for these don't differ from one another if it is not even so with intellect, whose activity accords more with its being than its being with its activity—so that it doesn't act as it | naturally does, nor will its activity and its life, as it were, be referred to its so-to-speak substance, but its something-like-substance is together with it and so to speak comes to be from eternity together with its activity and it makes itself from both, both for itself and from nothing.

8. But we look upon self-determination not as accidental to that Good, but self-determination itself in relation to itself by taking away the opposites from the self-determinations in the case of the others. We might say these things about

it, transferring to it lesser attributes from lesser things in our inability | to hit upon what is appropriate to say about it.

And yet we would find nothing to say that applies to it, let alone to speak strictly about it, since *all beautiful* and majestic things are later than that, for it is itself the originative principle of these, and yet in another way not an originative principle. For to those who put away all things, | even "being in its power" is later, as is self-determination; for already one speaks of an activity directed toward another and says that it is unhindered and that while others exist its activity toward them is unimpeded.

But we must say he is altogether unrelated to anything, for he is what he is even before them, since we take away even the | "he is" and so too any relation whatsoever to real beings; nor is there any "as he naturally is," for this too is later; even if this were said about those beings, it would be said about those that derive from another and so it is primarily about substantial being because it grew out of him, and, if nature (or growth) applies to things in time, it does not apply to substantial being.

Nor must one even say "it is not from itself," since | we take away the "to be," and "not from itself" would imply the agency of another.

So did it then just happen to be? No—no "happened to be" is admissible, for nothing happens to it or is directed to something else. "Happened to be" applies to many things when they exist and then something happens to them. How did the First happen to be? For | it did not "come" such that you could ask "how then did it come? What chance brought it or established it in existence?" since there was as yet no chance or spontaneity, for spontaneity derives from another and is found among generated things.

9. But if one should take "happened to be" as applying to the Good, one can't stop with the mere word but must understand what the speaker is thinking. What then is he thinking? That, having this nature and power, it is an originative principle, for if it had another originative principle, it would have been what | it was, and, if worse, it would have acted according to its own substantial being.

To this line of thinking we must reply that it is not possible for it, being the originative principle of all, to be what chanced to be—not that it is worse, nor even good, but good in another, as it were, lesser way. But the originative principle must be better than everything that comes after it, so that it is something | defined—I mean by defined that it exists uniquely and not out of necessity, since there was no necessity. For necessity inheres in things that follow the originative principle and even in these has no prevailing force, but this uniqueness is self-derived. So it is this and not something else, but what it must be. Therefore, it didn't just happen this way, | but had to be this way; and this "had to be" is originative principle of all that had to be.

Nor therefore could this be so as just having happened, for it is not what it chanced to be, but what must be. Rather, not what must be, but others have to wait until the king appears to them, and affirm that he is what he himself is, not appearing as he | happened to be, but as really king and really principle and really the Good, not just acting according to the Good—for he would thus seem to follow something else—but by being one, just what he is, so that he is not *in accord* with that, but *is* that. So even if "happened to be" doesn't apply to being—for if anything is to happen, it happens *to* | being, but being *itself* does not happen nor does "being like this" happen to be, nor does it derive its being like this from something else, but its nature is to be really being—how could one infer about that which is beyond being that it happened to *be* like this—that to which it belongs to have engendered being, which didn't just happen to be like this, but *is* | as its substantial being is, being what substantial being is and what Intellect is?

For in this way one might say that Intellect "just happened in this way to be Intellect" as if Intellect were going to be anything other than what the nature of Intellect is. Indeed that which does not deviate from itself but belongs unswervingly to itself, one would say is most master of | what it is. What would one say who ascended There and looked toward what is above this? That it *happened* to be as one saw it to be? No, it didn't happen to be in this or that way, rather it didn't happen *at all.* But what about "only in this way" and not otherwise, but "in *this* way"? But not "in this way"; for you would thereby define it as a definite individual, but | one who sees it can't say "in this way" or again "not in this way," for you would be saying it was one of the beings to which "in this way" applies, and then it is something else beside all the things that are "in this way."

But since you see it as indeterminate, you'll be able to speak of all that comes after it and affirm that it is none of those, but if it is | anything, it is total power of real self-mastery; it is this that it wills to be, and more so throwing off what it wills to be to the beings; itself greater than all willing, it sets willing after itself. So it did not then will the "in this way" so as to follow it, nor did another make it this way.

10. Now we must also question one who says "it happened to be like this." How would he evaluate that the "happened to be" was false, if there were something? And how would someone exclude "happened to be"? And if there were a nature, will he then say "happened to be" doesn't fit? For if he ascribes | to chance the removal of "happened to be" from other things, wherever would what is not by chance occur? But this originative principle takes away the "as it

chanced" from other things by giving them form, limit, and shape, and, among things generated according to formative principle, it is not possible to ascribe the cause to chance, but rather to make this very point, to ascribe the cause to formative principle, while | chance is in things that happen, not by antecedent and consequential causality, but by coincidences. But as for the originative principle of all formative principle and order and limit—how could anyone ascribe its reality to chance?

Chance is indeed mistress of many things, but not mistress of intellect, formative principle, and order in generation. In cases where chance seems to | be opposite to formative principle, how could it be generator of formative principle? So if chance doesn't generate Intellect, so too for what is prior to and better than Intellect, for it had no "whence" to generate from, nor was it at all in any way among the eternal beings. So if nothing is before That, but he is first, one must stop here and say nothing more about it, but inquire | how the things *after* it came to be, no longer how *it* came to be, because *this* really did not come to be.

What then if it did not come to be and is as it is without being master of its own substantial being? And if it is not master of its substantial being—but is what it is, not having brought itself into existence, but making use of itself as it is—it would necessarily be what it is and not | otherwise. No; not because it couldn't be otherwise, but because being like this *is* the best. For not everything has the self-determination to go toward the better, but nothing is prevented by another from going toward the worse. But that it did not go, did not depart from itself, is due, not to its being hindered, but to | its being itself that which did not depart. And the inability to go to the worse doesn't signify a powerlessness of what doesn't go, but its not going is from and through itself. And not to go to anything else signifies that it has the excess of power in itself, a self not constrained by necessity, but one which is itself necessity and law for | the others.

So did necessity bring itself into existence? No, it did not bring itself into existence; the other things after it came to exist because of it. Therefore, how could that which is prior to reality come into existence by the agency either of another or of itself?

11. But what is this that didn't come into existence? We must go away in silence and, acknowledging that we are at a mental loss, seek no longer. For why would one even inquire, having nothing further to go to, since every inquiry goes toward an originative principle and stops there? Moreover, one | must accept that every inquiry concerns what, or of what kind something is, or why or if something exists.

Now being, as we say it to be, is (known) from things that come after it. The question "why" seeks another originative principle, but there is no originative principle of the originative principle of everything. And to inquire what *kind* of thing something | is is to attribute something to what has no attributes. And the question "what is it" makes it clear that we must make no inquiry about it, that we should grasp it alone in intellect insofar as we can, in learning that it is not legitimate for us to attach anything to it.

Generally, we who reflect upon this nature seem to approach this puzzle by inferring a space and | place as some yawning gulf, and then, with a space already preexisting, we introduce this nature into an imagined or actual place, and, introducing it into this sort of place, just go on to seek, as it were, whence and how it has come there. Treating it as an interloper, we inquire of its presence and, as it were, its | substantial being, as if it were thrown here from some depth or some height.

Therefore one must eliminate the cause of the puzzle by excluding from our attention to it all place, and not put it in any place whatsoever, either as always lying in it | or being seated in it or having come into it, but as being solely as it is, saying—this is said by necessity of discourse—that place, like everything else, is later (than the Good) and later than everything.

So when we think as we do that this is placeless, and no longer circumscribe it with a circle, as it were, or can comprehend | its extent, we will not at all attribute extent to it, and certainly not quality, for there could not be any shape—even intelligible—around it, nor attribute to it any relation to another, for it exists as self-dependent before anything else.

So what further could the phrase "it happened to be this way" mean? Or how would we express this, since everything else said | about this is said by abstraction of attributes? So that it is more true to say "it did not happen to be in this way" than to say "it happened to be in this way," when in fact it did not even "happen" at all.

12. What then? Isn't he what he is? And is he himself master of his being what he is, or of his being beyond being? For again the soul, not at all persuaded by what has been said, is puzzled. So one must reply to these issues that each of us is far from substantial being in respect of the | body, but in respect of the soul and what we most are, we participate in substantial being and are a particular substantial being, and this is, a compound, as it were, of difference and substantial being. So we are neither substantial being in the strict sense nor substantial being just in itself, and so we are not masters of our own substantial being. For somehow substantial being is one thing and we | another, and we are not masters of our own substantial being; rather substantial being itself is master of us, since it is this also that adds the difference. But since in some respect we are what has mastery of us,

to that extent even here below we can be said no less to be masters of ourselves.

But where substantial being just itself is completely what it is, and its identity is not one thing and | its substantial being another, it is also master of this and no longer related to something else insofar as it *is* and insofar as it is substantial being. For again it has been set free for self-mastery insofar as it is what is first in relation to substantial being.

Now That which has made substantial being free is clearly of a nature to make free and would be called freemaker. To what might he | be a slave (if it is at all legitimate to speak thus)? To his own substantial being? But this freedom derives from him and is later than him, and it possesses no substantial being. So if there is some activity in him and we place him in the activity, he wouldn't therefore be other than himself and would not himself be his own master as author of the activity, | since he himself is none other than activity. But if we will not at all grant that there is activity in him, but that other things possess their reality by being active around him, then we will refuse even more in this case to grant mastery or being mastered.

But we didn't even grant "self-mastery," not because another is his master, but | because we gave self-mastery to substantial being, but placed him in greater honor than this.

So what would we place in more honor than what is its own master? It is because, since substantial being and activity are in this case somehow two items, and gave from the activity the notion of mastery, but this was the same as substantial being, for this reason what it means to be master came to be separate | (from the activity) and was said to be master of itself. But where there are not two as one, but just one—either activity alone or no activity at all—the term "self-mastery" is inappropriate.

13. But if one must incorrectly introduce these terms for what we seek, let it be repeated that some things (thus far) have been said correctly because we ought not to make it two, not even for the purpose of reflection, whereas we must in what we are now going to say deviate from proper thought for | the sake of persuasion.

For if we were to ascribe activities to him, attributing the activities, as it were, to his will—for he doesn't act without willing—and the activities, his putative substantial being, (then) his will and substantial being are the same. And if so, then as he willed, so also he is. It would be no more true (to say) that he wills and acts according to his | nature than that his substantial being is as he wills and acts. Therefore he is completely master of himself by having his existence also in his power.

Note this too: every being desiring the Good wishes to be that Good rather than what it (already) is, and thinks that it exists most of all when it participates in the Good, and in such a state each one will choose for itself to exist insofar as it has existence from the Good, since clearly the nature of the Good is for itself a much greater priority of choice, if whatever portion of the Good that is most to be chosen by another becomes its voluntary substantial being supported by its will, and is one and the same with its will and is established through its will. | And as long as each one did not possess the Good, it wanted something else, but when it had it, it already wants itself, and this sort of presence is neither by chance nor is its substantial being outside its will, and it is by this (the Good) that its substantial being is defined and is by this that it belongs to itself.

So if it is by this that each thing makes itself something, it doubtlessly | becomes clear that it (the Good) is primarily what it is by itself and is that by which other things exist by their own selves, and that the will to be such as he is goes together with his as it were substantial being and that he is not apprehensible without his own willing to be by himself what he is, and his willing to be himself by his own | agency is concurrent with his being what he wills, and he and his will are one and no less one by the fact that he is neither one thing that happened to be, nor another thing that he would have wanted to be. For what would he have wanted to be other than what he is? For even if we supposed he could choose to become what he willed and | were able to change his own nature into another, he wouldn't want to become something else or find some fault with himself as though he is what he is by necessity, this "being himself" which he always willed and wills. For the nature of the Good is really his will, neither corrupted nor attracted to its own nature, but choosing | itself, since there was nothing else to which it could be attracted.

And one might also say that not any one among other things contains in its being the reason (formative principle) for being satisfied with itself, for it might even dislike itself. Now in the reality of the Good, it is necessary that choice and self-will be included, or it would hardly be possible | for anything else to have leisure to be pleased with itself; such things are pleased with themselves either by participation in or imagination of the Good.

But one must agree to these terms if, in speaking of that Good, one necessarily uses for the sake of illustration terms that we don't precisely allow to be spoken. Let one take each | such term with an "as it were."

Given the reality of the Good and its coexistence with choice and will—for without these it will not be—and granted that the Good must not be multiple, its will and substantial being [and its willing] must be united, but <if> its willing derives from itself, it is necessary that its being is also from itself, so that | our account has discovered that it has made itself. For if his will is self-derived and as it were his own work, and this will is the same as his reality, then in this way he would be self-constituted, so that he is not what he happened to be, but he is what he himself willed to be.

14. And furthermore, one must see it also in this way: each of the things said to exist is either the same as its existence or different, as for instance this particular human being is one thing and being human another; of course, the human being participates in what it is to be | a human being. <And soul and what it is to be soul> are the same thing if soul is simple and not a thing predicated of something else, and a human as such is also the same as what it is to be a human being. Now one might chance to become a human being insofar as it is different from essential humanity, but essential humanity could not come to be by chance: and this means "humanity as such | is self derived."

So if essential humanity comes from itself and this is not by chance or contingency, how could what is above humanity itself and is the generator of humanity itself and source of all real beings be said to be by chance, a nature simpler than essential humanity and all being in general? Besides, as one approaches the simple, | chance is not brought along, so it is impossible that chance ascend to the simplest of all.

Moreover, it is appropriate to remember what has already been said somewhere, that each of the things that truly are have come into reality also by virtue of that nature, and if anything among sensible things is such (as it is), it is such | by virtue of derivation from those realities. By "such" I mean to include in their substantial being also the cause of their reality, so that the one who later beholds each thing can say the reason why for each of its constituents, for instance, why the eye and feet of such beings are as they are, and that the cause co-originating each part belongs to each | and causes the parts to exist because of one another. Why are legs and feet of such a length? Because this is as it is and because the face and legs and feet are of such a kinds. And in general the symphony of all (the parts) with one another is the cause of each, and the reason why for each is that this is what it means to be a human being, so that its very existence and its cause are one and the same. | And in this way these are both derived from a single source that didn't deliberate but provides both the "why" and the existence as a complete whole. So it is the source of being and the "why" of being, giving both at once, but, like things that come to be, that from which they derive is much more archetypal and true and more closely related | to what is better than they are.

So if there is nothing random or by chance and no "it happened to be like this" among things that have their cause in themselves as well as all that derives from him—for he is <Father> of formative principle and <cause> and causative being—indeed all of these things far from chance—he would be originative principle and as it were a paradigm of whatever has | no share in chance, really and primarily uncontaminated by chance and spontaneity and coincidence, cause of himself, and being himself from and through himself, for he is primarily and transcendently himself.

15. And he himself is loveable and love and self-love insofar as he is beautiful only from and in himself. For even his communion with himself could not be otherwise than if the conjoiner and the conjoined were one and the same. And if conjoiner is one with | the conjoined, and what so to speak desires is one with the desired, and what is desired is in accord with existence and a sort of substrate, it again appears to us that desire and being are the same. But if so, it is again he himself who makes himself and is master of himself and hasn't come to be as something else willed, | but as he himself wills.

Moreover, when we say that he doesn't receive anything into himself nor does another thing receive him, even by this we would put such a thing outside chance existence, not only by making him alone and pure of all things, but because, if sometimes we too see in ourselves such a nature that has | nothing in common with other things connected to us, so as to experience whatever might happen by chance—for all other things that pertain to us are enslaved to and at the mercy of fortune and approach us as by chance—it is only by this that one has self-mastery and self-determination, through an activity of a <well-formed> and | good light even superior to that of Intellect, whose superiority to Intellect is not extraneous.

Indeed, when we ascend to and become this alone, abandoning the rest, what can we say of it except that we are more than free and more than self-determining? Who would then constrain us by chances or randomness or happenstance when we have | become, or have come to be in, the true life itself, which has nothing else, but is itself alone?

For the other things, when isolated, do not have the autonomy to exist, but This is what it is even while isolated. But the first existence is not in a condition of soullessness or of irrational life, for such an existence is too weak to exist, a dispersion of formative principle | and an indefiniteness. But so far as it advances toward formative principle, it leaves chance behind, for what is in accord with a formative principle isn't by chance. But for us, as we ascend, That is not formative principle but more beautiful than formative principle, so distant is it from happening by chance. For it is from itself the root of formative principle and all things terminate in it, like the origin and basis of a very great | tree living according to formative principle, itself remaining self-dependent but granting existence to the tree according to the formative principle it has received.

16. But since we say—and so it seems—that this is everywhere and again nowhere, we must reflect upon this and, looking from this point of view, think out what one must posit about the subjects of our inquiry.

For if he is nowhere, he hasn't happened to be anywhere, and | if everywhere, he is as much as he is at every point, so that he *is* the "everywhere" and the "in every way," not that he is *in* that everywhere, but that he *is* this himself, and in this "everywhere" he gives existence to the others lying alongside him. But since he has the highest rank—or rather doesn't *have* it but *is* himself the highest—he has all | things as slaves; he is not contingent for them, but they are for him, or rather they surround him who does not look to them but they to him.

But he as it were tends toward his interior, loving himself so to speak—the "pure radiance"— being himself what he loves, and this is his self-constitution, if indeed he is enduring activity and | the supremely beloved, rather like Intellect. And Intellect is an actualization, so that he is an actualization, but not of anything else, so he is his own actualization. Therefore he is not as he happens to be, but as he acts.

Moreover, then, if he exists principally because he is so to speak fixed upon himself | and looks toward himself, and his sort of existence consists in looking toward himself, he would as it were make himself, not as he chanced to be but as he wills; and his will is neither random nor has it happened to be, for being the will of the best, it is not random.

But that such an inclination of himself to himself—being as it were his | activity and his remaining in himself—makes his being what he is, is confirmed by positing the opposite, since, if he were inclined to his exterior, he would annihilate his being what he is; so his being-what-he-is is his self-directed activity, but this is one and the same with himself.

Therefore he brought himself into existence, his | activity having been linked with himself. So if he didn't come into being, but his activity always was and was like an awakening when the awakener was not something else—an awakening and an intelligizing transcending thought that is eternal—then he is as he awakened himself to be. And his awakening is <beyond being> and Intellect and | <intelligent life>, but these things are he himself. He is thus activity above intellect and thought and life, and these are from him and not from another. His existence then comes by and from himself. Thus, he is not as he happened to be, but as he himself willed to be.

17. And still another viewpoint: We say that each thing in the universe and this universe are as the maker's choice willed it, and is maintained as if he, proceeding and foreseeing by reasoning things through, would have fashioned it according to providence. But | since things (here) are always like this and always come to be like this, so too their formative principles always rest among coexisting things that stand in a better order, so that there too (in Intellect), things transcend providence and transcend choice, and all things in real being exist evermore in intelligible stability.

So if one calls this arrangement of | things providence, then let him realize that Intellect stands before this All—this All which is from and according to Intellect. So if Intellect is before all things and such an Intellect is an origin, it would not be as it chanced to be; although multiple, it is concordant with itself as though organized into a unity. For this multitude and ordered | multiplicity, as well as all formative principles contained in a unity throughout the universe, is not as it chanced and happened to be, but is far from and opposed to such a nature, as much as chance, embedded in irrationality, is contrary to reason (or formative principle).

But if what is prior to such a thing (Intellect) is an origin, it clearly borders on this that has been rationally formed. And | this that is spoken of in this way accords with and participates in that Principle and is as it wills and is its power.

Therefore that Principle is dimensionless, one formative principle <for> all things, one number, and a One that is greater and more powerful than what has come into being, and nothing is greater or better than him. He has | neither his existence nor being what he is from another. He is thus by himself what he is, related and directed to himself so as not to be related to anything external or to anything else, but totally self-related.

18. And as you seek, seek nothing outside him, but seek within him all things that come after him, but let him be. For he is himself the outside, the comprehension and measure of all things. In depth, he is inside, while his outside, touching and stretched around him like | a circle, is all formative principle and Intellect, or rather would be Intellect insofar as it touches him and in the way it touches and depends on him insofar as it has from him its being Intellect.

Thus just as a circle <that> would touch its center round about might be agreed to have its power from the center and be as it were centriform | insofar as the radii in the circle, converging into a single center, direct their extremity towards the center to which they are, so to speak, led and from which they, as it were, sprout forth. The center is superior to the radii and to their extremities—the circumferential points of the radii themselves—and they are, so to speak, that (center), but they are also | dim traces of that (center) which enables them by enabling the radii that impinge upon it at every point. And what that (center) is is revealed through the radii, unfolded as it were without being unfolded.

Thus it is that one must apprehend Intellect and Being, having come to be from That and, as it were, | poured out, unfolded and suspended, attesting from its own intelligent nature that there is a sort of intellect-in-unity that is not Intellect because it is one. Just as the center there is neither the radii nor the circle, but is the father of the circle and the radii, giving traces of itself and with abiding power generating the radii and circle | not at any point detached from it by some (inner) force.

So it is also the case with That; the intellectual power moving around it as if it were the archetype of its image, an intellect-in-unity so to speak, conquered into multiplicity and because of this having become Intellect, while That remains before Intellect and <from> its own power has generated Intellect. What | chance concurrence—or spontaneity or happenstance!—could approach such an intelligence-creating and truly creative power? For in That One there is, so to speak, something like what is in Intellect, although in many ways greater, like a light dispersed from some single entity translucent in itself. What | is dispersed is an image, but that from which it derives is the True. The dispersed image—Intellect—is not at all an alien form, a happenstance; rather each individual part of it is formative principle and cause, but That is cause of the cause. So in a superior way he is as it were the most causative and truest cause, possessing all together | the intellectual causes about to emerge from him, and generative—not of what is as it chanced to be—but is as he himself willed. And his will is not irrational or random or as it "turned out" for him, but as it had to be, since nothing There is random.

Whence Plato spoke of <"what needs to be and the timely moment">, desiring to indicate that, | far from being "as it chanced to be," what it is *is* what is needed. And if it is appropriate, this is not irrational and, if timely, it has the most absolute mastery among the things that come after it and it has inherent priority, and is not what it, as it were, chanced to be, but as it so to speak *wished* to be, since he wills what needs to | be; and what needs to be and the activity of what needs to be are one. And needful is not like a substrate, but is like a primary activity manifesting itself as what it needs to be. For one must speak of him in this way since one is unable to speak of him as one would wish.

19. Roused up from what has been said toward That, let one accept That himself, and he too shall see—although unable to say—all that he wishes. But seeing that

That in himself, having abandoned every formative principle he will posit that That is from himself what | he is, such that—if he had substantial being—his substantial being would be his slave and be as if derived from him.

Nor would anyone seeing him still dare to say the "as it happened to be," nor would he be able to utter anything at all, for he would be astounded at his rashness. Nor, in his rapid flight, could he say about him "where" he is at all, since he appears to him | everywhere, as if before the eyes of the soul, and wherever one directs one's gaze, he sees That, unless, abandoning the god, he should gaze elsewhere, no longer thinking about him.

And likewise, one ought to know that it was in this way that the phrase "beyond substantial being" was mentioned by the ancients, in the form of a riddle not only that he generates substantial being, but that | he is enslaved neither to substantial being nor to himself, nor is his substantial being his originative principle. Rather he, being originative Principle of substantial being, did not make substantial being for himself but, having made it, left it outside himself, since he who made it has no need of existence, nor again does he make the "it is" | in accord with his existence.

20. What then? Might one say "Doesn't he *happen* to be before he *came* to be? For if he makes himself, in respect to *himself*, he does not yet exist, but in respect to the

making, he is already prior to himself since what is made is he himself." We must reply to such a claim that | he is not at all to be classified as product but as producer, by positing that his self-production is unconditioned, not in order that something else be completed by his making, since his activity is not the completion of something else, but is entirely him, for there are not two but one.

For we must not be afraid of positing that the first activity | is without substantial being; rather we must posit this very thing as his so-to-speak existence. And if one posited an existence without activity, the most perfect originative principle of all would be defective and imperfect. And if one adds activity, one does not preserve unity. So if activity is more perfect than being, and the most perfect | is the first, activity would be first.

So having acted, he is already this and he cannot be what he was before he came to be, for then he was not before he came to be, but already entirely was.

Indeed an activity not enslaved to substantial being is purely free, and thus he is himself from himself. For if he were kept in being by | another, he wouldn't be first from himself, and if he is rightly said to contain himself, he is himself, even the one who introduces himself forward, since what he contains by nature is what from the beginning he has made to exist. So then, if there were a time when he began to be, the phrase "he has made" would be most properly said; but now, if he were what |

he is before eternity was, let this phrase "he has made himself" be understood to mean the concurrence of the "having made" with his own self, for the being is one with the making and is, as it were, an eternal generation.

Whence there is also the notion of "ruling himself'; and if there are two, this is properly so, but if one, (then only) the "ruling," for he has nothing that | is ruled. How then to say "ruling" when there is nothing ruled? "Ruling" here pertains to what is before him, but there was nothing before him. And if there was nothing, he is First, and he is such, not in rank, but in mastery and purely self-determining power. And if he is purely so, it is impossible to grasp in that case what is not self-determining There. So in himself he is | wholly self-determining. Then what is there of him that is not himself? What is there that does not act, that isn't his work? For were there anything in him not his work, he would be neither purely autonomous nor omnipotent, neither master of that nor omnipotent, that is, he would have no power over that of whose making he is not master.

21. So could he have made himself something other than what he did make? Otherwise, we will not yet eliminate his making the good because he is incapable of making evil. For There, the ability to make isn't to make contraries but to make with unshakeable | and immoveable power, the superlative power, since it does not depart

from being one; for to be capable of contraries means lack of capability to remain with the best.

But his making of which we speak must be once for all, for it is beautiful. And who would alter something that has come to be by God's will and *is* his will? | By a will of something that doesn't yet exist? And what would be the will of That if he is without will in his very existence? Whence would a will accrue to him from a substantial being without activity? His will was in his substantial being, and there is nothing other than his substantial being. Or what was he that was not, so to speak, will? So he was entirely | will and there is nothing in him that does not will, nor anything prior to will. So he is first of all will.

And when we say that he willed, and speak about the way he willed, and what results from his will, what such a will generated—and it generated nothing further in himself—all this he already was.

And his containing | himself is to be understood, if one were to express it rightly, such that all else that exists is contained by him, since they exist by a certain participation in him and they all lead back to him. And from himself he has no need of containing or participation, but he is all things by himself, or rather none of them, since he doesn't | need all things to be himself.

But when you speak or think of him, abandon all other things. Abandoning all things and leaving him alone, don't seek anything you might add, lest there be something in your thought that you haven't abandoned. For even you can touch upon something else about which it is | no longer possible to speak or apprehend. Rather only this that is truly free lies far above, since it is not enslaved to itself, but is only itself and really itself, while each of the others is itself and something else.

Commentary

The Title

There are two versions of the title of our treatise. One appears in Chapter 5 of the *Life of Plotinus* as *peri tou hekousiou* ("on free will/the voluntary") and the other in Chapter 26 as *peri tou hekousiou kai thelematos tou henos*, which may be construed in two ways: "on free will and the will of the One" or "on the voluntary and the will of the One." We prefer the second, "on the voluntary and on the will of the One," primarily because the term *hekousion* is only once applied to the One (at Chapter 13, 18) and appears otherwise only in relation to human freedom in the first part of the treatise. However, the term *thelema* is also never used of the One by Plotinus, who prefers *thelēsis*. This indicates, as Leroux and Lavaud note, that the title comes from Porphyry, not Plotinus.

On the other hand, one might argue that Porphyry's title "on the voluntary and the will of the One" is as good as the title that has become customary, since it emphasizes in a down-to-earth way a real continuity between free human and divine willing. And, in fact, Plotinus makes this connection himself between human and divine *voluntary* activity, and, by implication, shows its primary applicability to the Good's free will in Chapter 13. Since VI.8 is a work about active freedom, we emphasize this in translating *thelema* in the title: "On the Voluntary and on the Free Will of the One."

How to Read this Commentary

VI.8 is an important but difficult work. To make it more accessible, we use headings adapted from our detailed outline in the Introduction. Each chapter in the commentary starts with an overall description that we put in both bold and italics. This is followed by sub-headings in bold. Then each item of commentary has the chapter and line numbers in bold (e.g. **1, 1–11**) followed by a portion of the text or headline (on occasion) to be discussed in italics before our actual commentary. We occasionally add Excurses with bold heading in an appropriate context to explain important terminology or to give a brief explanation of complex ideas as at **1, 15–16** (terminology); **3, 1–20** (terminology); **4, 24–28** (substantial being); **8, 25–27** (order, chance and spontaneity). Sometimes, we abbreviate the text in italics to be discussed to a few phrases, but sometimes we give a larger portion of the text and occasionally the whole text where we judge that the reader needs to have both to make sense of a difficult passage.

The Problem and Context

VI.8 [39] examines the nature and source of real agency in human beings, Intellect and, ultimately, the One or Good.

For Plotinus' earlier thinking about freedom in IV.8 [6], IV.3 [27], IV.4 [28], see Charrue, 2013; and for commentary on VI.8 or related questions see Benz, 1932; Rist, 1967, 130–138; Cilento, 1971 and 1973, 97–122; Westra, 1990; Leroux, 1990, and 1996, 292–314; Gerson, 1994, 155–163; Beierwaltes, 2001, 125–59; Lavaud, 2007 and 2012, 11–25; Horn, 2007; Collette-Dučić, 2014, 421–436; Corrigan, 2015, 131–149. On the vexed question of the discovery and history of the will see Dihle, 1982; Frede, 2011; for other references, Horn, 2008, 153n1–2. For a useful discussion on the nature of Platonism, see Gerson, 2013a, and for Neoplatonism generally, see Wallis, 1995.

As we suggested in the Introduction, freedom and agency became a real problem for Plotinus for many reasons: First, Jewish and Christian writings (and many Gnostic texts that will figure prominently in this work) describe a God who acts, gets angry, forgives and loves. In short, this is a God who does many real things, who intervenes in human history. By contrast, the Neoplatonic hypostases—Soul, Intellect, and the One or the Good—do not *do* anything. Action or *praxis* is specifically denied of them. What they make or produce is not at all like human production or making either, but is achieved only by the power of contemplation, as we see in III.8 [30]. So the question emerges with some force: are the

Neoplatonic spiritual principles really agents at all and in what sense could they be agents in any meaningful way that would successfully compete with the direct entry of God into history as in the Bible?

Second, Plato himself represents the Demiurge in the *Timaeus* as actually doing things. The Demiurge or Craftsman is the principal cause of order in the cosmos. He frames the World Soul and the World's body, but unlike the Creator God of the bible, he does not create but only brings order and geometrical form to precosmic disorder, for which he is not responsible, and in this way he makes a cosmos. Timaeus, who tells the tale, represents the Demiurge (a "likely story" as he famously puts it) as deliberating, framing, ordering, etc. However, against such anthropomorphic representation, Aristotle had insisted that his God, the Unmoved Mover, is a "thinking of thinking" not a thinking of doing or making—Aristotle's Unmoved Mover is a principle that moves only by being loved. Final causality, not efficient causality, is what appears to move the world. God moves not by doing, deliberating, loving, but by being loved. Furthermore, in VI.7 [38], the treatise written immediately before VI.8, Plotinus himself rejects any need for deliberation or action, that is, for any *praxis*, in the making of the universe. Instead, he argues that Plato cannot mean that the Demiurge actually reasons or deliberates, because such a representation of rationality in any form of creation would be a *defect*, not an achievement. Reasoning is necessary to work things out after the fact; but understanding grasps reality all at once without the need for deliberation (cf. VI.7 [38] 1–11 and V.8 [31] 6–7). If divine activity cannot be in any sense defective or incomplete (that is, demiurgic creation cannot be an Aristotelian incomplete motion, as Numenius had appeared to claim—Numenius fr. 12: the demiurgic God rules "as he goes through the heavens"), then it must be "whole and entire" and "in anything of those things that belong to the divine everything must inhere" so that we can unfold it later in temporal succession as a "this after this" (1, 45–55). In other words, the sensible universe eternally comes-to-be without deliberation or reasoning out of the perfect world of the divine Intellect.

However interesting or powerful Plotinus' solution to the anthropomorphic problem may be, he is left with one problem: the possibility of free agency seems altogether missing from his sophisticated account of the continual emergence of phenomenal reality. If agency means choosing between alternatives and willing something, how can phenomena that eternally unfold out of a non-deliberative Intellect involve agency? How then are we to explain the reality of freedom and free agency in a system of thought that seems to eliminate agency in favor of the spontaneous outflow of all being? We are left with a puzzle, then: is there a different way of understanding divine agency without anthropomorphism?

Third, is there any connection between human and divine agency that permits us to understand human agency as a genuine link to the divine without introducing intermediary anthropomorphic figures (as in many Gnostic writings)? Can we trace out a real connection without supposing either that the gods have nothing to do with us (as in the case of the Atomists and Epicureans) or that divine providence extends only to the level of the moon and not to all sublunary individuals, such as you and me, horses and dogs (as in the case of Alexander of Aphrodisias) or, again, that divine figures sometimes contemplate and at other times act (as appears to be the case in Numenius) or that they occasionally intervene in human affairs (as the whole of earlier religious thinking had held to be the case and as Alexander too seems to allow—as we shall see immediately below)?

This then is the broader context for the writing of VI.8.

Why is this treatise important?

First, it answers the series of questions outlined above by developing a new approach to creative agency. It is the first of Plotinus' works to pinpoint where agency is to be situated in the human being by working through some of the complex ambiguities of human existence and by means of an analysis of ordinary language usage.

Second, it develops an entirely new way of thinking about God—Plotinus is the first to argue, in the precise way he does it, that Will comes before Intellect and to posit the One as pure freedom, a self-establishing cause of Itself—and, third, it articulates a creative idea of agency and radical freedom by showing how such terms as desire, will, self-dependence, and freedom in the human ethical sphere can be genuinely applied to Intellect and the One in a way that nevertheless preserves the radical inability of all metaphysical language to express anything about God or gods. On the vexed question of the discovery and history of the will see Dihle, 1982; for other references, Horn, 2007, 153n1–2.

Chapter 1

Can we apply our idea that there is something "in our power" to the gods and can we even apply it to ourselves when we find ourselves overwhelmed by external compulsions and addictions?

Chapter 1, 1–13: *Setting out of the goal and scope of the work; what does it mean to say that something "has power?"*

The immediate context of Chapter 1

The immediate context of VI.8 can be seen in its first lines (*Ar' esti kai epi theōn ei ti estin ep' autois zētein . . .*), namely, Alexander of Aphrodisias' denial that the notion of "what is in our power" (*to eph' hēmin*) can be applied to the gods since their being what they are is necessary and, therefore, cannot be said to be in their power: "In the case of the gods being such [as they are] will no longer depend on them because being like this is present in their nature, and none of the things that are present in this way depends on oneself (*ep' autōi*)" (*On Fate* 204, 12–15; trans. Sharples). On the other hand, Alexander does allow the possibility of the gods having things in their power, if they have "the power (*exousia*) of also not doing them . . . if indeed they perform some actions concerning the things that can also be otherwise" (204, 22–23), that is, non-necessary actions in the sphere of change. So for Alexander, strictly speaking, the gods do not have things in their power since their natures are necessary; only in the case where the gods can do actions in the sublunary realm where the power of choice, to act or not to act, comes into play, could they be said to have such power. VI.8, Chapters 1–3 examine the sources of human freedom always in relation to the question whether we can apply our findings to the case of the gods (and "gods" can refer in Plotinus to Soul, Intellect and the One—as also to the visible gods, the stars and planets). VI.8, 4 then introduces the further question of whether freedom is coextensive with our will, that is, the power to act or not act. But if our will as a form of desire is led by something outside itself and our reason or intellect is determined by the necessity of its own nature, how can we ever link freedom through intellect/Intellect to the gods and the Good? In general, in the case of intellect in these earlier chapters it is not always clear whether Plotinus refers to divine Intellect (*nous*) or to the human intellect in some capacity; where this is ambiguous, we generally leave "intellect" uncapitalized.

1, 1–11 *Is it possible to inquire, even about the gods, whether there is anything in their power*: In VI.8.1, 1–11, Plotinus sets out the scope of the inquiry: Is it possible to apply the technical phrase that we find in Aristotle, the Peripatetics, the Stoics, etc., namely, *to eph' hēmin* (what depends on us or what is in our power), to the gods or does it only refer to the human sphere where there is weakness and ambiguity, or should we attribute to the gods omnipotence where everything depends on them, or should this only be attributed to the One and the rest of the gods only, proportionate to their stature? This brings out the question of having something or everything in one's power in the sense of "being able to do" something or everything (*panta dynasthai*), and Plotinus quickly sketches some of the ambiguities in the verb *dynasthai*. Does the "being able to" refer to power or potency, that is, to a potentiality that a subject has or can develop, or to a present or future power or activity (1, 11–13: *dynasthai. Kaitoi kai to dynasthai touto skepteon pōs pote legetai, mēpote houtōs to men dynamin, to d' energeian phēsomen, kai energeian mellousan*)? For a treatment of these issues see *Ennead* II.5 [25] "On what exists potentially and on what actually." We should also note briefly here that divine omnipotence could be significantly qualified in antiquity. For Theophrastus, god *is able to direct all things to the better,* but only to the degree possible (*Metaphysics* 11b8–10, Fobes). For Porphyry, god cannot become bad (*Against the Christians,* fr. 94, 23–24, Harnack; for examples see Beutler-Theiler, *HBT,* 4b, 361–362). More generally, for Plato in the *Timaeus,* the Demiurge does not make the Receptacle; he only brings order and form to its precosmic state.

1, 5–7 *one is required to ascribe omnipotence to the gods, such that not just something, but everything is in their power? Or is it that omnipotence and having everything in its power should be ascribed only to the One but with the other gods some things are this way and some that way (tois d' allois ta men houtōs ta d' ekeinōs)?*: We have translated this difficult phrase as literally as possible (though it still remains unclear). Henry-Schwyzer links *houtōs* to the previous phrase *to ep' autoi panta* ("having everything in its power") and *ekeinōs* to *tēn dunamin pasan* ("omnipotence"), but the difference between the two remains opaque. Other translators make *ekeinōs* a negation of *houtōs*; so, for example, Leroux translates: "pour les autres dieux, nous devons dire que certaines choses sont ainsi en leur pouvoir, d' autres non;" and Harder: "bei den anderen Göttern dagegen ist nur einiges in ihrer Verfügung, anderes nicht." Lavaud attaches *houtōs* to a power that extends to some one thing in line 5 and *ekeinōs* to a power that extends to all and translates: "pour les autres êtres, certains exercent leur pouvoir sur toutes choses, et d'autres sur une seule." He argues that the beings who exercise their power over all are "the One, Intellect and perhaps Soul Hypostasis"—or all souls together, while the beings who have power over particular things are individual souls (Lavaud, 244n5–6). Lavaud's textual solution is attractive, but his explanation cannot be correct because individual souls are not gods, while the heavenly bodies (which he leaves out of account) are "the gods in heaven" (cf. V.8 [31] 3, 27–29) who exercise their power with more particularized focus than the One, Intellect, All Soul—and perhaps also the World Soul. This seems to make best sense of the text, though Plotinus is unclear and never in this treatise clarifies precisely what he might have meant.

1, 13–30: *What does the expression "what is in our power" mean in relation to human experience?*

1, 15–16 *But for the time being, we must . . . first inquire as we usually do whether there is anything that happens to be in our power*: To determine whether the notion of "what is in our power" can be applied to the gods and, above all, to the One, we first have to determine "whether anything happens to be in *our* power" (1, 15–16). As so often (see for example III.8.1, 1ff.), Plotinus' writings start with "us," the members of his seminar—his philosophical friends and acquaintances—and, more broadly, the "us" or all philosophical addressees who "overhear" this dialogue. The "we" for Plotinus is not our contemporary "ego" or even "self" and not yet "person" in any modern sense, but a dialogical Platonic forerunner of something like a community of selves. As Plotinus says about finding an image for Intellect in VI.7.15, 25–26: "it (Intellect) is as a thing all faces, shining with living faces." On the self and the "we," see O'Daly, 1973; Gerson, 1994, 127–163; Beierwaltes, 2001, 84–122 (*Das wahre Selbst*); 2002, 11–40 (*Le vrai soi*); Ousager, 2004; Sorabji, 2006; Remes, 2007; Mortley, 2014.

Excursus on important terms: Aristotle, Alexander, and the Stoics

In VI.8, Plotinus will use several terms to express the notion of what we might call will or free will, many of them deriving from Plato and especially Aristotle's ethical works, the Stoics, etc.: *to eph' hēmin* (what depends on us or what is in our power), *hekousion/akousion* (voluntary/involuntary), *to autexousion* (self-determination), *exousia* (freedom), *boulēsis* (wish, will), *thelēsis* (will), *to eleutheron* (freedom), *proairesis* (choice). While *boulēsis* and *thelēsis* seem synonymous, *hekousion* and *to autexousion*, the voluntary and the self-determining, are different, since an action can be voluntary but not truly self-determined. Freedom is therefore closer to self-determination than to what is voluntary. In Aristotle, *proairesis* or choice very often refers to the choice of means to an end (and is discursive), whereas *boulēsis* is the will to the end, and is "inseparable from thought, *noēsis*" (Joachim, 1970, 104–105). For *to eph' hēmin* see Frede, 2007, 110–123; Eliasson, 2008. It is striking in VI.8 that Plotinus will use forms of the verb *hairein* to express positive choice, x chooses y exclusively for itself, but not in the sense of choosing between alternatives; and he never uses *proairesis* at all in the early chapters about purely human agency in its typical Aristotelian and Stoic senses—as choosing between alternatives or as means to an end. *Proairesis* is only used in the later chapters of Intellect.

Aristotle and Alexander

We will take each term in the order it first appears in the treatise, starting with what depends on us or what is in our power—*to ep' autois* or *to eph' hēmin*. A version of the phrase first appears in Aristotle's *Nicomachean Ethics*, where it applies specifically to *actions* in a discussion of which actions are voluntary and which not (*hekousion/akousion).* "Both the terms voluntary and involuntary must be used with reference to the moment of action (*hote prattei*). Now the man acts voluntarily (*hekōn*); for the principle that moves (*archē tou kinein*) the instrumental parts of the body in such actions is in him (*en autōi*), and the things of which the moving principle is in the man himself (*en autōi*), *are in his power* either to do or not (*ep' autōi kai prattein ē mē*)" (*EN* 1110a14–18; cf. 1111a22–24; 1113b20–21). In other words, for an action to be *eph' hēmin* or in our power, the origin of the action must be *in the agent*. Here it is unclear whether or not such an action must involve reason and judgment. But later in the Peripatetic tradition, with Alexander, for instance, who was active in the late 2nd and early 3rd centuries CE, what is strictly in our power is our unforced assent to something in accordance with reason and judgment: ". . . the voluntary and what is in our power are not indeed the same thing. For it is what comes about from an assent that is not enforced that is voluntary; but it is what comes about with an assent that is in accordance with reason and judgment that is in our power. And for this reason, if something is in our power it is also voluntary, but not everything that is voluntary is in our power. For the irrational living creatures too, which act in accordance with the impulse and assent (*kata tēn hormēn kai sugkatathesin*) in them, act voluntarily; but it is peculiar to man that something of the things that are brought about by him is in his power (*to ep'autōi*)" (*On Fate* 183.26–32; trans. Sharples adapted). Whether or not such unforced assent in accordance with reason and judgment is the result of choice (*proairesis*) in Alexander is the subject of scholarly debate.

The Stoics

But one can also see elements of the long Stoic debate about "what is in our power" in Alexander's choice of Stoic terms such as "impulse" (*hormē*) and "assent (*sugkatathesis*)." Though there is considerable variety in the many Stoic positions that we should not forget, we can set out the major differences or shades of opinion in the following chronological outline. Chrysippus (279–206 BCE) held that the principles that all things happen according to fate and that something is nonetheless in our power are compatible and he therefore defined what is in our power as "what comes about through us" (*SVF* II 979, 3–4/ Alexander, *On Fate*, 181, 14), "in impulse and assent" (*SVF* II 981; cf. II 986; Plotinus, VI.8.3, 1 and 7) or as "what is brought about by something or someone (*tinos*), according to its own nature" (*SVF* II 1006/Alexander, *On Fate* 211, 30–31).

For Seneca (4 BCE–65 CE), what is not in our power (*in nostra potestate*) are things in some sense external to the soul (*aliquid extrinsecus*; cf. *De Beneficiis* V.5.4), such as fortune, emotion or passion (*adfectum*; cf. *Ad Helviam* 17.1.13–15; *Letter* 85.10–12), even "inveterate vices of the human mind" (*Letter* 85.10); since both passion and reason can be directed "toward the better and the worse" (*De Ira* I.viii.3, 28–30), it is not easy to draw a simple line between what is or what is not in our power. Generally speaking, however, what is in our power is connected with the search for happiness, our control of our impressions with the use of reason and our ability to choose the philosophical life, by training our reason and freeing ourselves from faulty passions. For Musonius Rufus (c. 30–62 CE), Epictetus (c. 55–135 CE), and Marcus Aurelius (121–180 CE) later, while there is again considerable variety, what is "in our power" is ultimately only internal states of the soul, not actions at all: "only the correct use of impressions (*phantasiai*) is in our power" (Epictetus, *Diss.* I 1.7.2–3); "[happiness consists in] the use of imaginations/images (*phantasiōn*) . . . that happening correctly [results in] freedom, well-flowing life, good spirit, tranquillity . . . complete virtue (*eleutheria, euroia, euthymia, eustatheia . . . sympasa arêtē*) (Musonius, fr. 38.1–3, Hense); "assent (*sugkatathesis*), conception, impulse, desire (*hypolēpsis, hormē, orexis*), and, in a word, everything that is our own doing"

(Epictetus, *Handbook* I, 1, 2–3; *Diss.* IV.1.71.3–72.1); "choice and all the works of choice are in our power . . . [not] the body . . . [or] possessions . . . " (Epictetus, *Diss.* I 22.10. 2–11, 1; Marcus Aurelius, *Med.* VI. 41.1.1–6 ("what is in our power . . . are things within our choice (*proairesis*)"; XII.22.1.1–2). So important is this question to the Stoics that someone like Epictetus treats directly of what is in our power both in Book 1, Chapter 1 of the *Discourses* and fragment 1 of the *Handbook*. And we cite these examples here to give a sense of the vocabulary and range of Stoic thought, some of which is clearly present in the early chapters of VI.8.

In what follows, we can see Plotinus navigating a decidedly subtle Platonic position somewhere in between Aristotle and Alexander, on the one hand, and the Stoics, on the other. For Aristotle and Alexander, the question of what is in our power lies somewhere in between the subject acting and the action. For the Stoics, what is in our power is situated either between the agent's assent and action (Chrysippus) together with the correct use of impressions in accord with reason, choice or assent (Seneca, Epictetus, Marcus Aurelius), or, more strictly, in the assent only of the subject itself, since action can always be hindered and is not therefore properly in our power (Epictetus, Marcus Aurelius). Plotinus' solution, though it might look, in VI.8, Chapter 6, at first sight more Stoic and, though it has in fact been thought to situate *to eph' hēmin* outside action altogether, is rather a sophisticated development of Platonic and Aristotelian thinking than anything straightforwardly Stoic, as we shall see.

1, 22–33 *overwhelmed by compulsions, are we nothing?*: In ordinary life, Plotinus notes, we find ourselves besieged by opposing compulsions and passions, and we think that we, as subjects, are nothing. We hope that if we could escape from these compulsions, what we wish might be free (1, 22–33).

Note the simplicity of the starting point: "What then do we have in mind when we say 'being in our power' and why investigate it? I myself think that when we are moved by opposing chances and compulsions and violent passions possessing our soul, we accept all these things as our masters and, enslaved to them and carried wherever they take us, we are at a loss (*ēporēsamen*) whether we are not nothing and nothing is in our power—on the implicit ground that what would be in our power is that which we will to do and actually do, unenslaved by chance, compulsion or passion, with nothing opposing our wills" (1, 23–29).

We start in Plotinus' direct assertion of the apparent confines of our overwhelming experience of powerlessness (cf. VI.8.1, 2 above) and nothingness in the face of apparent external compulsions; this experience, nonetheless, has as its implicit other pole the supposition that we have some idea of what free and willed action is. Here, the construction, *hōs* with the genitive participle, signifies a supposition that is almost not that of the person experiencing nothingness (Goodwin, 1574), that is, if I am experiencing powerlessness, then the thought of my being able to experience powerlessness depends upon the fact that I must have some notion of what willed action in my own power might be; and thus the idea that it is because I *can* will something that I am able to have my present experience of *not being able* to will something may well seem foreign to me. It is, as it were, on the supposition of what another voice in the conversation asserts ("so you say"). We can only fear we are nothing ironically because our will *is* somewhere supposed to be something. So *boulēsis,* will, is mentioned for the first time and it emerges as the hidden condition of our being able to suppose that we are nothing; it, therefore, presents an avenue, and perhaps the only avenue, for further inquiry that can take us out of our painful perplexity.

But the moment we hold onto the vague idea of will as something opposed to the fluctuations of chance or passions, why should we suppose that the notion we have of what is in our power (*hē ennoia tou eph' hēmin*), that was previously enslaved to passion, should not now equally be enslaved to our will? Here we have perhaps *the* classic Platonic context for inquiry that may be outlined as follows.

In *Republic* 7, 524a–525a, Socrates argues that intelligible understanding (and the ascent through all the sciences to a synoptic view of being and truth) begins to be aroused in the self-contradictory evidence of sense-perception or experience, when we are "at a loss" (524a5; e4) how to interpret the opposing appearances of the one and the many, or the one and the great: "But if some opposition is always seen simultaneously in perception [or experience] so that it no more appears to be one or the opposite, then the soul would certainly need *the subject to judge* (*tou epikrinountos*) and would be compelled in this experience (*en autōi*) to be at a loss and to inquire, by moving [or waking up] the notion in itself (*kinousa en heautēi tēn ennoian*), and to ask whatever then is the one itself (*ti pot' esti auto to hen*), and so it would be a study, relating to the one, that leads and converts the soul to the contemplation of being" (524e2–525a2). This is implicitly the methodological guide for Plotinus here: caught in the midst of addictions and compulsions and yet vaguely understanding that one's dilemma is a dilemma of the will, the soul needs judgment, but is altogether at a loss and needs to rouse up thought; or, in its present experience, it needs to begin to clarify, articulate and validate our notion or idea of what is in our power in order to ask further questions about "the one." This is the cluster of meanings connected with Plotinus' usage of *ennoia* in VI.8 and Plato's usage in *Republic* 7: "moving [or waking up] the notion in itself." All commentators note that *ennoia* is a Stoic term and so it is, but much earlier it is a term used pivotally by Plato. For *ennoia*, see also on 7, 24.

This further series of questions, in order to clarify the notion of what is in our power and to draw out the consequences, Plotinus begins at VI.8.1, 30: but perhaps here too, he asks, the will is enslaved to itself and to the implicit dilemma of choice, i.e., it "would or would not happen to the extent we willed it" (*douleuei kai para tosouton an genoito ē mē, par' hoson boulētheiēmen an*)? Choice is only implicit at this point and there is as yet no mention of *proairesis*. For we say, Plotinus continues, that an action depends on us if it originates in the agent. And certainly, what is "voluntary" is what we do without compulsion and with knowledge; but "what is in our power" is what we are also masters of, or competent in, doing. Here he starts to think through the problem of Plato's "one" (in the *Republic* 7 as above) or what the free subject may be, with Aristotle and Alexander primarily in mind.

1, 30–44 *What is voluntary and involuntary and how does the voluntary differ from "what is in our power?"*: The use of the term voluntary—*hekousion*—recalls Aristotle's definition of the involuntary, *EN* 1109b35–1110a1: "those things are thought involuntary, which take place under compulsion or owing to ignorance; and that is compulsory of which the moving principle is outside, being a principle in which nothing is contributed by the subject acting or being affected (*ho prattōn ē paschōn*) . . . " or even closer to Plotinus' language here: "by voluntary, I mean . . . any of the things in his power someone does *with knowledge*, i.e., not in ignorance of the object, instrument or end (*ho an tis tōn eph' auto ontōn eidōs kai mē agnoōn prattēi mēte hon mēte hou <heneka>*) (*EN* 1135a23–25). But Plotinus is simultaneously thinking generally of Alexander's distinction between the "voluntary" and "what is in our power" since he goes on to specify: "and both terms may often coincide, even if their definition is different" (1, 33–35). Alexander defines the "voluntary," for example, as "unforced assent" and "what is in our power" as "assent in accordance with reason and judgment" (*On Fate*, 183, 27–29). Their definitions do differ, then, since what is in our power (*to eph' hēmin*) requires the more intensive criteria of reason and judgment; and so, of course, they might well not fit at all as in the famous case of Oedipus who unknowingly killed his father, Laius. Oedipus was competent or capable of killing but this can hardly be voluntary if he did not know Laius to be his father.

Again, Plotinus' thought shifts instantaneously here between Alexander and Aristotle, for in the *EN* 1135a28–33 Aristotle had taken up the same example: "The person struck may be the striker's father, and the striker may know that he is a man . . . but not know that it is his father; a similar distinction may be made in the case of the end, and with regard to the whole action (*homoiōs de to toiouton diōristhō kai epi tou hou heneka, kai peri tēn praxin holēn*). Therefore, that which is done in ignorance, or though not done in ignorance is not in the agent's power, or is done under compulsion, is involuntary." In this passage, Aristotle seems to distinguish the general from the particular case and yet at the same time to suggest that even the particular case (Oedipus knowing that Laius is his father) requires a broader context, that is, the goal, purpose or *telos*, together with the action as a whole. Earlier in the *Nicomachean Ethics,* however, Aristotle expressly states that what causes involuntary action is not "ignorance of choice (*hē en tēi prairesei agnoia*) . . . , not ignorance of the universal (for that men *are* blamed), but ignorance of particulars, that is, of the circumstances of the action and the objects with which it is concerned (*oud' hē katholou psegontai gar di age tautēn all' hē kath' hekasta, en hais kai peri ha hē praxis*). For it is on these that both pity and pardon depend, since the person who is ignorant of any of these acts involuntarily" (*EN* 1110b31–1111a2).

Plotinus is clearly including the thought of all these passages compressed in his own thought here, for, unlike Aristotle, he argues that we need more than knowledge of the circumstances or particulars, but a "general" knowledge—otherwise, like Oedipus, we will kill Laius, Oedipus' father, in supposed freedom but in ignorance either of the real circumstances or of what we ought to do. Commentators often take Plotinus to be arguing against Aristotle in favor of the Socratic maxim that "no one makes a mistake wittingly, or willingly" (*oudeis hamartanei hekōn—hekōn* means both "willingly" and "wittingly"), but while this is certainly in the background of the overall argument, we think Plotinus' meaning at this point in the argument is much simpler and actually in tune with part of Aristotle's thought: Oedipus' killing of Laius is involuntary and for that he deserves pity and pardon, but it is not a good example of what is, or should be, in our power for this really does require broader "knowledge of the goal and the whole action," in Aristotle's terms, or of "reason and judgment," in Alexander's terms. Indeed, if a characteristic of the authentic rational agent for which the agent is praiseworthy or blameworthy, is a stable, responsible, lifetime's commitment to the good, then a more holistic awareness must be necessary for Aristotle too. Therefore, Plotinus uses the more general adverb *holōs*, not the phrase *en tois katholou* (1, 39–40) or *hē katholou* (as in the passage from Aristotle cited above). In other words, Plotinus is arguing the general case in accord with one side of Aristotle's own argument.

So Plotinus concludes that such ignorance "would be incompatible with having something in one's power" and that the knowledge involved in the voluntary act, by which we think he means at this point any act that can be said to be voluntary in a stricter sense, must as knowledge not only be "in the particulars" but also "in the sense of the whole (*holōs*)." Plotinus is thinking through the question in his own mind but he is also insisting on the Aristotelian side of the question that both knowing the particulars and the broader, more universal context is essential to a stricter definition of *to eph' hēmin* culpability. For why should the action be involuntary if Oedipus does not know that Laius is related to him, but not involuntary if he does not know that one ought not to do it? Surely, Plotinus insists, this is because one *ought* to have learnt it (together with Epictetus, *Diss.* I.1.31: "This is what it means to have studied what one ought to have studied"). Not knowing that one ought to have learned something important is not voluntary in any meaningful way, nor is what leads one away from learning something important really voluntary.

1, 27–30 *hōs toutou esomenou/as if what would be in our power*: For this construction see Goodwin, 1574, on circumstantial participles: "they express the idea or assertion of the subject of the leading verb . . . *without implying* that it is also the idea of the speaker or writer." As, for example, in Plato, *Republic* 329a: *Aganaktousin hōs megalōn tinōn apesterēmenoi*—"they are indignant, because (as they say) they have been deprived of some great blessings." We can only recognize failure, perplexity, and disorder because of the order and intelligibility, however imperfect, of things. For Aristotle, for example, chance and even spontaneity or randomness are only discernible within the context of the intelligibility of nature ("for the most part," as Aristotle typically characterizes events in the sublunary world) or the regular structure of causality (Aristotle, *Physics* II 6 198a9–10: "Spontaneity and chance, therefore, are posterior to intelligence and nature"). For Plotinus, see III.2.4, 29–34: ". . . it is because of order that disorder exists . . . not that the better things produce the worse, but the things which ought to receive the better are unable to do so because of their own nature or because of some chance circumstance or hindrance from others." A major theme of VI.8, namely, the priority of the Good and intelligibility over chance and random spontaneity, emerges implicitly at the very beginning of the work.

1, 34 *what is in our power is that of which we are masters (kurioi)*: *Kurios*, to have power, dominion or authority over, to be master of, as opposed to being enslaved to something (VI.8.1, 25–27), is used by both Plato and Aristotle to signify authority over or responsibility for. In Plato, for example, *Alcibiades* I 130d, in examining what each thing is itself, "we surely could not say that anything of ourselves is more master (*kuriōteron*) of us than the soul"; *Republic* 9, 583a (in determining which of the lives is most pleasant—the lovers respectively of gain, honor or wisdom) the life of the person in whom the love of wisdom is master (*kurios*) is the most pleasurable; *Republic* 7, 534d: those children who cannot practice true dialectic and be properly tested "you will not allow them to rule in the city . . . and be masters of (*kurious*)/be responsible for the greatest matters." In Aristotle, *De anima* 410b10–15: (in the case of the principle that holds the elements of things together, a principle that is "most master"—*kuriotaton*) "there can be nothing more naturally prior or master (*kurion*) than intellect"; 433a5: "In general, the person who has the art of medicine does not always apply it; it is not knowledge but something else which is master (*kurion*) of making us act according to knowledge." For other usage, see *EN* 1113b32; *EE* 1223a4; see also Alexander in Leroux, 1990, 239; who thinks that Plotinus owes more to Stoicism than to Aristotelianism in these lines and he thus emphasizes Plotinus' emphasis on power—"souveraineté": "la marque de ces concepts est d' être determinés par une métaphysique de la force, qu'on peut contraster sur la construction psychologique du désir et du souhait délibéré qui caractérisait l'effort d' Aristote. Ce thème reflète la pensée de Plotin dans son traité sur le Destin, III, 1 et les traités III, 2 et III, 3 sur la Providence." Leroux is right to point to these three treatises, III.1 [3], III.2 [47], and III.3 [48], but he puts the wrong emphasis on Plotinus' thought. There is no such contrast here between a supposed "metaphysics of force" and "the psychological construction of desire and deliberative will that characterizes Aristotle." Yes, Plotinus does not speak of choice or deliberation, but he is certainly concerned with the complexities of the psychology of desire and its involvement in rational agency and action, as we will see in VI.8, 2ff., and he understands the subtleties of Aristotle's thought on this all-important question very well, as we shall also see below. Indeed, desire in its full range is such a force in Plotinus' broader thinking that he can say of the divine Intellect in III.8 [30] that "it is always desiring and always hitting upon the object of its desire" and in VI.7 [38] 35 that it is "intellect in love, when it goes out of its mind, drunk with the nectar [cf. *Symposium* 203b5] . . . and it is better for it to be drunk with a drunkenness like this than to be respectably sober" (trans. Armstrong, modified).

1, 34–35 *And both (the "voluntary" and "what is in our power" may often coincide, even if their definitions (logos) are different*: In context, this sentence illustrates the range of the term *logos* with many different but related meanings in different contexts: speech, discourse, expression, proportion, word (as in the prologue to John's gospel), meaning, even "tale," "story" or account (as in Plato's *Gorgias* 523a: "Listen to a very fine story [*logos*], which you . . . will consider myth [*mythos*], but I an actual account [*logos*]"), reason, reasoning, form, definition, intelligibility. For *logos* as "reason" see 2, 31–36; for *logos* as formative principle, see 10, 36–37.

How does *logos* come to mean definition? To define something, we have to employ a process of reasoning. In practice this means that if we claim to know something we can be asked to give an account (*didonai logon*) of our claim. This is what Socrates says the dialectitian can do in *Republic* 6–7 (and elsewhere). But as we see in a later dialogue, the *Theaetetus*, justified true belief (that is, correct opinion that such and such is the case, *plus* an account or *logos*) is not equivalent to knowledge or scientific knowing (*episteme*). The reason is that knowledge involves more than justified belief; it *is understanding* or *noēsis*, not justified opinion or belief; an "account" is something we provide after the fact, and so is more like a representation of understanding rather than understanding itself. If knowledge is to go beyond justified true belief, it must be knowledge of what x *is*, not of what x is *like*.

This will help us see how the meanings in *logos* are linked and how "account," "definition," "expression," "reason/

reasoning," "form," and "intelligibility" can cohere. When we define something, we put together the elements of the definition (e.g., genus and specific difference in Aristotle's case: animal + rational = human being); that is, we give a discursive account of what is in reality unified. Or in other words, we give the account that is a definition, not to look at the elements separately, but rather to see them conjointly as a single "expression" of what is real. The essence or what Aristotle calls in a very strange phrase—"the what it was to be" (*to ti ēn einai*)—is the unified totality of all the elements in the definition (genus and difference) *seized in a single act of thought* (cf. Tricot, 1986, 1.24; Ross, 1975, 1.127). What is collected and presented discursively by a process of reasoning is united by understanding or thought and becomes one with the real. A definition, therefore, represents discursively the world's intelligibility as understood by thought. So *logos* as *definition* is thought's encounter with *logos* as a principle or indwelling *form* really active in the world, a form that expresses *intelligibility* in things; this *logos* is the formative principle at Chapter 10, 6–11.

There is, of course, much more to the term *logos*, from Heraclitus, through the prologue to John's Gospel, to the Stoics, but this will provide for the time being part of a thought map to show how "definition" is a natural extension of other meanings—to be determined in different contexts. For *logos* generally, see Fattal, 2001; 2003 (ed.); 2015.

Conclusion to Chapter 1

The whole of this first chapter, first sets out the scope and goal of the inquiry, and then, starting from the experience of the painful perplexity of consciousness, caught between its apprehensive fear of being nothing at all, on the one hand, and its will that emerges even in this self-defeating anxiety, on the other, goes on to articulate the fuller meaning of what is in our power (*to eph' hēmin*) and assimilates the notion of what is "voluntary" to this stronger epistemic understanding of "what is in our power."

Chapter 2

To which faculty or power of soul should we trace "what is in our power?"

2, 1–12 *Should we trace it to desire, high spirit or anger, or to a combination of desire and reason?*: Chapter 2 turns more explicitly to the drives of the soul to determine where we should situate what is in our power. Throughout his argument in these early chapters, Plotinus is exploring many different perspectives open-mindedly and does not commit exclusively to any single view, since the whole range of ancient thought, reasonably enough, is open for his inquiry.

2, 1–9 *to what should we assign "what is in our power?"*: To what then should we assign "what is in our power"—"to impulse and some kind of desire—for example, what is done or not done out of high spirits or desire or out of rational calculation of what is advantageous together with desire?" (2, 2–4). Impulse (*hormē*) is a technical Stoic term (though common in Plato too) and Plotinus' use of the indefinite "some kind of desire" shows his awareness of the extension of meanings in the primarily Aristotelian term—*orexis*—ranging from "impulse" or "instinct" to "desire" generally (in which it may be closely akin to *epithymia*) and to "desire of the good or apparent good" which Aristotle identifies with will or *boulēsis* (cf. *EN* 1113a15–16; cf. *Metaphysics* A 980a1: "all human beings naturally desire—*oregontai*—to know"). Plotinus' example—"what is done or not done out of high spirits or desire or rational calculation . . . with desire"—can fit either a Platonic or Aristotelian model: in the former case, the tripartite soul (*ho thymōi prattetai ē epithymiai ē logismōi tou sympherontos met' orexeōs*) of *Republic* 4, 435c–441c, but the soul considered not as parts so much as forms, kinds, faculties or powers (as Plato also calls them in the *Republic*—see Corrigan, 2007, 100); in the latter case, *thymos* or *orgē* (anger), *epithymia*, and *boulēsis* are the three forms of appetition for Aristotle (*EN* 1187b37; cf. *EE* 1223a26ff.); Aristotle can distinguish the forms of appetition from *logismos* or rational calculation (cf. *Politics* 1334b22–24), but to the degree that *logismos* controls desire (cf. *EE* 1220a1) and wills the good, will and correct reasoning converge. This is what Plotinus has in mind here because at 2, 9–10 he asks whether we should rather assign what is in our power "to correct calculation and correct desire." That is, on the understanding that if we assign it to high spirit and desire, we open up a can of worms by effectively assigning such power to children, beasts, drug addicts and mad people, etc. But if we give it to rational calculation with desire, what happens if the desire goes astray? *Orthē doxa*—correct opinion—is, of course, Plato's phrase, but the phrases, *orthē orexis* and *orthos logos*, that is, correct desire and correct reason, are also used by Aristotle (*EN* 1139a24; 1138b20–34; e15). So the whole of this argument has a broad-based appeal to it.

It represents an attempt to reach right across the spectrum of different positions and different terms or emphases to a thought that is meaningful for any persuasion.

2, 2–3 *impulse, desire*: Because of the range of meaning from impulse to desire in *orexis*, Armstrong is right to translate *orexis* sometimes as "impulse" (e.g., IV.4. [28], 28) and at others "desire" (as in VI.8). There is, for example, "desire directed to intellect" in I.8 [51] 15, 21. For a classic definition of *hormē* and *orexis*, see Stobaeus, *Anthology* II.86, 17–87, 3 (*SVF* III 169): "*hormē* is a movement of soul toward something as to its genus; viewed specifically, there is the impulse that comes to be in rational animals and that in irrational animals . . . *orexis* is not rational impulse, but a form or species of rational impulse; and rational impulse is strictly . . . a movement of the discursive reason (*dianoia*) towards something concerned with action. . . ." The question of the link between impulse, fate and what is in our power Plotinus already poses in III.1 [3] 7, 13–22: if necessity governs everything, as the Stoics say, "our mental images (*phantasiae*) will follow antecedent causes and our impulses (*hormai*) will depend on our mental images, and 'what is in our power' will be a mere word; it will not exist any more just because it is we who have the impulses, if the impulse is produced in accordance with those preexisting causes; our part will be like that of animals and babies, which go on blind impulses and madmen, for these also have impulses—yes, by Zeus, fire has impulses too, and everything which is enslaved to its structure and moves according to it."

2, 5–8 *But if we assign it to high spirit and desire, we will grant that something is in the power of children, beasts, and madmen*: As Lavaud points out (2007, 248n24), Plotinus has Aristotle, *EN* 1111a24–27, in mind. After insisting that the source of a voluntary act is in the agent who knows the particular circumstances in which he is acting, Aristotle remarks: "For it is probably a mistake to say [as Plato had done at Laws 683b, linking anger and desire with ignorance as sources of wrong action] that acts caused by anger or by desire are involuntary. For first this will debar us from speaking of any of the other animals as acting voluntarily, or children either." According to Lavaud, Plotinus is continuing his polemic against Aristotle, skipping over the difference between what is voluntary and what is in our power, a difference he had made explicit in Chapter 1, 33–36, and effectively ruling out voluntary action for children and beasts. But, strictly speaking, this is not so. The acts of other animals and children can still be voluntary—even in a minimal sense. But here Plotinus is speaking of "what is in our power," not of what is voluntary. He can accept with Aristotle that an action not done by force or because of ignorance is voluntary, but these are only the minimal conditions for a certain kind of free action. By contrast, what is in our power is "that of whose doing we are masters." This requires rational responsibility of an entirely different order. In a similar way, Aristotle grants voluntary action to irrational animals and children (*EN* 1111a24–27), but *not* choice (*EN* 1111b9–10; cf.1099b32–1100a1). Plotinus does not use the word "choice" (*proairesis*), but his view is akin to that of Aristotle: "Mastery" implies the responsibility of authentic rational agency. In other words, mastery is where praiseworthiness or culpability is rightly in play, for this is where rational agency makes a difference to the expression of our desires.

2, 8–10 *If we assign "what is in our power" to rational calculation together with desire, is this so if rational calculation is erroneous? Then should we assign it to correct calculation and correct desire?*: Compare Aristotle, *EN* 1139a23–27: "Hence as moral virtue is a disposition related to choice, and choice is deliberate desire, it follows that if the choice is to be seriously good (*spoudaia*), both the reason must be true and the desire correct (*ton te logon alēthē einai kai orexin orthēn*), and that reason and desire must pursue the same aims." In other words, reason and desire have to work together.

2, 10–12 *And yet even here, one might inquire whether the calculation moved the desire or the desire the calculation*: If desire is the single cause of motion, however much it may combine with sense, imagination, practical reason, according to Aristotle in *De Anima*, Book 3, Chapters 9–10, what role does reasoning have as a motive force? Which is determinative? Surely mind in some capacity is a mover—even my mind at the level of reasoning? We might say, for instance, that sometimes the thought and calculation that an action is beneficial for me prompts me to act, though sometimes it does not—if, for example, a conflicting pleasure overwhelms me or something else intervenes, such as an unpleasant pain associated with the action or a moral obligation that causes me to do something else. But what happens in the case of desire? Desire can certainly impel me to work out the means to do something, but is it the same desire that impels me to do something base and to do something noble?

2, 12–35: *An examination of different possible relations between desire and reason.*

2, 12–16 *the soul and the compound*: And then, if one admits with both Plato and Aristotle that we can speak on two levels, that of the compound being and that of the soul—we don't say, for instance, that the soul blushes, but we do say that the human being blushes, then we will be referring to different levels of subject predication when we refer to the compound and when we refer to the soul. This might be equivalent to speaking on the level of physics or physical compounds (*kata physin*), on the one hand, and on the level of form or metaphysics, on the other hand—just as Aristotle says, about substance in *Metaphysics* 7, that its proper object is form, even if this is "most perplexing." If we trace motive force to the compound, then it will be subject to physical necessity (however complex or conditional such necessity may be), whereas if we trace it to the soul alone, many common sense notions of agency, such as that I, this psychosomatic complex, do things not only voluntarily but freely, will be called into question—and we'll have a ghost-in-the-machine responsible for my perfectly concrete and supposedly free actions.

2, 16–30 *how can we be masters where we are led . . . ?*: We are certainly moved by passion, for instance, and if reason moves desire or passion, what minimal reasoning can we suppose to precede the passions (if the passions are failed judgments as the Stoics claim)? Or if imagination and desire are the driving forces, then how can we be masters of ourselves or even generally in *any* case where we are led by something—an image, a desire, a notion, a thought, an intellect—how can *we* be in charge? Indeed, anything that needs fulfillment at any level of being (as, for example, Socrates speaks in *Republic* 9 of the life of wisdom being the most fulfilled and fulfilling or in the *Symposium* of love being always in need)—such neediness is surely not in charge *where it is being led*. And this is true surely of *any* principle, no matter how lofty—anything, in fact, that does not have its being from itself—you, me, all soul, intellect, etc., that is dependent on another for its very structure. How can it be "from itself?" For if this is true of intellect, why is it not equally true of inanimate things, like fire, that operate totally in conformity with their nature?

Alexander uses the example of fire to argue that the being of different things functions in different ways: "that of a living being in being a living being with impulse, that of fire in being hot and a thing with the power to heat," whereas "to be rational is nothing other than to be a beginning or originative principle (*archē*) of actions" (*De Fato* 184, 16–21). Something like this perhaps is in Plotinus' mind, since just because x has its being from something else does not mean that it has no *archē* or beginning principle in itself. I have my being from my parents and from many other things, no doubt, but I *can* move or do things. Where then should the power for freedom be located? Is it because, unlike fire, the living creature knows via perception what it does? But seeing something does not make one master of one's actions; and the same is true for knowing something: knowing simply knows; it does not *do* anything; "something else leads to action" says Plotinus in 2, 30.

2, 30–37 *But if reason or knowledge counteracts and controls desire, we must inquire what this refers to and generally where this occurs. And if reason itself makes yet another desire, then how must we understand this? But if reason stops desire and stands still, and here is what is in our power, this will not be in action, but this will stand still in intellect, since everything in action—even if reason controls it—is mixed and cannot have the 'being in our power' in a pure state*: Or is it really true that something other than reason or knowledge leads to action, since reason *can* act contrary to desire and control desire? And if it does so, then it itself may *do* something on an entirely different scale from the more limited scope of ordinary actions, like eating, drinking, getting angry, etc. It may in fact "make *another desire*." In other words, it may generate a new expression of desire—no longer lower forms of appetition like *epithymia* and *thymos*, but willed desire or *boulēsis*. Indeed, one could argue that whereas in *Republic* Book 4 *epithymia* is the lowest part or power of the tripartite psyche, by the time we get to Book 9 we have a different picture because the highest kind of life, the wisdom-loving life, is a life with its own vertical desire and its own purer pleasure (cf. *Philebus* 62e; 66c; 63d–e; 66a; I.1 [53] 5, 24–30). So the conversion of the soul to the Good that occurs in *Republic*, books 6–7 does result in "another desire." And something similar must be true for Aristotle, as we have seen, since to actualize one's rational being is to change the character and focus of one's desire and, ultimately, in *Metaphysics* 12 7 to share in the actuality of God's life which is the purest pleasure (for Plotinus' view of this desire see I.8.15, 21). So "how we are to understand this" is, as Plotinus indicates, a very big question, particularly because we are in danger of getting outside action altogether—at least, action in any normal sense. So for instance, if reason puts a stop to desire and comes to a standstill (a position very close not only to Stoic *ataraxia* or imperturbability of spirit, but also to Aristotle's closest thing to an Unmoved Mover in us, namely, the contemplative intellect), then this will not be situated in, or referred to, action, but in "intellect;" and the problem is that we may be seeking some "pure" sort of agency, but nothing that concerns action is unambiguous or pure. How then are we to locate "what is in our power" in a mixed condition, when such a notion, as is recognized in different ways by Plato, Aristotle, and especially the Stoics, must be "impassible" in the sense that it cannot be hindered or contaminated by external or even internal forces?

Lavaud distinguishes four relations in these lines between reason and desire culminating in the final relation in which reason puts a stop to desire and comes to a standstill; and he concludes from this that Plotinus will make it clear that "what is in our power" is strictly only in the contemplative repose of Intellect itself: "Seule la retraite intérieure dans la contemplation de l'intelligible pourra par consequent assurer à l'âme de ne dépendre que d' elle-même" (251–252n34–35). This may ultimately be true by the time we get to the end of Chapter 6, but it should not obscure the fact that this final suggestion at the end of Chapter 2 is not going to be Plotinus' entire position for the *agent engaged in action* (a subtle position worked out from Chapters 3–6) and that Plotinus' final position on this question in Chapter 6, while certainly not in agreement with the Peripatetic school's understanding of what is in our power as "totalement orientéé . . . vers l'action" (Lavaud, 251n34), situates embodied human action that is self-dependent and in our power *in between the inner activity and the outer action but referred to the inner activity.* We shall see what this means precisely in Chapter 6.

2, 32–37: *Plotinus' enquiry and Aristotle, De Anima 3, Chapters 9–10.*

Throughout the latter part of this chapter, Plotinus is thinking partly through Aristotle's *De Anima*, Chapters 9–10 (cf. *EN* 6, Chapters 1–2), in the broader context of Aristotle's metaphysics. It is not enough to recognize the tripartite soul, Aristotle argues in Chapter 9, that is, the reasoning, spirited, desiring parts or powers (*logistikon, thymikon, epithymetikon*) or divide the soul into the rational and the irrational, because we find other parts such as the nutritive, perceptive, imaginative, the power of desire (*orektikon*), reason and so on. Plotinus in Chapter 2 in a similar way has eliminated imagination, sense-perception and *gnosis* or *logos* as the locus of what is in our power (2, 16, 26, 28–31).

What is it, then, that causes movement in living creatures, Aristotle asks? Is it the nutritive and sensitive faculties or reason and desire? It cannot be the nutritive or sensitive faculties since each on its own moves nothing (432b14–20). And it is not imagination because it moves only when desire is present (433a20–21). Nor can it be reason because "even when the mind does command and thought bids us pursue or avoid something, sometimes no movement is produced; we act in accordance with desire, as in the case of moral weakness. And, generally, we observe that the possessor of medical knowledge is not necessarily healing, which shows that *something else is required to produce action* (*heterou tinos kuriou ontos tou poiein*) (cf. VI.8.2, 30) in accordance with knowledge; the knowledge alone is not the cause" (433a1–6). Nor can it be desire on its own that is cause of motion for desire, too, "is incompetent to account fully for movement (*kuria tēs kineseōs*); for those who successfully resist temptation desire and have appetite and yet follow mind and refuse to enact that for which they have desire." Aristotle goes on to conclude in Chapter 10 that there are not two sources of motion, since the practical intellect, namely, that which calculates the means to an end (and which is therefore directly equivalent to *logismos* in the context of VI.8.2), does not cause motion apart from desire, while desire does cause motion apart from reason. In other words, when we are moved in accordance with reasoning (*logismos*), we are moved in accordance with will (*boulēsis*), which is a form of desire (*orexis*) (*De Anima* 433a23–25). In other words, will is a higher form of desire actualized by the practical intellect in its pursuit of the good, akin to the idea Plotinus floats in Chapter 2—how are we to understand it if reason makes "another desire?"

So, in one way, there is only one source of movement for Aristotle, namely, *desire*. Yet, in another way, *the force of mind or reason* is such that it transforms the character of desire from simple impulse to *something willed*. Therefore, reason—or what Aristotle calls here practical intellect—plays a real part in forming the kind of desire that moves us. As Aristotle puts it in *EN* 6, Chapter 2, 1139a36–1139b7: "thought (*dianoia*) by itself moves nothing, but only thought directed to an end and dealing with action. This indeed is the moving cause of productive activity . . . since doing well is an end, and desire is of this. Choice is therefore desiring intellect or thinking desire (*orektikos nous . . . ē orexis dianoētike*)." And, indeed too, there is also the sense in Aristotle's metaphysics that we are ultimately moved by desire for the beautiful and the good—both the real good and what appears good (*De an.* 433a28–29), and not only the real good, but the Best, the Unmoved Mover. There is therefore a third way in which *the good*, or in Aristotle's case, *the Unmoved Mover, moves everything* "by being loved" (*Metaphysics* 12, 7).

This larger picture is what Aristotle picks up at the end of *De anima* Chapter 10. That which originates movement can be understood in various ways: "it may mean either (a) something which itself is unmoved or (b) that which at once moves and is moved. Here that which moves without itself being moved is the realizable good [and ultimately, the Unmoved Mover], that which at once moves and is moved is the faculty of desire (for that which is influenced by desire so far as it is actually so influenced is set in movement, and desire in the sense of actual desire is a kind of movement), while that which is in motion is the living being."

2, 35–37: *Preliminary Conclusion: nothing related to action can be completely in our power.*

In other words, Plotinus is aware of the subtle, organic relationship between reason and desire in both Plato and

Aristotle, and of the need for both reason and thought not only to generate a higher form of desire, but also to work together with this desire in a convergent way toward a larger, more intelligible goal. The problem here for Plotinus, however, is that on the face of things, this has little or nothing to do with *action*.

Chapter 3

From soul to intellect: if we trace "self-determination" (a new term introduced here) and "what is in our power" back through intellect rather than through imagination and other powers, we may be able to link them to the gods.

3, 1–20: *Can what is in our power be related to opinion or to imagination?*

That Plotinus has in fact been talking about the whole range of being, from intellect/Intellect to fire, in Chapter 2 becomes evident in the opening lines of Chapter 3: "That is why we must investigate these matters, for already we are also getting close to our discourse about the gods." The deeper consideration of the roots of agency necessarily leads to the contemplation of all being, from Intellect and Soul to fire, as we saw in Chapter 2. For we have traced this back to will—or led it up again to will (cf. the ascents that we find in so many of Plotinus' works—I.3 [20] 1, 5; III.8 [30] 10, 20; V.4 [12] 1, 2), putting will in reason (so that the criterion of reason is not outside desire or the impetus of desire outside reason), and then in "correct reason" (cf. Plato, *Phaedo* 73a8; 94a1; Aristotle, *EN* 1144b25–28) with the proviso that reason must be grounded in a truly stable disposition, namely, knowledge or science. Only in this way will we have the unambiguous power of self-determination.

Excursus on Terminology: self-determination

This is the first mention of self-determination (3, 6: *autexousion*) in VI 8. Bréhier translates the term "puissance sur soi-même," Harder: " Selbstbestimmung," Leroux: "l' auto-détermination," McKenna: "true freedom," Lavaud: "la libre disposition de soi" and Armstrong: "power of self-determination."

Where does the term come from and why does Plotinus choose this word rather than some other, such as *exousia*—freedom—that he also employs? The compound of *auto* and *exousia* intensifies the sense of freedom as self-dependence and, therefore, emphasizes agency. It is noteworthy that of all the terms Plotinus uses to characterize freedom, will, and self-determination, he only once (VI.8.15, 27 *autarkē*) mentions "self-sufficiency" (*autarcheia*), but it is never directly applied to the Good.

Plotinus uses the word *autexousian* on only three occasions before VI.8 [39] and then only twice afterward. In a famous early passage, V.1 [10] 1, 5, it bears a negative sense and is certainly related to Gnostic thought: how have the souls forgotten their Father, God? Plotinus replies: "The beginning of evil for them was audacity (*tolma*) . . . and the willing to belong to themselves (*to boulēthenai heautōn*). Since they were clearly delighted with *their own sense of self-determination* (*toi autexousioi*) and made use of movement *from themselves* . . . they were ignorant even that they themselves came from that world . . ." In other words, *autexousion* intrinsically denotes the state and activity of being a self-mover, that is, an agent, even when this is negative. Next, in IV.3 [27] 16, Plotinus argues that we should not think of the order of the universe and the exercise of self-determination as somehow external to each other: "one must not think that some things are contained in the order, while others are let loose for the operation of self-determination [or free will] (*autexousion*)" (16, 13–15). Again, although this one word occurs in a massive set of treatises (IV.3 [27] and IV.4 [28]), the overall sense is that, however we are to think about everything that happens in the cosmos, rewards or punishments for deeds done—"what goes around comes around," self-determination remains an integral part of the order of the universe.

After VI.8, we have only three further uses: I.4 [46] on happiness and III.2 [47], the first of two works on providence. In I.4.8, 9, Plotinus insists that no matter how many pains the good person (*ho spoudaios*) may have to endure, they will not take away his power of self-determination. For Plotinus' sage or *spoudaios*, see Schniewind, 2003 and Remes, 2014, 453–470. Here there is a definite Stoic coloring: even if one is about to be swallowed alive by the agonies of material existence, self-dependent agency is real. And in the very next treatise, III.2.4, 37 and 10, 19, Plotinus emphasizes the freedom of self-determination for either good or ill: when something has its order from outside, it may fail to hit its own balance: "but living beings which have a movement of self-determination (*kinēsin autexousion*) might incline sometimes to what is better, sometimes to what is worse."

Finally, at III.2.10, 19, Plotinus emphasizes a point made by Aristotle in the *De anima* 3, 9–10 (see above) and also in the *Eudemian Ethics* (1199b2), in the context of *exousia*, that human beings are originative principles or *archai*: if the structured universe was exactly as its makers, the gods, fashioned it, so called evil men would not be able to oppose the divine structure. But we see that human beings are "from themselves": "Given a first principle, it accomplishes what follows in the chain of causation of all the principles there are; but human beings too are beginning principles; at any rate, they are moved to noble actions by their own nature, and this is a self-determining principle" (*archē hautē autexousios*).

Here we can already begin to see why Plotinus chooses *autexousion* for such prominent treatment in VI.8. Unlike other words, such as "the free," "voluntary," "what is in our power," etc., *to autexousion* denotes not just the subject agent *but what it is to be a subject agent*—with a range of possibilities, not simply as a steadfast originative principle, but as an agent in motion—even at levels higher than the human in V.1.1— capable of choice for good or ill. But this is only part of the reason, we suggest, for Plotinus' choice of *autexousion*.

The term is never used by Plato or Aristotle (though *exousia* is), but it is used frequently by the Stoics (Chrysippus, Epictetus) and on three occasions by Alexander of Aphrodisias, who is thinking about Stoic determinism (for references see Leroux, 257–258; Lavaud, 252n37; and for overview, Harl, 1960, xxvii–xxviii). What is definitive, in our view, is its usage in Christian, Jewish, and Gnostic texts; in Philo, for example, it appears fourteen times (TLG) and invariably designates divine freedom; Origen seventy-eight times; Clement of Alexandria fifteen; Clement of Rome fifteen; the *Corpus Hermeticum* four.

Exousia/autexousia occurs throughout many Gnostic texts: so, for example, *passim*: the *Apocryphon of John*, the *Hypostasis of the Archons, On the Origin of the World, Eugnostos the Blessed*, the *Sophia of Jesus Christ*, the *Apocalypse of Adam, Apocalypse of Paul, Paraphrase of Shem, Second Treatise of the Great Seth, Apocalypse of Peter, Testimony of Truth, Letter of Peter to Philip, Interpretation of Knowledge, Trimorphic Protennoia*, and *Gospel of Mary*—where it can designate hostile authorities, along with powers, archons, magnitudes/majesties, principalities, archangels (*archai, dynamai, daimones*).

The Greek *autexousia* is rendered in Coptic as *tmntautexousios* and occurs three times only in the *Nag Hammadi* corpus, all in the *Tripartite Tractate* (NHC I 5, trans. Thomassen, *Nag Hammadi Scriptures*):

Tripartite Tractate 69, 25–31: "They became fathers of the third glorification, which was produced in accordance with the free will (*kat' tmntautexousios*) and the power they had been born with, enabling them to give glory in unison while at the same time independently of one another, according to the will of each" (i.e., individual free will and self-production of each aeon rather than of Pleroma as whole).

Tripartite Tractate 74, 18–23: "The aeons were brought forth according to the third fruit, (cf. 69, 24–70, 19 = 3rd glorification?) by using the freedom of the will (*tmnntaut-exousios*), and the wisdom (*sophia*) the Father had graciously given them for their thoughts" (i.e., having wisdom, perhaps as the cardinal virtue of distinguishing good and evil, and free will means being able to turn oneself toward a higher level of *gnosis* in order to be fertilized by it).

Tripartite Tractate 75, 17–76, 23: "It came upon one of the aeons that he should undertake to reach the inconceivability of the Father, and to give glory to it as well as to his ineffability. It was a Word belonging to the unity, [although] it was not one that arose out of the union of the members of the All, nor from him who had brought them forth—for he who has brought forth the All <is> the Father. For this aeon was one of those who had been given wisdom, with ideas first existing independently in his mind so as to be brought forth when he wanted it. Because of that, he had received a natural wisdom (*ouphysis nsophia*) enabling him to inquire into the hidden order, being a fruit of wisdom (*oukarpos nsophia*). Thus, the free will (*piouōše nnaute{u}xousios*) with which the members of the All had been born caused this one to do what he wanted, with no one holding him back."

We can compare also in the *Tripartite Tractate* 9 occurrences of *exousia*, almost always meaning "power" or "authority," including pages 53 and 56: "boundless greatness, his inscrutable wisdom, his immeasurable power (*exousia*), and his sweetness that is beyond tasting"; see also the *Gospel of the Egyptians* IV 2, 79, 5–8: "O Perfect one, who art self-begotten and self-determined" (*eujpo e[bol mau]/aaf pe euex[ousia ebol m]/mof mauaaf*).

In other words, the range of the term from the divine to the human (especially in Jewish, Christian, and Gnostic texts) and its specific application to agency make it particularly appropriate for Plotinus' purpose here, namely, for an inquiry that will lead us through our own experience of the meaning of freedom to the gods. The faintest hint of a Gnostic sub-text is the first indication in this treatise of its kind. The term's Jewish, Christian, and Gnostic provenance, therefore, is important.

Reason, desire and intellect

We have emphasized that rather than taking up polemical positions, Plotinus seems to be thinking somewhat open-mindedly through the problems of "what belongs to us" and probing where to situate this in the drives of the soul itself and the psychosomatic being that he calls the "composite." Leroux argues that it is only Plato and Plotinus who make will identical with reason but Aristotle, not Plato, who makes will a form of desire. For Leroux (256–257), Plotinus' emphasis on the "impassibility" of intellect (see especially *Ennead* III.6 [26]) makes it impossible that there should be "any desire or *orexis* in the life of Intellect" (as Plotinus does say, for example, in IV.7 [2] 13, 3). We have argued instead that for Aristotle also, desire, reason and will converge in the life of rational agency. The highest form of desire, namely, the will, takes on a new energy in the life of the practical intellect and reason itself both transforms and is transformed by this convergence: "if the choice is to be seriously good (*spoudaia*), both the reason must be true and the desire correct (*ton te logon alethē einai kai orexin orthēn*), and . . . reason and desire must pursue the same aims" (*EN* 1139a23–27, cited above in comment on 2, 8–10).

Furthermore, if Aristotle's God—the Unmoved Mover—moves everything "by being loved" (*Metaphysics* 12, 7), that is, as a final cause of all desire, then desire must be a motive force not only for the 47 or 55 Unmoved Movers of the celestial spheres (*Metaphysics* 12, 8) and the psychic unmoved movers of *Physics* 8, but also, in some sense, of every intellect, contemplative and practical (that is, yours and mine). This must also be the case for Plotinus, however different his thought may be, for otherwise how can *eros* characterize the life of Intellect (as we have noted above in VI.7.35) or *orexis* be fundamental to the good life? See for example VI.5 [23] 1, 16: ". . . the ancient nature and the desire of the good . . . leads to what really is, and every nature hastens on to this, to itself" (cf. IV.4 [28] 35, 36; I.8 [51] 15, 7; and see also

VI.8.3, 26: "and we will say that this power is present in the gods . . . [as many as live by desire in accord with Intellect]").

From one viewpoint, then, intellect/Intellect—and all truly incorporeal entities—is impassible, with the imperturbability of a Socrates or a Stoic sage, and such impassibility is freedom, more or less, from passions and external things; from another viewpoint, intellect is not freedom *from*, but freedom *for* desire, that is, the awakening of a higher kind of desire, namely, a life that is intrinsic to desire of the Good.

3, 5–36: *body and intellect*

In 3, 5–36, Plotinus sets up a broad contrast between these two different perspectives, the sphere of body and the life of intellect. We will not grant self-determination to someone who does not know why he acted, even if he happens to get it right by chance or by some imagination; while there is a higher form of imagination based on opinion (III.6 [26] 4) and another even higher (V.3 [49] 11), imagination in the strict sense, Plotinus argues here, is body-based, since it follows bodily images (cf. Alexander, *On Fate* 178, 19) and is aroused and shaped by the bodily passions. And the same is true of inferior or bad people whose actions cannot really be called "in their power" or even voluntary, since they may do the good as it appears to them but they do it unknowingly (as Socrates had claimed—see, for example, *Republic* 589c). But we do grant self-determination to those who are free of the bodily passions and act through the energies of intellect (i.e., the contemplative intellect, presumably, in us). And the premises that come from here, through what is presumably our practical intelligence, are truly free and "the desires awakened from thinking" are not involuntary (as in *Republic* 7, 523a–524d, when out of opposing appearances, thought wakes up in us through perplexity into inquiry). This power of self-determination, Plotinus concludes, must be present in the gods where reason and desire converge in the life of intellect/Intellect.

At this point, the very notion of "intellect" is still undetermined. Is it my mind, your mind, and the convergence of practical and contemplative mind when we live according to something higher? Or is it the heavenly gods (the planets and stars) living in accord with the immaterial divine Intellect? Or is it ultimately the intellect of soul—of our souls? Or do we tentatively approach the divine Intellect here through all of the above perspectives? If the text is undetermined, that is perhaps how we should leave it and avoid capitalizing entities such as "intellect" before we know more and before we have to do so. Even "tracing up what is in our power to a fairest originative principle or *archē*" (3, 21–22) remains ambiguous, for as we have seen in both Aristotle and Plotinus, we human beings are originative principles because of mind, both practical and contemplative. Yet, at the same time, we are also originative principles by virtue of a universe of higher originative principles, all dependent on the First.

3, 10–11: *imagination*

Plotinus distinguishes two kinds of imagination in III.6 [26] 4, 18–23: "It should, then, be obvious to anyone that the mental picture is in the soul, both the first one, which we call opinion, and that which derives from it, which is no longer opinion, but an obscure quasi-opinion and an unexamined mental picture, like the activity inherent in what is called nature in so far as it produces individual things . . . without a mental image." The higher type of imagination appears to be related to judgment and the lower to images arising from the body. But they are probably both connected with the lower soul, as Blumenthal observes (1971, 93), and there is a still higher form of imagination. For higher and lower forms of imagination see IV.3 [27] 31 and Blumenthal, 88–94. And for the hint of imagination in the height of Intellect, see V.3 [49] 11, 7–9: Intellect or pre-intellect "desired one thing, having vaguely in itself a kind of image of it (*phantasma ti*), but came out having grasped something else which it made many in itself." This strange pre-intellectual image is probably suggested by an association with Plato's verb "to divine" as in the *Republic* (6, 505e–506a; and for the continuation of the image: 7, 531d; 538a–b that is, to divine that the Good is something) and in the *Symposium* (192c4–d2) in Aristophanes' speech to divine a deeper purpose (in the soul) in the passionate attachment of the divided halves to their original unity.

3, 18: *phaulos*

Not always "bad" but inferior, by reference to the "good" or "mediocre" (see Leroux, 260; Lavaud, 254). For Plato's frequent usage, see *Symposium* 174c5–7 (in the larger context of 174a–d) and *Republic* 6, 496a.

3, 21–26: Free self-determination must be traced primarily through our intellect to Intellect itself, for the premises derived from Intellect and the desires that Intellect awakes in us are not involuntary.

3, 22 *premises . . . truly free*: For the practical syllogism and two kinds of premises, one relating to the universal and the other to the particular case, see Aristotle, *EN* 1146b35–1147a10—if Plotinus has this in mind. The distinction seems broader, however, between premises flowing from intellect or the contemplative mind (mentioned later in 6, 32) into the practical intellect, on the one hand, and premises derived from the passions or a "mind" that is in some sense passive. See, for example, IV.4 [28] 44, 6: "But in practical life [as opposed to contemplation] there is no being of oneself, and reason does not produce impulse, but an origin also of the irrational is the premises derived from passion"; cf. I.3 [20] 4, 19; 5, 17; V.8 [31] 4, 49; I.8 [51] 2, 11.

Chapter 4

Objections: how can desire be compatible with freedom? How can intellect/Intellect be free if it acts out of necessity? How can intelligible things be free if they have no practical action? If our desire is led by something outside ourselves and intellect is determined by the necessity of its own nature, how can we link freedom through intellect/ Intellect to the Good?

4, 1–11: *How can desire that needs something outside itself be compatible with freedom? And how can intellects/Intellect be free if they must follow the necessity of their natures (according to Alexander of Aphrodisias)?*

4, 1–7 *And yet one may also inquire how that which comes about in accord with desire will ever be self-determined when desire leads to what is outside oneself and experiences neediness, for that which desires is led, even if it is led to the good*: The provisional conclusions of Chapter 3 Plotinus now proceeds to think through in more detail, setting out objections and replying to the objections as a way of taking the argument through a series of problems or *aporiae*. On the side of desire, in the first instance, there is necessarily neediness and dependence on something outside of itself; and even if there is desire of the good, as we implied at the end of Chapter 3, nevertheless desire experiences a kind of passivity, since it is being led to the good. On the side of intellect, on the other hand, we have the opposite problem. If intellect can act only in accordance with its nature, how can it be free, especially when it appears to lack the power *not* to act? We saw at the beginning of the treatise how Plotinus had in mind Alexander of Aphrodisias's denial that the notion of "what is in our power" (*to eph' hēmin*) can be applied to the gods since their being what they are is necessary and, therefore, cannot be said to be in their power: "In the case of the gods being such [as they are] will no longer depend on them because being like this is present in their nature, and none of the things that are present in this way is in one's power (*ep' autōi*)" (*On Fate* 204, 12–15; trans. Sharples). We also saw that Alexander allows the possibility of the gods having things in their power, if they have "the power (*exousia*) of also *not doing them* . . . if indeed they perform some actions concerning the things that can also be otherwise" (204, 22–23), that is, non-necessary actions in the sphere of change. Both of these problems, namely the necessary being of the gods and the fact that they do not appear to have the power not to act, are precisely the point of Plotinus' inquiry here. And they are important for many reasons, not least because it is far from clear how we are to think of desire in relation to the gods or how we are to apply notions that are action-related to the gods without yielding to the anthropomorphisms of popular religion or without populating the divine world with Gnostic and other super-entities.

4, 4–9 *activity* (*energeia*), *action/practical action* (*praxis*), *and making/doing* (*poiesis*): But the problem is also pressing in a different way for Plotinus, and we shall italicize the crucial Greek terms below in order to show this, since it is not obvious in any translation: "We must be at a loss about intellect itself," he says, "if when it actualizes what is in its nature and acts (*energōn*) according to its nature, it might be said to have freedom and 'what is in its own power,' when it does not have it in its power not to act (*poiein*); and then, in general, [we must be at a loss] whether "in their power" can strictly be said of those beings for whom there is no practical action (*praxis*)."

The three terms italicized are (1) *energoun* (*energeia*): to act; (2) *poiein* (*poiēsis*): to make, do or act; and *praxis* (with its infinitive verbal form: *prattein*): practical action or to act. Both (2) and (3) refer primarily to making and action in the physical sense of actually *doing something*, although (2), that is, *poiein* or *poiēsis*, can also in the *Enneads* mean making or producing in a spiritual sense as when Intellect-hypostasis generates or makes Soul-hypostasis. While (1) can also mean to act in a general sense, because of Aristotle's philosophy, among other things, it comes to mean the energy or action of intellect/Intellect or soul, that is, the spiritual energy of pure thought or contemplation, which is fully generative at the heart of intelligible reality. Aristotle also classified the sciences according to these three terms (*poiēsis, praxis, theōria/energeia*), starting with the productive sciences, in which subjects/artists make objects different from themselves, the practical sciences, such as ethics, economics and politics, in which subjects organize themselves, and culminating in the theoretical sciences, such as physics, mathematics, metaphysics and first philosophy or theology, in which subject and object are united in contemplative understanding. And Plotinus in III.8 [30] argues that *poiēsis* and *praxis* are at root forms of contemplation or intelligible activity, no matter how derivative or subsidiary they may be.

If we look at 4, 4–9 in the light of these different terms, we can see more acutely the problem Plotinus poses. According to Plotinus' many classic statements about the generation of spiritual principles in the intelligible world, Intellect's energy of pure thought necessarily *makes something else*. Spiritual energy necessarily gives from itself a second energy, an efflux, that, in turning back to, and seeing, its source, becomes something different from its source, that is, something "made" (*poioumenon*) or generated, something that has come-to-be (*genomenon*). So Plotinus' puzzle here is about his own thought: how can the divine Intellect, and indeed any intellect, be really free, if it is intrinsically productive—if its energy *cannot but make*? This is an important question that goes to the heart of so-called Neoplatonic emanation theory, that has so often been taken to be the opposite of free production—a quasi-mechanical or spontaneous reflex that involves, therefore, no agency or agent. What subject is it that can be said to act or do anything freely at this level?

Plotinus poses the problem even more acutely in his second *aporia*: "and then, in general, [we must be at a loss] whether 'in their power' can strictly be said of those beings for whom there is no practical action (*praxis*)." Can we really talk about Intellect and Soul or any of the gods having things in their power if they cannot *do* anything, that is, if they do not physically act?

4, 6 *to eleutheron*: This is the first appearance of the phrase *to eleutheron*, that which is free/freedom. *HBT* translates it as "Freiheit" (compare Chapter 5, 33). Here it is opposed to slavery (*to douleuein*) immediately in what follows according to the classic Greek conception: to be slave or master of one's being. This political notion pervades the treatise (Leroux, 264). See also in Plotinus: III.1 [3] 8, 10; III.3 [48] 4, 7.

4, 9–11: *external necessity*

Physical or practical action is also beset by an obvious related problem: external necessity. Action is necessarily goal-directed and other-directed. I always act in relation to something outside of me: I need food, sleep, a book or to get somebody else to do something. Of course, I may not achieve my goals. Something else might intervene; I may have conflicting motives; something totally unexpected might happen or might occur to me even as I act. But I am still dependent upon external or even internal forces; as Plotinus puts it, how can there be freedom if "these too are slaves to their own natures?" In other words, if spiritual realities are compelled by their own natures, why should physical agents be better off, if they are compelled by the physical systems of themselves and others?

4, 11–32: *Reply to the objections: For intelligible things, if being and acting are not separate, and if their nature and necessity are identical, then one cannot be enslaved to the other.*

In reply to the above objections, Plotinus argues that if we take a less determinist view of everything, we can say that if a subject is not compelled to follow another, there is no slavery involved here; and the desire of something that is led to the good is surely voluntary if it knows what it is doing and that its goal is something good. For we define the involuntary in ordinary language as an action that leads us away from our good by force toward something that is not our good. And we define slavery along similar lines as that which, being not in charge of its own good, is led away from its own good under the power of something or someone stronger. And this is why we find slavery blameworthy, not when someone has no power to do the bad, but when one has no power to do one's own good, but is compelled to do the good of another. In other words, we do not find slavery reprehensible because the slave has no power actively to choose what is bad for himself, but because he cannot choose his own good.

What Plotinus seems to be implying here is that freedom of choice, in life and death situations, does not mean actively choosing what is bad for us; freedom of choice, properly understood, means our ability to choose our own goods. Presumably, this is why Plotinus has not used the word *proairesis*, choice or purpose, so far. Though *proairesis* does not essentially involve choice between alternatives, it does involve in Aristotle's ethics a "weighing of alternatives" (see Joachim, 1971, 102–110).

Here in the case of slavery, we are immersed in the physical world where we are enslaved to passions, drugs, people, and even ourselves. Plotinus now suddenly transposes the argument onto the intelligible level, undoubtedly to show, first, that Intellect, and all intelligible beings, cannot be enslaved by the necessity of their being and, second, that what it means to be an agent even in the sphere of action has to be understood simultaneously by what we mean by intellect/Intellect. To be enslaved to one's nature involves two elements in the relationship: something that does the enslaving and something else that is enslaved. But a simple nature such as intellect/Intellect that does have a distinction between potentiality and actuality within it must be free, Plotinus argues, for it could not be said to be active by nature, if its activity was one thing and its substance another. Why should this be so? And how can there be a distinction between potentiality and actuality in the divine Intellect? Or is this the human intellect? And what does Plotinus mean by substantial being (*ousia*)?

4, 24–28: Excursus: *substance/substantial being*

Let us take substance, first, as a way of answering our other questions—we normally translate "substance" (*ousia*) as "substantial being." For Plotinus (and Aristotle), individual things like you and me, or dogs or horses, are substances and subjects that bear qualities, quantities, relations, etc. Individual substances are made of stuff (or matter); they grow into their distinctive forms (formal cause) in the sense that their forms develop toward a mature state or goal (final cause, *telos* or "that for the sake of which"). But they are not fully self-causing, since they need parents and the right conditions for a flourishing existence. In other words, we individual substances are not simply identical with substance; our substantiality is derivative—transmitted through our parents—and composite—made up of matter and form. But what is most substance in us is the form that gives us our definite nature, as Aristotle also argues in *Metaphysics* 7–8. And, in us, this form is the soul and our capacity for mind/intellect. However, if we were simply identical with our form, we would be identical with substance, since all immaterial forms simply *are* their substance. In the case of pure Intellect, therefore, and even of the "intellect" in us, the "intellect" of our souls, as it were, intellectual activity and substance are simply one; there is no distinction between a subject and the attributes it bears, as there is in any composite entity such as you or me. Here, being is "simple," not composite.

potentiality and actuality/activity

Can there be a distinction, then, between potentiality and actuality/activity in the divine Intellect, if Intellect is identical with its substance? Surely potentiality means the potentiality or power to develop over time into something—and this could not be attributed to the divine world? We have to realize that while intellect may be "simple" in the sense articulated above, it is not an indiscriminate melting pot, but a duality of subject thinking and object thought in unity, on the one hand, and a unity in multiplicity of all intellects—everything, on the other, each distinct and yet each not just containing, but *being* all. How this can be so is problematic since we can hardly imagine such a holographic unity in multiplicity, but Plotinus uses many examples that build on our own experience of having minds.

From Aristotle on, for instance, there is something like a distinction between potentiality and actuality in intellect: intellect is a kind of potentiality that is instantaneously actualized in thinking the object of thought, which, of course, is identical with itself; and, indeed too, there is something analogous between divine and human thinking, as we see in *Metaphysics* 12, 7, insofar as intellect is receptive of the object of thought and becomes actualized in thinking it. Aristotle here talks of intellect's "participation" in the object of thought and makes it clear that the whole of our experience, from thought to joy, derives its worth from intellect. So for Aristotle (and Alexander of Aphrodisias, who distinguishes a "material" intellect, an intellect *in habitu* and an active intellect; on this see Schroeder and Todd, 1990), the potentiality/actuality distinction in intellect is not strictly temporal, though the mind allows of development, but an instantaneous actualization of a capacity, power or openness to thought. Plotinus, of course, in some places rejects (physical) potentiality in the intelligible world (V.9 [5] 10, 15; VI.4 [22] 4, 39; II.5 [25]), but elsewhere he includes it as a way of explaining how the multiplicity of intellects can yet be one, like the intimate relation between genus and species, or of the theorems of a science or even the multiplicity virtually in seeds. Thus he tries to show how the whole may be said to possess the parts potentially or in power and how each part may be said to possess the whole potentially. For this see IV.8 [6] 3; IV.9 [8] 8; IV.3 [27] 2; VI.2 [43] 20; VI.4 [22] 4, 39; 16; II.9 [33] 2; I.2 [19] 4 and A. Smith, 1981, 99–107. Lavaud omits any mention of this distinction, preferring to emphasize that that there is no potentiality in intellect/Intellect. In other words, potentiality-actuality as it pertains to intellect, broadly speaking, stretches from our intellects and can be articulated as a hierarchy of "parts," each one of which is also the whole—in however attenuated form this might be—even the horse here, for instance, Plotinus observes in VI.7 [38] 9, 34–37, is "the last and lowest [manifestation] of this particular intellect."

This is why Plotinus here gives a single reply to the two objections he had raised above, namely, the objections that the gods are compelled by their own natures and that in pursuing external goals we are enslaved to our own natures. Neither the one nor the other is enslaved because the nature of intellect/Intellect is simple in being and activity, with a duality of power/potentiality and actuality. There is one reply to both extremes of the problem. To be an intelligible agent means not to be enslaved to one's own nature or to anything else, because one is simply oneself, at one with one's being. It therefore does not apply only to Intellect-Hypostasis in the strict sense, but to the divine Intellect with all intellects, which necessarily in a broader sense includes your intellect and mine—and much more besides, as we have seen.

So in these final lines of the chapter, Plotinus is certainly talking about the divine Intellect: "Being and acting there are the same thing." This identity is characteristic of all intelligible reality for Plotinus. See, for example, VI.6 [24] 6, 10–11; VI.7 [38] 40, 15–16; VI.2 [43] 15, 6–11; V.3 [49] 5, 40–41; 7, 18–20; 12, 5. But his focus remains broader as he weaves together different viewpoints. Such activity is neither because of another nor in the power of another; therefore, it must be free—even if we are speaking inadequately about something higher than what we normally mean when we say something is in our power. Nothing else is master of intellect's activity or its substance, if it is an originative principle. However, of course, intellect/Intellect does have another principle, namely, the Good, from which it derives (cf. V.1 [10] 11, 7; III.8 [30] 9, 39; VI.7 [38] 16, 32). How then are these two different statements compatible, namely, that intellect/Intellect has no master and yet that the Good is its principle?

4, 32–40: *To be in one's own power is to be in the Good and, therefore, to be more free.*

For Plotinus, the Good is not outside intellect, but is its inner foundation. Intellect is in the Good, for the Good is the light by which intellect sees (see V.5 [32] 7, 33–34). And so to act in accord with the Good is to be even more free and in one's own power. In fact, this is what "anyone" seeks in acting in accord with the Good (4, 36).

The chapter's final lines try to capture the inner reflexive nature of Intellect or of any thinking subject (see 5, 1–3) in relation to its source ("for it already has the object of its vision toward which it is directed and from which it has come in itself too [if it is to it], which is better for it to be in it, if indeed it is directed to it")—and they are therefore difficult, quite apart from the fact that the text is corrupt, presumably as the result of the confusion of several copyists in its earlier transmission.

4, 35 [*to*] *ep'autō*: It seems necessary to accept Kirchoff's addition of [*to*] *ep'autō* (*<to> ep'autō kai to eleutheron*):

"much more does it have 'the being in its own power and what is free.'"

4, 38–40 *hormōmenon/ horōmenon*: First, there are two different readings at line 38; Kirchoff's *hormōmenon* ("stirred up," "impelled") and the manuscript reading *horōmenon* ("that which is seen"). And, second, the phrase *eiper pros auto* ("if it is directed to it") occurs twice between lines 38–40 and is probably a scribal error—dittography. The whole sentence reads: *ēdē gar echei to pros auto ex autou hor<m>ōmenon kai en autōi, eiper pros auto, kai en autōi, ho ameinon an eiē autōi en autōi an einai, eiper pros auto* (37–40).

Kirchoff's reading *hormōmenon* may, in fact, pick up the Stoic notion of impulse (*hormē*) introduced in 2, 3, but transposed here onto a higher level. Armstrong, with Bréhier, Igal, *HBT*, accepts *hormōmenon* and translates it as "goes": "for it has already what *goes* from itself to it, and in itself what would be better for it, being in it, if it is directed towards it." Against this view, there is no direct parallel in the *Enneads*, although *hormōmenon* does occur in VI.1 [42] 20, 4, whereas *to horōmenon* occurs sixteen times. In general, therefore, it seems preferable, wherever possible, to retain the manuscript reading.

What about the repetition of *eiper pros auto*? Armstrong brackets the first (38–39), whereas Lavaud eliminates the second. BHT eliminate the final words of the chapter: *en autōi an einai, eiper pros auto.* We prefer to bracket the first *eiper pros auto* on the grounds that the repetition of the phrase results from the puzzlement of a copyist. And we translate accordingly, with Lavaud: "for it already has in itself too the object of its vision toward which it is directed and from which it has come, which is better for it to be in it, if indeed it is directed to it [the Good]."

Chapter 5

Self-determination and being in one's power are not only in intellect/Intellect but also in soul. How then are freedom and virtue related? Can self-determination be related to action?

5, 1–27: *Is the virtue of soul that governs action really free? If virtue is compelled and only the inner determination is free, then freedom will be outside action.*

Chapter 5 looks critically at the question of how self-determination can be related to action. We see again how Plotinus interweaves concurrent perspectives into his argument, that of "intellect," broadly conceived, that of the divine Intellect itself, that of "anyone" seeking the Good, and here in 5, 1–3 three further precisions: are self-determination and being in one's power in intellect only when it thinks and, and in intellect that is pure, or are they also in soul when it acts (*energousēi*) in accordance with intellect/Intellect and engages in morally good practical actions (*kata aretēn prattousēi*)?

5, 1–3 *Are then self-determination and being in one's own power in intellect alone when it thinks and in an intellect that is pure, or is it also in soul when it acts in accordance with intellect and engages in practical action in accordance with virtue?*: As we saw above, Plotinus distinguishes two layers of activity: *energeia* is the inner intelligible *activity* and *praxis* the outer *practical action*. We can compare Alcinous, *Handbook* (Dillon, 1993, 153, 2–5): "Contemplation (*theōria*) . . . is the activity (*energeia*) of the intellect when intelligizing the intelligibles, while action (*praxis*) is that activity (*energeia*) of a rational soul which takes place by way of body." However, as we see in III.8 [30] 4, *energeia* or intelligible activity is the deeper reality of what practical action tries, or fails, to express: we do things, however unconsciously, in order to contemplate; compare VI.8.5, 9: *tēn tote energeian* refers to the particular activity of being virtuous during wartime. The three further precisions Plotinus introduces seem to be as follows: first, we refer to an active, not a potential intellect. This seems to be the sense of the phrase "intellect only when it thinks." Second, we refer to the "pure" intellect. Here Plotinus certainly seems to include what he calls elsewhere "the purified intellect in us" (cf. V.8.2–3). And, third, we refer to the soul, properly speaking, that acts in conformity with intellect/Intellect as a morally good agent. The soul here seems to be lower than the "pure intellect" but we should note that Plotinus' thought is often elastic. In VI.7, for instance, the soul can "become intellect" (35, 4–5) and, "being carried on the swell of the wave of the divine Intellect," it can see the light of the Good itself (36, 15–20). In other words, under the influence of the ladder of ascent from Socrates-Diotima's speech in the *Symposium*, the hierarchical order of three hypostases (the One, Intellect, and Soul), with our individual souls lower still, can be subverted by the experience of any soul being catapulted above everything to the Good. On what it means for us or our soul to become so transformed by and into Intellect (*noōtheisa*) see Beierwaltes, 2001, 84–122.

5, 3–7 *Now if we grant this to the soul in its practical action, first we need not grant it to the accomplishment of the action, for we are not masters of the outcome. But if this refers to doing well and doing everything from oneself, perhaps one might rightly claim this*: In 5, 3–7, Plotinus thinks through the practical action of the soul in relation to Stoic thought. If we grant that the soul's practical action is free, we do not need to include the outcome of the action, for anything can intervene and prevent the intended outcome—for example, a breath of wind can interfere with the archer's hitting the target, but we would include everything that relates to the archer's skill and execution of the shot. Epictetus, for instance, excludes the outcome or accomplishment (*teuxis*) from what is in my power (*Handbook* II, 5, 8), but the proper virtuous execution is in our power (cf. Cicero, *On the ends of good and evil* III, 6, 22).

And yet—implicitly against the Stoic position, surely the exercise of moral virtue always depends upon circumstances: a war calls for a certain courage that would never have been actualized otherwise. But if one gave virtue a choice (*hairesis*) whether there should be war so that it could exercise bravery, and injustice so that we could define justice, on the one hand, or to lead a restful life, on the other, it would surely choose restful quiet from practical actions (*heloito an tēn hēsychian tōn praxeōn*). Here for the first time Plotinus puts a strong emphasis upon choice, and the notion of restful quiet (*hēsychia*) is introduced—a significant notion in relation to virtue elsewhere (see, for example, I.2 [19] 5, 28–30; cf. II.3 [52] 9, 18ff.).

Lavaud sees this argument as directed against the Stoics who emphasized the interiorization of freedom and what is in our power but, in maintaining a relation between interior freedom and action, did not go far enough for Plotinus. Lavaud, therefore, characterizes Plotinus' view as much more radical: "Plotin pour sa part accomplit une intériorisation radicale de la liberté: elle relève purement et simplement de l'intelligible . . . et doit être dissociée de tout rapport avec l'action" (260, 69). We see this differently: Plotinus' arguments here are dialectical, that is, they look at a problem from different viewpoints and, as yet, do not adopt a final position. It is therefore a *problem* for him that if we place will and reason before action, and consider action as something "compelled," then self-determination and "what depends on virtue" will be outside action. There is then no complete dissociation of interior freedom from action, though the final line of Chapter 5 appears to state just this: ". . . being in our power does not occur in action, but rather in intellect quietly at rest from actions." This, however, is not Plotinus' own final position, as Chapter 6 will make clear. What Plotinus stresses is the problem: while our embodied freedom cannot be entirely outside of action and, therefore, cannot be purely free, nonetheless, if we cut our freedom completely away from action, it will not be *our freedom*. And he thinks through this problem—first, in relation to the Stoics, and a few lines later with reference to Plato, Aristotle and the ancient tradition—before finally coming in Chapter 6 to a precise statement of his own position. Plotinus is, therefore, reviewing different available options prior to making his own determination.

5, 27–37: ***But if virtue organizes practical life, has no master, and establishes freedom, perhaps this makes it "another intellect" and a "habit" that organizes the soul—and then still this is outside of action in the restful quiet of intellect.***

5, 27–28 *and what of virtue itself . . . in accordance with habit and disposition?*: See Plato, *Philebus* 11d4–6: "it is a condition and disposition of the soul (*hexin psuchēs kai diathesin*) which can make life happy for all human beings"; Aristotle *Nicomachean Ethics* 1106a22–24: "excellence or virtue in a man will be the disposition (*hexis*) which renders him a good man and also which will cause him to perform his function well"; compare Plotinus II.5 [25] 2, 34). In *Categories* 8b28, Aristotle holds that "habit (*hexis*) differs from disposition (*diatheseōs*) in being more lasting and more firmly established." For *diathesis* see Plotinus I.5 [36] 10, 13; and for *hexis* and *diathesis* together see Philo, *leg. all.* 3, 210.

5, 28–30 *is the work of virtue in our power?*: The point is implicitly this: if the soul is in a bad state and then becomes good by virtuous action, is this work not in its power?

5, 30–31 *virtue . . . without a master*: In what way do *we say* that virtue is without a master? The reference is primarily to Plato, *Republic* 10, 617e (*aretē de adespoton*) in the sense there that the virtue of one's soul alone determines one's future life. The formula can also be found in Epicurus (Diogenes Laertius X 133), and in later Platonism, for example, Plutarch (*Quaestiones Conviviales* 740d2), Alcinous (*Didaskalikos* 27, 179, 10ff.) and Proclus and Olympiodorus later. For references and comment see Romano, 1999, 151–191; Sorabji, 2000, 324ff.; Horn, 2007, 176–177. Plotinus refers to the formula twice in VI.8 at 5, 31 and 6, 6, and twice elsewhere in IV.4 [28] 39, 2 and II.3 [52] 9, 17.

5, 32–37 *In what way do we say that being good is in our power and "virtue has no master"? Yes indeed, this is so for those who will it and choose it! Or that when (virtue) comes to be, it establishes freedom and being in our own power and no longer allows us to be slaves to that to which we were previously enslaved?*: When we (Platonists) speak in this way, we mean that it applies to those *who will and choose it*. Or do we also mean that when virtue comes to birth in us, it establishes freedom and being in our power and frees us from previous slavery? If then virtue is another intellect, so to speak—that is, another way of thinking and being, different from our previous slavery or mixed condition; and if it is a habit that makes the soul intelligible, that is, something that transforms the soul into mindfulness, then "being in our power" is not in action but in an intellect at rest from action, Plotinus concludes. Here we should note that to put "what is in our power" in intellect, and not action, does not mean that such freedom has *no relation* to action whatsoever.

Since true virtue is found only in intellect, the soul must be freed and calmed from the realm of worldly deeds governed by the civic virtues, that is, "intellectualized" by the contemplation of intellect/Intellect. For the word "intellectualized" elsewhere see VI.7 [38] 35, 5. Lavaud, 262, refers to Plotinus' discussion of contemplative virtue in I.2 [19] 6, 11–15: "What then is each particular virtue when one is in this state (i.e., assimilated to God; cf. *homoiōsis theōi kata to dunaton, Theaetetus* 176b)? Wisdom, theoretical and practical, consists in the contemplation of that which intellect contains; but intellect has it by immediate contact. There are two kinds of wisdom, one in intellect, one in soul." See also Beierwaltes, 2001, 84–122.

Chapter 6

What is free human agency? To what in us do we attribute it and what does it include? Resolution of the impasse between inner freedom and external action; the definition of human freedom as including both. Soul through virtue, and intellect even more so, is self-dependent. So we refer what is in our power and self-determination in actions not to action as such but to the inner activity, thought or contemplation that makes the outer activity in that focus free.

6, 1–26: *Only virtue—identified with the inner activity of thought—and contemplation are free.*

6, 1–18 *So how did we previously refer this to will when we said "what would happen to the extent that it was willed"?*: This chapter draws the major conclusions of the first part of the treatise on the basis of the first five chapters. Plotinus refers first (6, 1–3) to Chapters 1, 32–33 and 3, 2, that is, with reference to tracing back what is in our power to will (or here, perhaps, to "a" will) and the power to will something either to happen or not to happen. We can compare Aristotle, *EN* 1113b9ff: ". . . if it is in our power to do something when it is fine, it is also in our power not to do it when it is shameful." Second, Plotinus refers (6, 3) to the findings of Chapter 5, namely, that being in our power belongs to intellect primarily, and he argues that if these two different strands—will as the root of choice and intellect as the root of freedom—are consistent (6, 4), then freedom, what is in our power and mastery are to be referred to moral virtue and intellect. They are both "without a master," but there is a slightly different emphasis in either case: intellect is simply self-dependent, free in a primary sense, while moral virtue wills to be self-dependent and assumes the responsibility to make the soul good and free (6, 4–10). What Plotinus seems to mean is that moral virtue involves two additional perspectives, if we can put it this way: it has to will the good and it has to assume a certain kind of care for the soul in order to draw it up into freedom. In other words, what we actually experience in the life of the soul is the transforming, dynamic power of virtue; and this gives us freedom, so that, as we saw in Chapter 5, virtue is a question of decision, that is, of will and choice: being good is in our power "if we will and choose it" (5, 30–32). This freedom in the soul, by contrast with that of intellect, is only *mekri toutou* (line 9): up to this point, that is, a necessarily ambiguous freedom, restricted by the power to stand over the whole soul and to provide freedom.

By contrast, when we are attacked by compulsive passions and actions—the position we started from in Chapter 1, 23ff., even though we have not willed these things (cf. 5, 13–24), the soul maintains its self-dependence even in such conditions by referring back to itself, not yielding to the particular circumstances, even if its refusal to yield looks impossibly heroic and definitely Stoic (6, 10–18). And this certainly is the Stoic side of Plotinus' position: to have as its goal its own beauty, not the existence of what is subject to it (line 18). Note throughout this passage a kind of ambiguity in Plotinus' thinking about intellect, soul, and composite existence, even though he will emphasize the priority of the immaterial, he includes embodied existence throughout.

6, 12 *beboulēsthai*: We read *beboulēsthai* ("be willed") with manuscript J, Lavaud and HS_2, instead of *bebouleusthai* ("be deliberated"), as in the majority of manuscripts.

6, 26–32: *What is free and self-dependent is the immaterial and to this we make ultimate reference in us. But everything that comes from and because of our will is in our power—both everything external and everything self-dependent. What it wills and actualizes without hindrance is primarily in our power.*

6, 19–31: *What is free human agency?*

What Plotinus argues for next is a precise Platonic-Aristotelian formulation of how this is to be understood, and he concludes the first part of his argument about human free will in Chapter 6 as follows:

"... so that both self-determination *in practical actions* and what is in our power *is referred neither to practical action nor to the outward activity but to the inner activity, that is, the thought and contemplation of virtue itself*.... So it is still clearer that the immaterial is free, and it is to this that being in our power is to be referred and the will itself that is master and self-dependent, even if something directs it to what is outside of necessity. Everything therefore that comes from and because of this will is in our power, *both everything external and everything self-dependent.* What it wills and actualizes without hindrance, this too is primarily in our power" (6, 19–31).

It might well seem that the above passage excludes action from true free will. But this is clearly not so. Plotinus specifies that he means *in practical actions* and that we refer *everything* self-dependent and in our power, *both external and internal,* to free will rooted in the immaterial. What is real in action is the inner activity, *noēsis* and *theōria,* as we saw in III.8 on nature, contemplation and the One. And only the free subject truly acts or makes in the physical world, since his or her *praxis* manifests externally the inner energy that forms one reality with it; and the inner activity is the action's formal and final cause, *"the thought and contemplation of its healthy functioning."* "Its intrinsic healthy functioning" is another possible translation of "virtue itself," for the word *arêtē* signifies the good, healthy or excellent functioning of anything whatsoever—ranging from pruning forks and hands, through bodily systems and psycho-somatic organic complexities, to psychic drives, and moral and intellectual capacities. Free agency, therefore, is a fully real, historical fact, grounded in each subject's firm orientation to intellect/ Intellect and the Good through which it wills, orders and makes the world to be good. But still, one might reply, does this not make the agent an intelligible entity rather than an embodied person like you or me acting in any real situation? We in the modern world want to make the agent a fully real unity (or multiplicity of various constructed egos) rather than some abstract ghostly presence, however "intelligible" such an agent may be.

There are two helpful and important features of the above passage that do not immediately suggest themselves to the modern reader, but that would have been more apparent to knowledgeable readers in Plotinus' school. First, the phrasing of the above passage shows that while Plotinus frames his conclusion in the terms of Aristotle's thought (e.g., *noēsis, theōria, energeia*)—and for reasons we will examine immediately below—he is plainly thinking of a crucial passage in Plato's thought where the union of the inner and the outer dimensions of life is given classical expression. When Socrates finally defines justice as characterizing the whole soul (and not just the different parts or powers) in *Republic* 4, 443d–444a, he defines it as follows:

". . . justice is something of this kind, not about the external action of the things of oneself (*ou peri tēn exō praxin tōn hautou*), but about the inner action (*peri tēn entos*), truly about oneself and the things of oneself (*peri heauton kai ta heautou*), not allowing each kind in the soul to do alien things or to meddle with one another (*polupragmonein*) . . . . He regulates well what is really his own and rules himself, puts himself in order (*arxanta auton hautou kai kosmēsanta*), is his own friend . . . and from having been many things he becomes entirely one, moderate and harmonious. Only then does he act (*prattein*). And when he does anything (*prattēi*), whether acquiring wealth, taking care of his body, engaging in politics, or in private contracts—in all of these, he believes that the action is just and fine which preserves this inner harmony and helps achieve it, and calls it so, and regards as wisdom (*sophian*) the knowledge that oversees this action (*epistatousan tautēi praxei*). And he believes that the action that destroys this harmony is unjust, and calls it so, and regards the belief that oversees it as ignorance."

Here we have a classic Platonic formulation in terms of *action* of how the inner self-relation of the agent is the precondition of any just action. Action is not excluded from this self-relation; instead, just or appropriate action comes into its proper focus in and because of this relation, since the inner and outer have become unified in an agent that "from many [has become] one." Plotinus adopts this position but changes the inner and outer *action* (*praxis*) to the Aristotelian notion of *activity* (*energeia*) precisely because, after the time of Aristotle, *praxis* came to mean principally *practical action* (which it does not in Plato) and also because Aristotle's complex notion of activity is more subtly adapted to Plotinus' thought.

As is well known, Plotinus adapts Aristotle's notion of physical causality to explain the derivation of

Intellect-hypostasis from the One and Soul from Intellect (cf. V.4 [7]); Rutten, 1956, 100–106; Lloyd, 1990, 98–106). There is the act of an entity and the act from the entity, like fire and the warmth that comes from the fire. In this relation, Intellect "makes" something else, just as fire makes warmth that becomes distinct from the fire. They are not cut off from each other; in fact, they constitute a single activity but from different points of view: fire and its warmth, Intellect and Soul. Just as teaching and learning, for instance, involve two different subjects, but constitute a single activity (*energeia*) from different perspectives (Aristotle, *Physics* 8, 255a33–b5; 3, 202a13–21), so also what is an action or an external motive force from one viewpoint is a manifestation of the deepest reality from another. The same activity involves two distinct aspects (Aristotle, *Physics* 3, 202b7–8; cf. Plotinus, VI.8.6, 19–22; compare the argument of IV.4 [28] 28 culminating in 28, 69–72; for the two-act theory, Rutten, 1956, 100–106; Lloyd, 1990, 98–101) but is nonetheless a single activity seen from two different viewpoints. What is divine from one aspect may be quite human from another! At the same time, the Aristotelian scale of nature embodies a hierarchy of different developmental forms, the lower forms always requiring the higher forms for their fuller actualization and explanation. All lower forms, therefore, require the energy of higher-order forms to give them their proper meaning. God is not therefore an explanation or cause remote from worms, butterflies, hopes, and thoughts, but their ultimate and yet proper meaning present to them from the beginning.

This is also true here, but in a particularly intimate way, for while Plotinus specifies two different perspectives (inner and outer), there is effectively a single *energeia*, since it is not a question of x making something different from itself, but of x doing something that is intrinsic to itself. For Aristotle too, the maker produces something beyond the producing; and the goodness of the production is embodied in the product. However, while practical action also covers all forms of doing something, especially a "doing" which is directed to and defined by an external goal, not all *praxis* has its end outside itself, for *praxis* as an *energeia* has its end only in so far as it is active. Joachim (1970, 207) gives the following examples: seeing, thinking (*phronēsis*), intellection (*noēsis*), the good life and happiness. "All of these are *energeiai* or energies of that which is perfected—not transitions *to* completeness, but manifestations *of* completeness" (cf. *Metaphysics* 8, 1048b23). Unlike the craftsman, therefore, whose works of *technē* "have their value in themselves," the success of the ethically good person (the *phronimos*) is the *acting well itself*. The "works" of the ethically good person are what they are in his or her "living them" (Joachim, 207). Or in Aristotle's terms (*EN* 1100b9–10), "the active exercise [of our faculties] in accordance with virtue is master of happiness" (*kuriai d' eisin hai kat'aretēn energeiai tēs eudaimonias*).

Plotinus' thought is different here in VI.8.6, not least because he extends this understanding of *praxis* as *energeia* to "everything external" that is actualized from this perspective, but his thought is certainly colored by this understanding of both Plato and Aristotle. Graeser in his book *Plotinus and the Stoics* (1972, 112–125) introduces into his discussion the anachronistic (Kantian-like) distinction between the "metaphysical" and "empirical" selves, roughly analogous to the distinction between the intelligible and sensible worlds. Although these terms are anachronistic, what we actually find in VI.8.6, 19–31 is the precise point in Plotinus' thought where the metaphysical and empirical "selves" unite in a single agent. And in the final sentence of this entire sequence at 6, 30–31, Plotinus enlarges the focus finally to include all such unimpeded activity/action: what it wills and actualizes (i.e., what it *actually does* in this active way) without hindrance, this is primarily in our power. This is not simply the absence of internal constraints (Leroux, 279 on 6, 31), but both internal and external. However, "without hindrance" applies properly to freedom in the full sense (see 7, 1 and 8, 12; cf. 7, 39). For the two terms together, unhindered (*anempodiston*) and unimpeded (*akōluton*), see Epictetus, *Diss.* II.19.32.4–33.1). For the term *anempodistos* and cognate forms, see I.5 [36] 4, 3; I.4 [46] 1, 3; I.8 [51] 4, 3.

The emergence of real freedom, therefore, is a manifestation or actualization of the intelligible dimension of agency in empirical life. This manifestation transforms the whole range of practical life, unites the inner and the outer forms of agency, and extends the power of that agency to everything that was hitherto merely external. This is possible only because such a new dimension of agency is no longer that of a solitary ego, caught in the oppositions of life, but a world of possibility in which the self becomes, for the first time as it were, pervaded by the discourse of "intellect/Intellect" and the activity of intelligible insight that makes intelligent activity in the world possible—no matter how difficult. This is not just a function of rationality, but of one's whole being—everything, in fact, that one really is.

6, 23–24 *not counted along with the passions . . . enslaved or measured by reason*: Compare Aristotle, *EN* 1106b15–26; and see Leroux, 278 ad loc.; "not counted . . . with the passions:" perhaps against Aristotle; cf. *EN* 1115a6ff; 1115b11ff. As *HBT* observe, "[enslaved] nach der stoischen Apathie, [measured] nach der peripatetischen Metriopathie" (370).

6, 24–25 *Plato*: Compare Plato, *Republic* 7, 518d10–e2: "Then the other so-called virtues of the soul risk being akin to those of the body, for not truly preexisting, they are created afterwards by habit and practice. But the virtue of thought (*phronēsai*), it seems, is certainly of a more divine quality, a thing that never loses its power."

6, 32–40: Transition from the (implicit) practical intellect (under discussion), through the contemplative intellect, to Intellect in the full sense, and the will of the Good.

6, 32–36: *Aristotle—contemplative intellect*

It is perfectly appropriate in relation to Plotinus' method of ascent throughout to introduce the contemplative intellect (*theōretikos nous*) at this point: Aristotle, *De anima* 432b27–29: "For the contemplative mind contemplates nothing in the realm of practical affairs and pronounces nothing concerning what is to be avoided or pursued." Plotinus has moved up implicitly from the sphere of the practical intellect in the earlier chapters and a meditation on *De anima* 9–10, through truly free human agency in 6, 19–31, to the contemplative intellect that contemplates nothing *practical*, but from which truly free premises are derived (3, 23). For the contrast between the contemplative and the practical intellect, see V.3 [49] 6, 35ff. Lavaud, 264, rightly refers to *EN* 10, 6, 1177b19–21: "the activity of the intellect is felt to excel in serious worth, consisting as it does in contemplation, and to aim at no end beyond itself, and also to contain a pleasure peculiar to itself, and therefore augmenting its activity; and if accordingly the attributes of this activity are found to be self-sufficiency, leisureliness, such freedom from fatigue as is possible for mankind, and all the other attributes of blessedness, it follows that it is the activity of the intellect that constitutes complete human happiness." But this is precisely where the difficulties—indeed, the apparent incompatibilities between the practical and the contemplative lives—seem most to emerge. Joachim, 1970, 288–297, points out some of the major problems of Aristotle's views in the

EN, *De anima*, and other works: does the contemplative life annihilate or break with the practical life or does the former complete the latter? Again, "is intellect itself divine—i.e., whether it is God in man, whether there is one intellect only, viz. God—or whether it is only that in us which is most akin to God—at any rate it seems to be viewed as pure form and not as a form of the body. It is in us without being of us" (Joachim, 1970, 288).

Some of these ambiguities are also to be found in Plotinus and Alexander of Aphrodisias. There is a sharp distinction in Plotinus between the rational or dianoetic level and the intellectual level of true understanding, but as we have seen here in VI.8.1–6, there is a gradation of intellect ranging from intellect in soul, the purified intellect in us, to the unity of inner and outer energy in agency, reaching into various discourses about "intellect/Intellect" itself. Indeed, for both Alexander and Plotinus, Intellect in the strict sense is both "ours and not ours." We belong to it rather than it belonging to us. For a different view of the difficulty but necessity of moving from the practical to the contemplative ideal in Aristotle, see Lear, 1988 152–302.

6, 36–38 *And its will is thinking . . . for we do say that "will imitates what accords with its mind"*: Armstrong points out that Plotinus is playing on the common meaning of *kata noun*—so minded, "according to one's mind" (244n2). The thought of Alexander of Aphrodisias (against the self-sufficiency of virtue) is very close to that of Plotinus at *Mantissa*,

24, 165, 3–5: "Moreover, if we say that someone acts as he is minded, not because he acts in whatever way he does having a mind, but because he acts as his mind wishes . . . just so the person who acts in accordance with virtue will act . . . because [he acts] as virtue wishes." However, we are not simply in the sphere of the "Divine Intellect" because Plotinus here, as earlier and later, continues to interweave different narrative possibilities. For example, "intellect wants the Good and is in the Good"—this probably refers to the Divine Intellect. But the following sentence is more nuanced: "So that intellect has what its will wants, and when it attains this, it becomes thinking (*hou tychousa an tautēi noēsis ginetai*)." Yes, Plotinus can talk of the Divine Intellect "always desiring and always attaining (*tychanōn*) its object." The same verb "attain" (*tuchanein)* is used in both cases. And, of course, Plotinus can also speak of Intellect as coming to be out of the One. But the context is a little different here, and much more like that in Aristotle's *Metaphysics* 12, 7, 1072b20–21, where Aristotle too weaves together different discourses, one about God and the other about intellect generally where intellect "becomes intelligible in touching and thinking" its object (*noētos gar gignetai thigganōn kai noōn*). "Touching" in Aristotle and "attaining" or "happening upon" in Plotinus are semantically related. Since this ambiguity between different levels of discourse runs right throughout these chapters and beyond (as we will see in Chapters 7 and 8), we prefer to avoid capitalizing "intellect," unless we are compelled to do so.

Chapter 7

Transition: presentation of "the rash argument from a different viewpoint." There are degrees of freedom in soul, intellect, and the Good, but what if the Good is not free because it is not master of its own nature?

7, 1–11: *Degrees of freedom in soul, intellect/Intellect and the Good.*

The first eleven lines of Chapter 7 effectively sum up the argument so far and transpose it into a new key as an introduction to the major problem that will be the subject of the rest of the treatise.

Soul becomes free when it hastens *through intellect* unhindered to the Good (and, as we have seen, soul does just this in VI.7, Chapters 34–35) and what it does *because of intellect* is in soul's power. By contrast, intellect/Intellect does this *through itself.* Soul, as Plotinus will say, is "in" Intellect, whereas Intellect is "in" the One. Therefore, the immediate object of desire for Intellect is the Good. There is "nothing in between" them, as Plotinus says frequently, and as Aristotle says of the agent's activity, that is, the teacher: "[it] is not cut off from the experience of the patient or learner—[the activity] is *of* something *in* something else" (*Physics* 202b7–8l; cf. Lloyd, 1990, 100). *HTB* 4b, 371 see the three Plotinian hypostases here—Soul, Intellect, and the Good—rightly insofar as "they are also present in us" (V.1 [10] 10, 1–10), but Plotinus includes more than the hypostases, as we have seen.

7, 4–6: *The One and the others—Plato's Parmenides*

When Plotinus says next that the Good is also "that through which the others have what is in their power, when one is able to attain it without hindrance and the other to have it"—when he frames it in this way he is thinking broadly (as we have seen implicitly throughout these early chapters) of a distinction between the Good or the One and everything else ("the others"). In the second part of the *Parmenides*, the Athenian Stranger in dialogue with a young Aristotle (probably not the Aristotle we know) sets out a series of chains of arguments to explore the consequences of assuming either that there is or there is not a one/One and if there is or is not a "one" what are the consequences for the "others" (*ta alla*—as here in 7, 4). Two things are noteworthy here: First, Plotinus' interest from the start has been implicitly to find the "one" or real agent in us and trace it back to the One itself. Second, this implicit framework of "the One" and "the others" shows us that when Plotinus thinks of everything other than the One, he includes everything at whatever level of existence: intellect/Intellect, soul/Soul, body, etc. For what is, or might have been, included in "the others" for the Neoplatonists, see Morrow/Dillon, 1992, xxiv–xxxiv; for Plotinus specifically, Corrigan, in Turner/Corrigan 2010, 2.35–48).

7, 6 *when one is able to attain it without hindrance and the other to have it*: In the immediate context, the one who is able to attain it—presumably through intellect/Intellect—is the soul, whereas the other who is able to have it is intellect/ Intellect. But the language of attaining and having could so easily in a different context mean something very different: intellect is itself by "having" its object, while in touching upon or attaining the Good in its desire for its real source, it is higher than Intellect (III.8.11, 23–25) or it becomes a loving, even "daft" intellect in its more intensive desire for the Good (VI.7.35).

7, 6–11: *But surely we cannot apply the expression "in its power" to the Good?*

7, 7 *the wish to ascend*: This ascent is emphasized throughout VI.8 (at 6, 44; 9, 35; 14, 16; 15, 21). Cf. VI.9 [9] 3, 21; VI.7 [38] 25, 19–24; see also Plato, *Republic* 6, 519d1; 7, 524e2–525a2 and following; *Symposium* 209e5–212c2.

7, 8 *the others . . . depend (exērtētai) on it*: Everything desires the Good and everything depends on it. The term is common in Plato (*Theaetetus* 156a4; *Meno* 88e8; *Laws* 5, 729e4; 732e6), conspicuous in a famous passage in Aristotle (*Metaphysics* 12, 7, 1072b13), appears elsewhere (e.g., Seneca, *Quaest. Nat.* II.45, 1ff.), and is found everywhere in Plotinus of the relation of Intellect, or everything else, to the One (VI.6 [34] 18, 48; VI.5 [23] 10, 2; VI.7 [38] 16, 5), or of soul to intellect (III.5 [50] 2, 30), or of inferior to superior (III.3 [48] 4, 8). For overview see Leroux, 285–286; Atkinson, 1983 on V.1 [10] 1, 14).

7, 8–11: *the problem of anthropomorphism vs. divine freedom*

Here Plotinus acknowledges a major difficulty in his whole approach; how can we presume to trace what is in the power of the Good through our understanding of what is in our power without reducing the Good in some sense to our viewpoints, that is, without avoiding anthropomorphism or own preferences. Even in the case of intellect in Chapters 5 and 6, he adds, we could only trace self-dependence to it with difficulty and not without violence to intellect/Intellect's own nature. We are therefore in a major dilemma: the challenge of anthropomorphism, or at least, the prism of our own viewpoints, on the one hand, or the need to give some real answer to the question of the Good's freedom, on the other. We need an answer that overcomes the objection that the Good is simply determined by its own nature and that it is therefore something that just happened to be (a kind of singularity brought about by chance or super spontaneity).

7, 11–15: *The rash argument: the Good is not free since it "happens to be" and is not master of its own nature.*

This leads Plotinus to formulate the "rash argument from a different viewpoint," that is, "from a different way of thinking" or simply "from the other side of the question"—an argument to the effect that the Good acts by chance, being neither master nor cause of itself, and therefore has no freedom or self-determination: "Since (the Good) happens (*tychousa*) to be as it is and since it is not master and does not have its being what it is from itself, it would not have freedom (*to eleutheron*), nor would its doing or not doing what it is compelled (*ēnagkastai*) to do or not do be in its power."

Where does this argument come from? Six major candidates to explain it have been proposed (and for overview, Leroux, 1990, 104–123; Lavaud, 266n105–267n106):

1) Plotinus is replying to a materialist position, perhaps an Epicurean or a materialist Peripatetic, according to which the gods are the result of chance or necessity (Bouillet, 1857–1861, note to translation).

2) He is replying to a Gnostic position (Bréhier, 1924–1938, notice to 6 8, points to a Nassenian formulation "I become what I will" (Hippolytus, *Ref.*, V 7, 142, 3); Cilento, 1973, 97–121; more recently Narbonne, 2011, 129–142, who cites many more examples, 130–131). The problem here is that the position Plotinus argues *for* looks very like a Gnostic position itself, and so how can he be arguing against the Gnostics?

3) The objection does not come from any school of thought but is a pure thought-experiment [*Gedankenexperiment*] initiated by Plotinus himself (BHT 4b, 372).

4) Plotinus is replying to a Christian objector (Armstrong, 1982, 397–406).

5) He is replying to a Peripatetic, such as Alexander of Aphrodisias from the Aristotelian school (Lavaud, O'Meara, 1992, 345–349).

6) Plotinus may well be in dialectical argument with himself (O'Meara, 1992, 345–349 and obviously compatible with 5 above—and possibly 3).

Both views, a dialectical Plotinus and a "visitor," are not incompatible. For such dialectical contrast between correct thinking and persuasive argument elsewhere, see VI.7 [38] 40, 2–5; V.3 [49] 6, 8–10; O'Meara, 1992, 343–349; Beierwaltes, 1991, 202–205. Any visitor could certainly have proposed this objection, but it actually does emerge dialectically through Plotinus taking up the other side of the question. We suggest that several of the views above can be plausibly linked. The treatise argues from the beginning against the position of Alexander that "what is in our power" cannot be granted paradigmatically to the gods. Since, as Lavaud points out, the principal proposition here in Chapter 7 is that the Good has neither freedom nor "what is in its power," then it is reasonable to suppose that Plotinus has Alexander in mind. Since too Aristotle had argued in *Metaphysics* 12, 1072b10–11 (cf. Szlezák, 1979, 162), that the Prime Mover is a "necessary" being and since this necessity in divine natures is the reason Alexander argues against giving them anything "in their power," then clearly Plotinus wants to overcome this side of Peripatetic thought, perhaps by finding a different way through or an interpretation of other aspects of Peripatetic thought.

At the same time, Plotinus' response to the objection in the fourteen subsequent chapters is much more far-reaching than this, since what is at stake is not simply Peripatetic thought, but the intelligibility of a universe founded upon an ultimate principle, the Good, that is itself no longer intelligible as such. Plotinus therefore does need to overcome other claims such as the primacy of chance or, again, material-like determinism. But the scenario we are sketching here is broader still since it is not too difficult to imagine Christians or Jews (perhaps a Gnostic known to have frequented Plotinus' school or simply a visitor) asking Plotinus over the course of the eight works leading up to VI.8 (from the "anti-Gnostic" works, treatises 30–33 [III.8, V.8, V.5, II.9] through treatise 38 [VI.7]), the following questions with increasing urgency: "Yes, your One is good, but surely It cannot do anything other than produce by spontaneous reflex, and this will be indistinguishable from necessity or blind chance? In addition, if the One does not need anything, it must be indifferent, as the Epicureans suppose? In fact, it is neither a believable subject nor a meaningful agent. By contrast, the Biblical God is a real creative agent, intervening and caring for his people and, in the New Testament, sending his only Son to die on His people's behalf. Your Good/One and your Demiurge cannot even compete. Besides, even if we grant that God does not deliberate, how can we have a God who doesn't even *will anything*? A will-less God will be a chance event, completely incompatible with a Biblical, Gnostic or Peripatetic notion, and, in fact, even with Plato's notion, of the primacy of freedom ("virtue is without a master"). How do you answer?" Compare Armstrong, 1982, 401.

We therefore suggest that Ennead VI.8 [39] 7–21 is Plotinus' answer to such critical questions both from himself and, perhaps, from someone internal or external to the School, but someone familiar with Platonic, Peripatetic, Jewish, Christian and generally Gnostic thought. So the rash argument from a different viewpoint arises dialectically out of Plotinus' own thinking but applies to the whole range of thought that embodies a "different viewpoint." This includes Epicureanism, Skepticism, certainly, and some elements in Peripatetic thought; but also from an opposing view, critical of apparent weaknesses in Plotinus' thought, it includes Jewish, Christian, and Gnostic thinking which emphasize the will and self-determination of God or divine figures. The question of chance and randomness that Plotinus argues against in later chapters shows too that generally Epicurean views are included in his broad focus. Nonetheless, Plotinus may well have someone in mind—possibly a visitor or auditor in the school—who made such an objection (as the rest of the chapter may indicate), but it remains plausible to suppose that this could be anyone who knows something about many different kinds of thought. No special adherence to any one school is necessary to lodge such an objection.

7, 12–15 *necessity*: Cf. Aristotle, *Metaphysics* 12 1074b11–12: "Thus it (the Prime Mover) exists of necessity; and *qua* necessary it is good, and is in this sense a principle (*archē*)."

7, 16–30: Reply: not to give freedom to the Good eliminates for everything the possibility of free agency and the meaning of "what is in our power;" moreover, this rash argument thinks, on the level of nonexistent things, making up notions that have no basis in the realities: Soul, Intellect, or the Good.

7, 24 *for the notion does not busy itself with the substantial being*: This is a difficult passage. Which notion does Plotinus refer to? Is it the notion in the mind of the interlocutor or the notion of what is in our power mentioned several lines earlier (17–18)? In addition, Stoic "common notions" may form part of the argument here, as they are elsewhere—for example, the common notion that the god in each and everyone of us is "one and the same" (VI.5 [32] 1, 1ff.)—and as might well be plausible in this context (see Lavaud, 268–269)? However, a Stoic notion or *ennoia* is derived ultimately from sense–perception (cf. *LS* 238, 39E–F), and this fits Plotinus' concern in context that an *ennoia* does not busy itself with the substantial being.

If it is derived from perception and concerned only with perception, then it cannot be concerned with the substantial being of reality. For the *ennoia* of substance see VI.2.4–5 and Corrigan, 1996, 317–319.

We think, despite the difficulty of the passage, that the thought is relatively straightforward. According to Plotinus, the objector's argument effectively reduces our use of such notions or concepts to empty talk or "sounds about nonexistent objects." Yes, he argues that the "notion" or *ennoia* (compare VI.8.1, 17 and 31 above) "fits" things the objector says it doesn't fit (*epharmozomenēs hois epharmottein ouk ephē*), not in the sense that the notion or concept (*ennoia*) is actually busy about the substance of anything or that it includes or grasps the substance over and above that. Our notions do not make themselves nor does anything bring itself into existence just because we want it to exist. Instead, our notions fit with things or substantial beings in the sense that our reflection (*epinoia*) upon the notion (*ennoia*) of "something being in our power" wants or wills to see the connection between itself and the world—or, as Plotinus puts it, our reflection wants to examine or contemplate, in its concrete experience of reality, what has self-determination and what doesn't, and what is itself master of its activity, something that with full plausibility applies properly to eternal things and derivatively, or more broadly, to all beings who pursue or have the good without hindrance.

Ennoia (41 instances) and *epinoia* (22) in Plotinus have a similar semantic range: thought, idea, notion, concept (see SP, 386 and 414), but *epinoia* (see also VI.8.13, 3) here must mean something like reflection. Plotinus uses *epharmottein* with *ennoia* only on two other occasions, in VI.7 [38] 29, 19 and III.7 [45] 7, 14. In the former, it is a question of an objector, as here, who doesn't understand the meaning of "good" or supposes it to be money or something perceptible; but even in despising such things, Plotinus argues, the person must admit that he *does* posit some good for himself, and even in his perplexity how the good is good, "he fits (*epharmottei*) these things to his own notion/idea (*ennoia*) of it." But if he applies his mind (*prosballōn*) to the Good or Intellect and still does not recognize them, "let him come to some *ennoia* of them from the things opposed to them." So, for instance, in *Republic* Books 8–9, Plato contrasts the "*mathēma*" of the Good in Books 6–7 with its genealogical deconstruction through the timocratic, oligarchic, democratic, and ultimately tyrannical constitutions and individuals that lead to its disappearance in phenomenal life but to the necessity of its rediscovery at the end of *Republic* 9 and in Book 10.

In the latter passage (III.7), we try to fit our opinion (*doxa*) about time, Plotinus argues, to the *ennoia* we have acquired of it (Armstrong, 1966–1988 *ad loc.*: "to the interior awareness which we have"). So the general sense in VI.7.29, and VI.8.7 (much less so in III.7.7) appears to be this: we fit either things to our notions or ideas or our notions to things so that we "apply our mind" (VI.7.29) or "reflect" (VI.8.7) upon the entire range of our experience to get a better, reality-based idea of what it is we need to recognize.

In Chapter 7, 30, we have, with Armstrong and Leroux, left "the good" uncapitalized (unlike Lavaud) because it is the good that at least some beings "have" and it is therefore "their good" as well as "a good" or even "the Good" that is pursued by some or all beings. In other words, all the goods that are pursued or possessed by the different beings cannot be logically or rationally entirely different from or independent of the Good itself. This is the point, then, of Plotinus' argument at 7, 31–32: but since the Good itself is beyond all these goods, it would be absurd to go on seeking some other "good" apart from it. In other words, our concepts do fit the nature of real things and reflection leads us to the principles themselves. As in Aristotle, we reach the Good through the goods that others either have or pursue: everything desires *to kalon* (the apparent or real beautiful/good) as the final cause of its movement, development and completion (*Metaphysics* 12, 7), but ultimately we desire the *one* Good or "best" as the ultimate object of any active love: "one ruler let there be" (*Metaphysics* 12, 10).

The verb *polypragmonein* is used especially by Plato in the *Republic* to denote meddling in other people's affairs or professions rather than "doing the things of oneself"—which is one of the city's founding principles: each person should do what he or she is best suited to do by nature. We can see this principle applied in the case of justice in *Republic* 4 (cited above in connection with 6, 19–22): ". . . justice is something of this kind, not about the external action of the things of oneself (*ou peri tēn exō praxin tōn hautou*), but about the inner action (*peri tēn entos*), truly about oneself and the things of oneself (*peri heauton kai ta heautou*), not allowing each kind in the soul to do alien things or to meddle with one another (*polypragmonein*) . . . ." Plotinus often applies the verb with this meaning, as, for example, in the case of the soul's preoccupation with organizing the multiplicity of the sensible realm: IV.8 [6] 4, 15; IV.4 [28] 6, 8; III.7 [45] 11,14; V.3 [49] 3, 17.

7, 31–46: A further series of replies: do we seek another "Good" apart from the Good? How can it be by chance, if chance applies only to things in the physical world? If it is as it is, is this because it has not come to be (unlike everything else)? But this uniqueness or singularity of its nature does not mean that it is hindered by anything, but that it is uniquely self-determining.

7, 34–38: *causation and chance*

The Good therefore cannot exist by chance since it has not come into being. Chance is posterior and applies to generated multiplicities. Lavaud, 269, rightly refers to Aristotle, *Physics* II 6 198a9–10: "Spontaneity and chance, therefore, are posterior to intelligence and nature" and III.1.8, 9–13: "When the soul is without body it is in absolute control of itself and free, and outside the causation of the physical universe; but when it is brought into body it is no longer in all ways in control, as it forms part of an order with other things. Chances direct, for the most part, all the things around it, among which it has fallen when it arrives at this middle point."

Equally, to say that it is determined by its own nature (as Alexander asserts of the gods), and therefore to imply on Plotinus' supposition that it could be free only if and when it acted contrary to its nature, is absurd.

7, 38–42: *Uniqueness*

Nor does the fact that the Good is unique and that there is nothing we can compare it with take away its freedom (*exousia*)—if its uniqueness is not a restriction by anything else, but signifies only a unique singularity, its, as it were, "being pleased with itself, " and its having nothing greater above it—or else, Plotinus concludes, we should strictly take away self-determination from everything that pursues the Good. Perhaps Plotinus has in mind here Aristotle's observation that the impossibility of defining individuals in the case of eternal beings escapes our notice, especially when they are "unique individuals like the sun or the moon" (*Metaphysics* 7, 1040a29), for he is obviously concerned to make a case here that this uniqueness can be understood, not just negatively but positively. And he adds the corollary: why give self-determination to everything that pursues the Good if we take it away from the Good itself?

We should also compare the "uniqueness" of God in the Valentinian *Tripartite Tractate* NHC 1 51, 9: "For he is first and he is unique, though without being solitary"; 56, 24: "Of him it may be said that he is a true father, incomparable and immutable, because he is truly singular and God" (cf. VI.8.9, 10, 13). Here uniqueness does not mean deprived of anything, such as to be "solitary." *Exousia*, as Leroux notes, is a Gnostic term (*Tripartite Tractate* 53, 4) and Leroux also points to the idea in Gnosticism that the First is "alone," cut off from every link with other things (*Tripartite Tractate* 51, 9 and 24). But "aloneness," like "uniqueness," in this context does not mean a deprivation, but rather the mystery of uniqueness, intimacy and beyond-ness. On this see Peterson, 1933, 30–41; Theiler, 1930, 134; Cilento, 1973, 108–110; Atkinson, 1983, 130; and Corrigan, 1996b, 28–42.

7, 46–54: If its being and its activity, so to speak, are even more one than in Intellect, how can it be other than eternally self-making self-dependence?

Plotinus argues something similar against the Good being "solitary" in 7, 44–54 in two different ways. First, while the Good remains self-dependent with no need to move to anything else, the others *move to it*—in other words, it may be unique but it is not solitary in the sense of being left on its own. Second, here for the first time in VI.8, Plotinus moves definitively into the field of figurative, non-literal language about the Good, marked by his typical *hoion* ("as it were," "so to speak") in conjunction with nouns or noun phrases, for example, its "quasi-reality" (*hypostasis*), its "quasi-activity" (*energeia*). The outcome of this improper, and therefore appropriately, qualified language is precisely that the Good is not a deprived solitary entity, but a kind of supremely *generative and self-generative togetherness* (compare *Tripartite Tractate* 56, 1ff: The Father "is self-generation, where he conceives of himself and knows himself"). In this case we do not refer actions or activities back to another principle, as we have been doing in all the earlier chapters; instead, "its something-like-substance *is together with it* and, so to speak, *comes to be eternally together* with its activity and *it makes itself from both*, for itself and *from nothing*" (7, 52–54). Strictly, of course, there can be no multiplicity whatsoever in the Good, but Plotinus' argument shows anyway: 1) that there is no solitariness in the sense of privation; 2) that there is no black hole of inactivity, but a supreme self-generative togetherness; and 3) that there is no pre-existent matter upon which such a principle might depend; instead, the Good is *self-producing and its production is out of nothing.*

There is a debate in contemporary scholarship about whether we can properly call the emanation or production of hypostases from the One "creation," even if we cannot go so far as to speak of "creation out of nothing." Strongly against any talk of creation in Plotinus there is O'Brien, 2012, 72–76; and in favor, most recently, there is Zimmerman, 2013, 55–105. For "creative" power, see Wilberding, 2006, 102, who points to Alcinous, *Didaskalikos* 15, 2, 2–3; Ammonius Saccas *apud* Photius *Bibliotheca* 461b8–9; Origen, *De Principiis* 3, 6, 6 and *Contra Celsum* 5, 23, 22. Here at the conclusion of

VI.8.7, we have the strongest statement there could be that *the Good eternally creates itself out of nothing*—even if we have to understand this with an "as it were."

Chapter 8

All our language is inadequate to say anything of the Good, which cannot be determined by anything or meaningfully conceived as existing by chance or random spontaneity.

8, 1–3: *The Good is not subject to the attribution of properties, but if we remove the power for contraries that characterizes lesser things [the power for good and bad, for instance], we can see that the Good must be pure self-related self-determination: "itself to itself."*

8, 1–3 *not an accident*: We *see/look upon* (*theōroumen*) self-determination not as an accident of the Good (cf. 7, 26: ". . . reflection wants to *see*/contemplate . . .), that is, the self-determination of the Good is not a relation between a substance, or subject, and an accident, or attribute, that can be predicated of it or attributed to it (as in Aristotle's substance/accident model, where categories, like quantity, quality, relation, etc., qualify primary substances such as this dog, horse or human being). Compare *Ennead* II.6 [17] 3, 20–21: "Everything which is accidental and not activities and forms of substance, giving definite shapes, is qualitative." On the distinction between qualities as accidents and activities and forms of substance, see Wurm, 1975, 252ff., Corrigan, 1996, 189–193.

Plotinus goes on to argue that we can see self-determination in the case of the Good as “itself in relation to itself” (*auto eph’ heauto*) if we take away the power for opposites from all other forms of determination. According to Aristotle (*Metaphysics* 9, 1046b3ff.), every science and every rational power is a power for opposites, namely, a power for good or evil, positive or privative state—for example, “the medical art can produce either health or disease” (1046b6–7). The Stoics argue that if what is in our power depends upon our capacity to do the opposites too, then being really good and wise, etc. will not be in our power since we will be too virtuous to do their opposites (cf. Alexander, *De Fato* 196, 13–197, 2); and Alexander argues against them that in *coming to be* good and wise, we do have the capacity to do the opposite, whereas *in being* good and wise, that is, in being already what is and has already come to be in us (an activity or *energeia*, as opposed to a *kinēsis* or process of development), this is a higher and more developed state of “what is in our power” (ibid. 197, 3–198, 3). What Plotinus emphasizes here, therefore, is that just as the positive state of something, rather than its privation or weakness, is what we look to in determining what x is and should be, so if we take away the opposites altogether (something that is not entirely outside our experience, since we can sometimes will only the good for those we love), we can understand what pure self-determination without relation to any otherness, but simply in relation to itself, might be.

We might, therefore, call this notion of self-determination supremely "self-relational" (*auto eph' heauto*) and note that it bears a certain continuity with the character of human agency, as outlined in Chapter 6, 19–31, that is, as a self-relation in which the inner and outer dimensions of activity are united and harmonized. This self-relational character of will is also consistent with the Good's self-generative togetherness of will at the end of 7, 38–42.

8, 4–23: We remove every characteristic or relation including self-determination and "in its power."

8, 4–9 *an originative principle . . . and yet . . . not an originative principle*: But even if we transfer lesser powers from lesser things to try to "hit" or "chance" (*tychein*) upon it, we can still find nothing to apply to the Good (*kat' autou*—that might be said or predicated of it), since everything is later (that is, caused by or dependent on it); for it is the originative principle of everything, "and yet in another way not an originative principle." Compare V.2 [11] 1, 1: "The One is all things and not a single one of them" (*to hen panta kai oude hen*); cf. Plato, *Parmenides* 160b2–3: ". . . if there is a one, the one is both all things and nothing whatsoever." Since the Good is not an item in any system, but that which makes all later things possible, every positive statement must also be negated. This has been characterized as "negative theology"—one can compare III.8 [30] 10, 29–31; V.3 [49] 4, 5–8.

Indeed, too, the negations themselves must also be negated. "Cut away everything," are the concluding words of V.3 [49] 17.

8, 9–14 *what is in our power* and *self-determination*: However, to talk about "self-determination" and "being in its power" is strictly not correct, because these terms are drawn from realities later than the Good and, in language and thought, they are necessarily relational terms ("for already one speaks of an activity *directed toward* another and says that it is *unimpeded*"), whereas the Good "is altogether unrelated to anything." Nonetheless, Plotinus will relate both terms to the Good in Chapters 13, 11 and 20, 32.

8, 23–27: *Chance, spontaneity and "it happened to be": all these designations are later than the Good.*

8, 14–25 *we take away the "he is" and "as he naturally is"*: For the removal of "he is," see Plato, *Parmenides* 141e9: since the one is not in time, "the one in no sense *is*. It cannot then *be* even to the extent of being one . . ."

The phrase *hōs pephyken*, "as he naturally is," echoes earlier usage at 7, 50 and 4, 5 and 26 and is only with extreme difficulty applied to the Good, since to have or to be a nature relates only to things that have a principle prior to them—that they can "grow out of," as Intellect's substance is said to have "grown out of" the Good (17–18). *Phyein*—to bring forth, produce, grow, and *physis*—origin, growth, nature, constitution, can be used in many different ways. For Aristotle, *physis* can be seen from three different perspectives: 1) as the matter or material constitution of x; 2) as the compound of form and matter itself; 3) as the form, namely, that which in the compound makes it what it is (*Physics* 2, 1); and the form, Aristotle says, is more "nature" than the matter since actual perfection is more a definite nature than potentiality (193b6–8). It makes sense, then, for Aristotle to link God and *physis*, as in *De Caelo* 4, 271a33: "God and nature do nothing in vain"; for Alexander to apply *physis* to the gods, as we have seen (*De Fato* 204, 14: being such as the gods are "in their nature" this will not be in their power). Consequently, it also makes sense for Plotinus to call nature, not only the lowest contemplative phase of soul in the cosmos (III.8 [30] 4, 15–16), but also to apply it to Intellect itself (see III.7 [45] 6, 1–2: Intellect is "a nature of such a kind, altogether beautiful and eternal around the One").

This is the distinction Plotinus has in mind in VI.8.17–19. To say of the Good "as he naturally is," as if the Good is determined by its own nature, is to misunderstand that if we are talking of nature in a primary sense, then we are actually referring to the substance of Intellect, not to the Good; and if we restrict the term "nature" to the temporal sphere, then it does not even apply to intelligible substance, and the terms we employ that seem in this case to restrict the Good's agency are all misapplied. This is especially so with the question: Did it just happen to be (*synebē*)? The verbal form *synebē* is related to the Aristotelian word for "accident" (*symbebēkos*), and we can see the connection in a passage from the *Metaphysics* 5, 30, 1025a24–29 (cited by Lavaud 274–275): "there is no definite cause for an accident (*symbebēkotos*), but a chance cause. Going to Aegina was an accident for someone (*synebē tō eis Aiginan elthein*) if he went not in order to get there, but because he was carried out of his way by a storm or captured by pirates. The accident has come to be or exists not in virtue of the subject's nature, but of something else."

Here in 8, 24–25, Plotinus seems to refer directly to the accidental coming and going in this text but in relation to the Good: "it did not 'come' such that you *could ask* 'how then did it come?'" There is a hint here of a direct interlocutor ("you could ask"; cf. 9, 39–45), representative of the "rash argument," but this could also reflect a natural reflexivity of Plotinus' own thinking. Most importantly, the concreteness of Plotinus' language indicates, we suggest, that he does not so much adapt the physical model and language of causation from Aristotle's *Physics* to his own spiritual vision, since he sees its primary application stemming properly, in Aristotle too, from theology and metaphysics to every other series of forms in the physical world. So the language of the One's coming or not coming elsewhere in the *Enneads* is a perfectly concrete usage even in the case of mystical experience: "the One neither comes nor goes away anywhere" (V.5 [32] 8, 2) . . . "but he did not come as one expected, but came as one who did not come, for he was seen, not as having come, but as being there before all things, and even before Intellect came" (8, 14ff.; cf. V.8 [39] 11, 19–25 and VI.7 [38] 15, 13). It is, instead, Intellect that "comes and goes" because it cannot simply "remain" in the "nothing" where the One resides.

8, 25–27: *Excursus on chance and spontaneity in 8, 25–27.*

Plotinus, at least in this chapter, has rejected self-determination of the Good and also the necessity of it being bound by its nature. He now concludes that the Good could not have come to be either by chance or by spontaneity. Chance and spontaneity are, as Aristotle argues in *Physics* 2, 6, 198a9–10: "posterior to intelligence and nature."

Chance events, according to Aristotle, are restricted to the sphere of agents capable of deliberation: Though I went to Athens to see my family, I happened to discover some treasure on the way. While this discovery could have happened for a reason, in fact it just happened by chance.

Although we typically use the word "chance" to cover all events that escape our understanding of regular causality, the class of spontaneous—"automatic"—events (and, therefore, roughly equivalent to our notion of randomness) is broader for Aristotle than chance events, since it extends to everything that happens outside the sphere of possible deliberation, that is, to inanimate things, lower animals or children who are "incapable of deliberate intention" (*Physics* 2, 6, 197b8). Thus, while spontaneous events are only intelligible within the sphere of regular causality, they in fact fall outside it: they belong to the general class of events that may come to pass for the sake of something, but that do not happen for the sake of what actually results and that have an external cause—for example, "the stone that struck the man did not fall in order to strike him; therefore, it fell spontaneously, because it might have fallen by the action of an agent and for the purpose of striking" (*Physics* 197b30–32).

Therefore, at VI.8.8, 27, Plotinus says that "spontaneity derives from another" (i.e., it has an external cause) and is found among generated things" (*Physics* 197b33: *en tois physei gignomenois*). So even though chance and spontaneous events *do* exist and have real effects, they would be unintelligible without regular causality. There is an indefiniteness about their role: "of these the multiplicity is indefinite" (*Physics* 198a4–5: *toutōn to plēthos aoriston*). They cannot *themselves* generate higher-order complexities of form. Aristotle concludes *Physics* 2, 6, as follows: ". . . however much it may be that the cause of the heaven is the spontaneous, it will still be true that intellect and nature will be prior causes of this all and of many things in it besides" (198a10–13). Events in the celestial and sublunary worlds can just happen, but this could only be meaningfully determined through intellect and nature. There is, therefore, no intelligible basis for the hypothesis that the Good, cause of intellect and nature, could have "happened to be" by chance, spontaneity, or some pure singularity that is coincident with randomness. See on this question generally in Aristotle, Lear, 1988, 36–42.

Finally, the major text in antiquity that rejects chance, spontaneity or randomness as an explanation for the world and that is worth keeping in mind throughout these subsequent chapters of VI.8, is Aristotle, *Physics* 2, Chapter 8. Aristotle formulates the strong case for randomness, spontaneity, a kind of natural selection, and, strangely to our modern way of thinking, mechanical necessity as follows: "why should not nature work, not for the sake of something . . . but out of necessity? Why then should it not be . . . that our teeth should come up of necessity—the front teeth sharp, fitted for tearing, the molars broad and useful for grinding down food—since they did not arise for this end, but it was merely a coincident result; and so with all other parts in which we suppose there is purpose? Wherever then all the parts came to be just what they would have been if they had come to be for an end, such things survived, being organized spontaneously in a fitting way."

We think of a necessary process as the opposite of spontaneity, but for Aristotle a spontaneous event is one that appears to be for an end, but is not. So he links spontaneity and brute necessity, and, of course, spontaneity seems to undermine the primacy of form, activity, and intelligibility. So, he goes on to reject the primacy of the spontaneous as follows: "It is impossible that this should be the true view. For teeth and all other natural things either invariably or for the most part come about in a given way; but of not one of the results of chance is this true . . . if then, it is agreed that things are either the result of coincidence or for the sake of something, and these cannot be the result of coincidence or spontaneity, it follows that they must be for the sake of something."

As Jonathan Lear argues in his commentary on this passage (1988, 36–42), order cannot be the result of spontaneity or randomness, for it is an expression of form all the way down, and the order that exists at any level of matter is insufficient to generate the order required at the next level of organization. In other words, the complexity of order cannot be the absolute result of brute necessity or spontaneous appearance; it must spring from form; otherwise, to say that living order is nothing but a property of certain peculiar combinations of atoms is like saying that Shakespeare's *Hamlet* is nothing but a property of a peculiar combination of letters or that, because an inkwell was pushed over, the Torah emerged.

Plotinus, of course, faces a different set of concerns in VI.8, for the free will and self-emergence of the Good cannot be explained in terms of order, form, or activity since the Good is not order, form, or activity (though Plotinus will talk of its activity). The Good rather guarantees order and form (see his argument at 10, 1–21). Instead, the Good looks as though it is a spontaneous entity and perhaps determined by the necessity of its own nature, if it has a nature. But how could it have a nature if it is a unique singularity? Plotinus therefore must distinguish the Good from coincidence, happenstance, and necessity by showing that if it gives rise to the complex organization of Intellect, Soul and the physical world, it must be a unique singularity utterly different from randomness and necessity.

Chapter 9

What does the objector think he means? Continued refutation of applying chance and "it happened to be" to the Good. The objector means that though it has a nature, this just happened or chanced to be the case. But this cannot be so, for chance is later than Intellect. Order cannot be a function of chance, but rather the other way round. A chance event is possible only to the extent that it might have happened for a reason or purpose, but actually didn't. So our interlocutor is not really thinking anything at all.

9, 1–17: *When someone says the Good just chanced or happened to be, he means that though it has a nature, this just happened or chanced to be the case. But this is to make the Good in some sense deficient, whereas it is unique and, though necessary, it is not bound by necessity; instead, it constitutes necessity for others. It is "what had to be" not "what happened to be."*

In these Chapters 9–10, Plotinus tackles some of the central issues that have come to dominate contemporary cosmological debates (as, for example, the 2012 debate between Richard Dawkins and Chief Rabbi Jonathan Sacks on Science and Religion) and he does so with an uncanny understanding of what is at stake, an understanding that has been taken to characterize modernity alone. His terminology, however, belongs to late antiquity.

From its most rudimentary appearance as material structure, and through its more developed appearances, first, as organic compound, and second, as the form controlling the developing organism (see on 8, 14–25 above, on Aristotle primarily), *physis* or nature means, or refers to, something ordered—something that, in principle, manifests meaning or design. In Plotinus, the term can also designate soul in one or more aspects (e.g., III.8.4, 15–16) and Intellect (e.g., III.7.6, 1–2). A nature or substantial being in the physical world is something to which accidents (*symbebēkota*) can be attributed (qualities, quantities, relations, etc). An accident (*symbebēkos*), related to the verbal form Plotinus uses here—*synebē* ("happened to be")—does not define the substance of something; it simply characterizes the substantial being in a certain way. It may be accidental in the sense of "chance" but it may be more closely related to the nature of the substantial being (whiteness of skin, for instance). In each case, an accident or characteristic feature of something presupposes a nature or substantial being, just as our recognition of a purely chance event presupposes the existence of (some) order or intelligibility.

Notice that intelligibility or apparent design does not necessarily involve a designer, that is, someone deliberating and working out some pattern. Nature manifests lesser and more complex patterns, not because of chance, randomness or spontaneity, but because it too is moved non-deliberatively by desire for Soul and, ultimately, for the Unmoved Mover (in Aristotle). And for Plotinus, Soul and, even more so, Intellect are meaningful and intelligible, but they do not need to deliberate or think like human agents sometimes have to.

So the objector of Chapter 7 thinks that the Good is bound by necessity or that it just happens to be, because he assumes implicitly that it is, or has, or is derived from, a nature or power; in the *Sophist* 247c, it is argued that anything that cannot act upon or be affected by something cannot be said to *be* in any sense at all. A primary mark of being, therefore, is the *power* to act upon or be affected by something, as later for the Stoics. In other words, the objector unknowingly assumes the intelligibility of things in order to deny it. He effectively contradicts himself without realizing it.

In this chapter, we can see Plotinus thinking his way through mutually conflicting designations of the Good—that it is defined and yet really undefined or infinite (compare lines 10 and 43), necessary and yet not necessary (lines 11 and 15). The idea that it could be "defined" arises, in context, from the thought-connection with the objector assuming that it has a "nature" ("so that it is something defined—I mean by defined that it exists uniquely and not out of necessity"). To have a nature is to be a definite something or other (see below at 9, 39 on *tode ti*), but the Good could only have a definite nature, Plotinus makes clear, in the sense that it is unique, that is, that it is *unlike* anything else; and this obviously means that it cannot be or have a nature, since it cannot be compared with anything else so that we could form any notion of a "nature" for it and the other; to be or have a "nature" requires at least some other with which things might be compared. Furthermore, it has not "grown out" of anything else, as we saw above, because there is nothing before it from which it might have grown (*phyein*: to grow/ *physis*: growth or nature).

Thus, the Good must be infinite, that is, undetermined by anything; and it must constitute necessity rather than be conditioned or be structured necessarily as any natures derived from a higher principle typically are. The Intellect has its own freedom necessarily because it derives from the One/Good, whereas we human beings have necessary structures (hands, feet, hearts, and brains) that make us capable of thought and of many remarkable things because we derive from the structuring perspectives that come from Soul and Intellect. For uniqueness, see on 7, 38–42 in relation to Aristotle and the Gnostic *Tripartite Tractate;* for necessity, see below 9, 10–16.

9, 5 *archē*: Kirchoff suppresses *archē* of line 5 as either dittography or *homoioteleuton*.

9, 10–16 *necessity*: As Lavaud, 278, points out, there are here two senses of necessity: that imposed on derived entities by their antecedent cause, which is excluded by the absolute solitude or singularity (*monachon*) of the One, and the necessity that an entity cannot be other than it is (cf. Aristotle, *Metaphysics* 1015a34–35: "what cannot be otherwise we say is necessarily so. It is from this sense of 'necessary' that all others are somehow derived"). The second sense might apply to the Good as beyond any derivation from a higher principle or any contingency. In this sense, that is, from different perspectives, the Good can be paradoxically both determined (*hōrismenon*, line 10) and indeterminate (*aoriston*, line 43, necessary (*edei*, line 15) and without necessity (*oude gar ēn anagkēi*, line 11).

9, 11–12 *For necessity inheres in things that follow the originative principle and even in these has no prevailing force*: Necessity not only makes things possible (because I have a certain frame derived from Soul and the Intelligible, I can run fast); it is also a limiting condition, a privation that is not a positive condition of my derivation (I cannot run at seventy miles per hour). Necessity in the Intelligible World is an entirely empowering feature of intelligible life, but in the Sensible World things are limited by their capacity for opposites, potentiality, and privation. We translate "*bian*" "prevailing force," that is, violence, which is an unfortunate condition of physical existence that does not derive from the Intelligible World.

9, 13–16 *So it is this and not something else, but what it must be. Therefore, it didn't just happen this way, but had to be this way; and this "had to be" is originative principle of all that had to be*: Plotinus uses the verbal forms "it must be," "what it must be" (*echrēn—hoper echrēn einai*) and "it had to be" (*edei*) to emphasize the special sense of "must-ness" involved, not necessity since the Good makes necessity for others. The choice of *echrēn*, we propose, is suggested to him by Fragment 1, 31–32 of the Presocratic philosopher Parmenides, where the young man learns from the goddess "that the things that appear *must genuinely be*, being always, indeed, all things" (*hōs ta dokounta* chrēn *dokimōs* einai *dia pantos panta perōnta*)—with the appropriate change that Plotinus puts the "must be" one tense further back—*echrēn* or "had to be/must be," since this characterizes not Being, as in Parmenides' poem, but the Good "beyond being" (cf. 9, 28). And then he negates even this: "Rather, not what must be, but others have to wait until the king appears to them" (lines 17–18). Throughout this section, Plotinus is thinking through different possibilities and either rejecting or refining them.

9, 17–23: And not even is the Good what "must be" but as the King appears to his followers, not following the lead of anything, but really "what he is."

9, 18 *the great king*: For this image of the great king see also V.1.8, 2; V.5.3; II.9.9, 34; V.3.3, 44; and I.8.2, 8, a term Plato uses to designate, not only the king of Persia in several of his dialogues, but also the principle of all things (*Letter* II 312e; *Philebus* 28c of intellect; *Cratylus* 396a of Zeus as cause of life and king of all things). On the new sense of the term in Plotinus, see Dörrie, 1970, 217–235.

9, 19 *touton auton thesthai*: We follow Igal in moving this phrase from line 20 to line 19: "affirm that he is what he himself is . . ."

9, 23–35: *And "happened to be" cannot even apply to Intellect, for chance is later than Intellect; and therefore it applies even less to the Good.*

9, 23–26 *So even if "happened to be" doesn't apply to being—for if anything is to happen, it happens to being, but being itself does not happen nor does "being like this" happen to be*: "Being" is *to on*, that is, real being or the intelligible being of Intellect. Yet there is an ambiguity here, since Plotinus just for the present moment thinks of real being as including all individual substantial beings, "for if anything is to happen, it happens *to* being" (that is, it happens to characterize substantial beings or subjects in different ways), before switching back to his earlier thought: "being *itself* does not happen nor does 'being like this' happen to be . . . ." Being itself, together with whatever substantial character it might have, cannot happen to be. It is not a predicate in any sense at all.

9, 27–28 *beyond being*: The first instance in this treatise of the famous phrase from Plato's *Republic*, Book 6, 509b9, the Good is beyond being (*epekeina ontos*), a phrase that is adopted in many Christian writers such as Origen, *Contra Celsum* 6, 64.

9, 30–32 language from Plato's *Sophist*: In line 27 Plotinus applies to the Good ontological terminology drawn from Plato's *Sophist* 240b3 (*ontōs . . . on*) and *Republic* 509b (*epekeina ontos*). In *Sophist* 240b7–12 one finds the sequence *ontōs on, ouk ontōs ouk on*, and in 254d1 *ontōs mē on*. In *Parmenides* 161e3–162b8, where the infinitival *einai* is used instead of the participial *on*, one finds the series *einai on, einai mē on, mē einai mē on, mē einai on*. Interestingly, Aristotle too makes the same distinctions, using *aei* instead of *ontōs* in his *On the Heavens* 282a4–b7 (reflected also in the *Categories*). Similar speculation on these modes of being also occurs in Marius Victorinus, *Ad Candidum* 11,1–12; Proclus, *Commentary on Plato's Timaeus* I. 233,1–4; and in the Sethian Platonizing treatises *Zostrianos* (NHC VIII 117, 10–14) and *Allogenes* (NHC XI 55, 17–30), as well as in Codex Bruce, *Untitled* 237,19–23.

9, 34 *it belongs unswervingly to itself*: That is, the Good cannot deviate from its own perfect stability rooted in itself. There are two other instances of *aklines* (unswerving) in the *Enneads*: II.9.2, 3 and III.7.11, 4. Note here, as throughout, that our treatise is effectively a prolonged philosophical meditation on what it means to be a "self" or an "itself" as opposed to "a self and an other" (cf. Chapter 21, 32–33), a pure unity as opposed to "the others" (of the second part of Plato's

Parmenides), something that "belongs to itself" (*oikeios*), "is of itself and through itself" rather than something that is mixed with other-ness in the case of Intellect and Soul or alienation in the case of the physical world. VI.8, therefore, develops the Platonic (and Stoic) contrast of "own-ness" and "other-ness," that is fundamental to the *Republic*, in terms of the well-known Platonic categories of "self-related" and "other-related" and, especially, of the hypotheses of the *Parmenides*, the "one" and the "others."

9, 36–49: *To characterize the Good as happening "in this way" is to determine it, when it is above even "willing."*

9, 35–39 *What would one say who ascended There and looked toward what is above this? That it happened to be as one saw it to be? No, it didn't happen to be in this or that way, rather it didn't happen at all. But what about only in this way and not otherwise, but in this way? But not "in this way"; for you would thereby define it as a definite individual*: Note here Plotinus' concern that there should be not just a vision of the Good but, as with the Gnostics, a saying or announcing of that vision (compare V.8.12, 3: "what does it announce?"), that is, a vision *and a production* of something new. In the ladder of ascent in Plato's *Symposium* (210a–212a), for example, at each level there is not just a new appreciation of beauty but the generation and nurture of beautiful discourses. However, there is also a difference from the Gnostic reliance on authoritative human visionaries: the vision of the Good is not "as [someone] saw it to be" and it is not to be given specific characteristics or qualitative dispositions "in this or that way." Such dispositions do not even characterize the Intelligible World, but are later still, and the same is true, but even more so, for "happening to be."

9, 39 *a definite individual*: "A definite individual," *tode ti*, designating a definite entity or substance, is an Aristotelian term, *Categories* 3b10: "every substance (*ousia*) seems to signify a definite thing (*tode ti*)." Plotinus also calls Intellect a *tode ti* at V.5 [32] 7, 5–7, and so we do not translate the term as "particular" but rather "a definite individual," that is, a definite individual substance at whatever level of complexity, from horses and human beings to the Divine Intellect. There is, of course, indefiniteness in the making of Intellect: intellect or pre-intellect comes from the One as indefiniteness, "the first otherness," indefinite duality, and becomes defined as Intellect in turning back to the One (see II.5 [25] 5; V.1 [10] 6–7; VI.7 [38] 16); and there is also "unshapedness" as a first moment of Intellect's being (VI.7 [38] 33), but Intellect itself as Intellect is a definite individual even if it is everything, that is, the "one-many" (V.1 [10] 8, 24ff.). Plotinus maintains the concrete individuality of Aristotle's primary substances even in the truly primary substance of all, the Divine Intellect itself. On the difficult question of substantial being, see Wurm, 1975; Corrigan, 1996a; Chiaradonna, 2002 and 2014, 216–230. See also commentary on 12, 3–11 below.

9, 38–48 *But what about "only in this way" and not otherwise, but "in this way"*: Michael Sells, 1994, 20, observes of lines 38–48: "The argument can be diagrammed as follows: (A) Because it is free, no other makes it what it is. It is what it wills itself to be. (B) But it cannot even be said to be limited to what it wills itself to be. (C) We should say that it projects the being, the quiddity, the 'what' that it wills itself to be, out into the realm of beings. It always remains beyond its own being and its own willing. This series of apophatic withdrawals is an explication of the dense expression *dynamin pasan hautēs ontōs kyrian*, 'power of absolute ontological self-mastery.' The 'projection' of being outside of itself is the prime Plotinian symbol. Later, even the notion that 'it projects' will be transformed, since the subject of such a predication implies an actor or being, but 'being' is precisely what is being projected out." For Plotinus, the Good is normally the "power of all things" (*dunamis pantōn*) other than the Good itself (V.4 [7] 2, 38 ; V.1 [10] 7, 9; III.8 [30] 10, 1; VI.7 [38] 17, 33; VI.2 [43] 20, 25; V.3 [49] 15, 33), but here, its power is reflexive, directed toward its mastery of itself as its will to be itself. Just as Plotinus posits two sorts of activity (*energeia*, e.g., V.1 [10] 6, 28–35; V.3 [49] 49, 44–45), one internal, self-contained, and intransitive (i.e., absolute in the sense of the Good's absolute making [*apoluton tēn poiēsin*] that effects nothing outside of the agent in 20, 4–8), and the other external, outer-directed, and transitive, so too he seems to posit for the Good a single will that is simultaneously both internal and yet externally effective, as in 13, 20–33, and a paradigm of the unity of inner and outer activities in the model of human free agency developed in Chapter 6.

9, 44–48 *but if it is anything, it is total power of real self-mastery; it is this that it wills to be*: As Lavaud observes, the two terms Plotinus uses here—*dynamis* (power) and *thelein* (to will)—are perhaps the only appropriate terms thus far. Plotinus calls the Good *dynamis pantōn, the power for all things*, in V.4 [7] 2, 38; V.I [10] 7, 9; III.8 [30] 10, 1; V.3 [49] 15, 33; and he says that it is *epekeina energeias* (beyond activity) in VI.7 [38] 17, 10. In Plotinus, *dynamis*, power, takes on a new note that it never possesses in Aristotle. For Aristotle, activity and intellect are supreme, and power/potentiality strive for fuller realization in what may be characterized as a steady state universe of determinate things. In Plotinus, by contrast, power/potency/possibility opens up the universe of determinate things and creates new ways of representing the dynamism of a universe in which indeterminacy or hyperdeterminacy plays a fundamental role: "The One is power of all, a fountainhead "in which the rivers that rise from it, *before each of them flows* in a different direction, remain yet together, though each of them knows already, as it were, where *they will let their streams flow*" (III.8.10, 5–10). On this strange use of tenses to characterize the emergent dynamism of pre-Intellect from the Good/One and Plotinus' development of the languages of indeterminacy/hyperdeterminacy, see Corrigan, 2004a, 163–174.

Here in VI.8, Plotinus defines power at its most intense in the Good as purely reflexive: it is "total power of real self-mastery," linking back to his concerns in Chapter 1, 1ff. Here, too, is the first attempt in the treatise (at first, unsuccessful) to introduce the concept of will on the level of the Good. As Leroux notes, the later Christian tradition will reserve the verb *thelein* for the Divine, while restricting the term *boulēsis* to the human will. Plotinus will be more daring here.

Chapter 10

How could the objector either refute or confirm the "happened to be" hypothesis? The continued refutation of applying chance and "it happened to be" to the Good, partly through an examination of the nature of causality.

10, 1–3: *How could our interlocutor evaluate his own position, for he has no principle by which either to refute or to introduce his "happened to be?"*

The critique of the previous chapter (that we can only deny intelligibility in the name of intelligibility) is here deepened by the related insight that the objector *cannot even evaluate his own position*, for he has no criterion by which to do so. In other words, the question of God or meaning is not just a question of your assumptions—for example, I assume that the universe arose by randomness out of nothing, not by design or God, and you assume that the big bang explosion was not so much an explosion, as in our present experience of bombs or volcanoes, but a highly structuring, however uniquely cataclysmic, experience, compatible with the existence of God. Plotinus might favor some version of the latter alternative. But he makes the extra claim in Chapter 10 that the first alternative is not just an implicit—perhaps unconscious—contradiction; it is in itself *incoherent*, because if the objector affirms that everything, including the Good, is entirely by chance, how could he *really* think this, when in order to make such a claim, he has to introduce some criterion of evaluation or exclusion, and when in order to think at all, he has to be a meaning-maker? And if he can neither affirm nor refute such a claim, there can be no evidence whatsoever for a position that is functionally *unthinkable.*

10, 2–3 *How would he evaluate (axiōseie) that the "happened to be" was false, if there were something?*: We understand this to mean that if something, however indefinite, exists, how might the objector evaluate that it wasn't by chance. And at 10, 3, in such a case, how could he definitively exclude chance? We follow HS_2 at lines 2 and 3–4 and regard Igal's slight corrections as unnecessary. The verb *axioō* means to evaluate, to think, to give a certain value to—see LSJ.

10, 4–6 *And if there were a nature, will he then say "happened to be" doesn't fit? For if he ascribes to chance the removal of "happened to be" from other things, wherever would what is not by chance occur?*: On "nature," see above commentary on 9, 1–17. In the case of something indefinite, the objector cannot evaluate or eliminate chance. But in the case of a definite "nature," he will have to say that chance doesn't fit the notion of a nature; but then on his hypothesis he will be forced to attribute the removal of chance from the nature he has just admitted *to chance,* and he will have nowhere to put any nature that is not by chance.

10, 5–21: How can that which is cause of Intellect, formative principle and order exist by chance? Order cannot be a function of chance, but rather the other way around. A chance event is possible only to the extent that it might have happened for a reason or purpose, but actually didn't. So our interlocutor is not really thinking anything at all.

On this generally, see commentary on 8, 14–25 (on nature and chance) and 8, 25–27 (on chance and spontaneity), and especially, Aristotle, *Physics* 2, 6: "Spontaneity and chance are causes of effects which, though they might result from intellect or nature, have in fact been caused by something incidentally (*kata symbebēkos*). Now since nothing incidental is prior to what is per se (*to kath' auto*) [in or through itself], it is clear that no incidental cause can be to a cause per se. Spontaneity and chance, therefore, are posterior to intellect and nature. Hence, however much it may be that the cause of the heaven is the spontaneous, it will still be true that intellect and nature will be prior causes of this all and of many things in it besides" (198a5–13).

10, 6–11 *But this originative principle takes away the "as it chanced" from other things by giving them form, limit, and shape, and, among things generated according to formative principle, it is not possible to ascribe the cause to chance, but rather to make this very point, to ascribe the cause to formative principle, while chance is in things that happen, not by antecedent and consequential causality, but by coincidences:*

One of the fundamental principles of Plotinus' philosophy is that the Good gives "what it does not have" (cf. V.3.15, 35–36). In giving form, limit, and shape, therefore, the Good is without form (*aneideon*, cf. V.5.6, 4; VI.7.17, 36–41). At the same time, however, there is in us and in Intellect something of the Good, so much so that in VI.7.32, Plotinus can argue that the originative principle and limit of beauty "makes that beautiful of which it is the principle, and makes it beautiful not in shape; but it makes the very beauty which comes to be from it to be shapeless (*amorphein*), but in shape in another way" (34–36).

We translate *logos* "formative principle," though its semantic range is much wider: meaning, discourse, reason, definition, etc. Typically, *logos* is translated as "la raison" (Lavaud, Bréhier), "rational forming principle" (Armstrong), "la forma rationale" (Cilento), "die rationale Formkraft" (HBT). Though the Latin "ratio" is intimately connected with *logos*, we prefer "formative principle" to avoid the impression that *logoi* are some kind of reasoning entities. They are not rational in the sense that they reason, for they are prior to reason, but they are rational in the sense that they are intelligible, permitting us to unfold in reason and definition the meanings enfolded in them. See 1, 34–35: *logos/definition*.

Lavaud, 282–283, helpfully outlines the three implicit levels of reality involved here: 1) the Good itself that gives to others form, limit, and shape, without itself being form, limit, and shape; 2) the real beings so produced (intelligible

Forms and perhaps the *logoi* contained in souls); and 3) everything that exists in conformity with these *logoi* (that one can identify in the sensible universe to the degree it is ordered). He concludes: "Plotinus' thesis is therefore that chance has no place in any of the levels of this descending series" (283). Thus, "chance is in things that happen, not by antecedent and consequential causality, but by coincidences."

For the phrase "antecedent and consequential causality" (*en tois . . . proēgoumenois kai . . . akolouthōs*) [e.g., the Good = antecedent causality, whereas Intellect, Soul, you, me, and individual things in the sensible world = consequential causality], HBT cite Marcus Aurelius, *Meditations* III.2, 5 but see also Alexander of Aphrodisias, *De Fato*, 178, 12–15: "and yet if nature does nothing of what is primary (*tōn proēgoumenōn*) in vain, and man's being a living creature with the power of deliberation is a primary product (*proēgoumenōs*) of nature (and not something that merely accompanies and happens along with the primary products [*ou kat' epakolouthēma ti kai symptōma tois proēgoumenōs ginomenois*]), the conclusion would be drawn that men do not have the power of deliberation in vain" (trans. Sharples). For "coincidences" (*symptōmasin*), in addition to Alexander, see Aristotle *Physics* 2, 8, 198b36–199a5: "We do not ascribe to chance or coincidence the frequency of rain in winter, but frequent rain in summer we do. . . . If then it is agreed that things are either the result of coincidence (*apo symptōmatos*) or for an end (*heneka tou*), and these cannot be the result of coincidence . . . it follows that they must be for an end."

10, 19 *but he is first*: Plotinus switches gender from neuter (*auto*) to masculine (*autos prōtos*) abruptly—as he often does.

10, 21–25: *Even if the Good were not master of its own substantial self-generation, but had an instrumental relation to itself, it would still necessarily be itself and not otherwise.*

10, 21–25 *What then if it did not come to be and is as it is without being master of its own substantial being? And if it is not master of its substantial being—but is what it is, not having brought itself into existence, but making use of itself as it is—it would necessarily be what it is and not otherwise. No; not because it couldn't be otherwise, but because being like this is the best*: For Alexander and for the Stoics, necessity is superior to freedom. As we have seen, for Alexander, the nature of the gods is not in their power (*De Fato* 204, 10–14) and for Aristotle, necessity for something involves not being able to be otherwise than it is (*Metaphysics* 1015a34–35). For Plotinus, by contrast, even if the Good is not brought into existence as it is and is not master of itself, but has an instrumental use of itself (*chrōmenos de heautōi hoios estin*), that is, in some analogous way perhaps as soul uses body or intellect soul, as in Plato's *Alcibiades* I (e.g., 129e), even then its existence is not subject to necessity; and this does not mean that it cannot be otherwise than it is, but that it establishes what is best. Its self-determination (*autexousion*—see commentary on 3, 6 above) does not mean that it wills to go to the better or the worse (as between alternatives—a voluntarist position), but that it did not depart from itself—not that it couldn't do it, that is, as a privation, inability or powerlessness, but rather that "its not going is from and through itself." Here and throughout, we do not, as does Lavaud, see Plotinus' argument against the rash interlocutor as directed against Peripatetic thought exclusively. Rather, Plotinus employs Peripatetic-Aristotelian and Gnostic thought to combat a real position that could have been formulated by anyone—not simply a specific Epicurean or Stoic or Aristotelian or Gnostic thinker.

Note Plotinus' insistence upon the *best* in the absolute sense, that is, something that cannot be coordinated with other degrees of goodness. This notion is evidently what Plato means by the Good, namely, a principle that cannot be coordinated with substantial being or intellect. However, it is also implicit in Aristotle's train of thought in *Metaphysics* 12, 7–10, since in *Metaphysics* 12, 10 1075a11–12, Aristotle specifies that in talking of the Unmoved Mover, he is talking not only of something beautiful (*kalon*) but also something good (*agathon*) and, indeed, best (*ariston*). He then indicates that this principle can be understood in two different ways, either as something separated and in itself (*auta kath'auta*) or as immanent to the order (*taxis*) of the universe. But the primary sense of what is best is *auta kath'auta*, for the order depends on the Good rather than vice-versa and the Good in itself cannot be reduced to the order (10, 1075a13–16).

10, 25–38: No, the Good is not constrained by necessity but is necessity and law for the others, being brought into existence by the agency neither of another nor of itself.

Necessity did not bring itself into existence, but the Good is before reality (*hypostasis*) and, therefore, not really *hypostasis* at all (despite the Porphyrian title of treatise V.1 [10]: "on the three primary hypostases"); nor is it subject to agency by itself or by something else. Here Plotinus ends up denying apophatically the very agency he seeks in order to make more precise the singularity of the Good, by contrast with Stoic and Peripatetic notions. For *hypostasis* see Dörrie, 1976, 35–92, who argues cogently that it only receives a technical sense in Porphyry. For a comprehensive history of the development of the term, see Narbonne, 2012, xcvii–ccxlviii.

Chapter 11

How do we think, represent or speak about the Good? The problem of thinking about something that did not come into existence prevents any scientific enquiry and provokes us to imagine falsely that it is somehow thrown into a pre-existing empty space, when in fact it is prior to all space, and neither quantity nor quality nor relation nor accidental happening can be attributed to the Good.

11, 1–13: The problem of something that did not come into existence reduces us to silence, since every enquiry stops at an originative principle and cannot go any further. The same is true with all the other questions we pose (the "what" something is, "what kind" it is, "why" it is, and "if" it is); we cannot attach anything to it.

As many others, including Thomas Aquinas, will argue powerfully much later, we can admit plausibly *that* God exists (Aquinas, *Summa Theologica*, Part 1, Question 1, article 1) and we can say many meaningful things *about* God (the rest of the *Summa Theologica*), even if we are severely limited beings who cannot know ourselves completely and who know *nothing* of God's nature or essence. Scientific enquiry can only go so far, but it has nothing, and can have nothing, to say about a divine principle that did not, in any way, in time or before time, come into existence. If an originative principle that did not come into existence is still important to us, then we have to find a different way of speaking about it. Scientific enquiry, whether ancient, medieval or contemporary, is always in need of a broader interpretative perspective.

11, 1 *But what is this that didn't come into existence?*: Here, as at 12, 1 ("What then? Isn't he what he is?"), Plotinus confronts one of the central questions of Neoplatonism: if the Good is no thing, neither Intellect nor substantial being, neither Soul nor any kind of existence, neither chance nor spontaneity, what is it? On this problem, see Narbonne, 1999, 25–51.

11, 1–13 *We must go away in silence and, acknowledging that we are at a mental loss, seek no longer. For why would one even inquire, having nothing further to go to, since every inquiry goes toward an originative principle and stops there? Moreover, one must accept that every inquiry concerns what (ti), or of what kind something is (hoion), or why (dioti) or if something exists (ei esti)*: Silent acknowledgment of the puzzle (*siōpēsantas*, 11, 1) is our only recourse, not the silence of contemplation that we find, for instance, in front of Nature's contemplation in III.8.4, 3–5 (cf. V.3.10, 46) but silence of the utter perplexity of one who no longer knows what to say or do (as Lavaud indicates, 286n196). One cannot seek a principle of a first principle (according to both Plato and Aristotle), for an originative principle is by definition a non-hypothetical starting point (cf. *Republic* 510b–511b; *Metaphysics* 1005b11–16). Moreover, for Aristotle in the

Posterior Analytics 89b, 21–25, "The kinds of questions we ask are as many as the kinds of things we know. They are in fact four: whether the connexion of an attribute with a thing is a fact (*hoti*), what is the reason of the connexion (*dioti*), if a thing exists (*ei esti*), and what is the nature of the thing (*ti esti*)."

Thus, in lines 6–13, Plotinus argues that none of these questions of conventional enquiry is possible about the Good. Is the Aristotelian context sufficient evidence that the interlocutor "is influenced by the Peripatetic school" or that this chapter is principally directed against the Peripatetic School (as Lavaud argues throughout, see 286n197, and 288n206)? Influenced certainly, and partly directed against, but not exclusively Peripatetic—the objection itself remains potentially broader, and could have been leveled by anyone, including Plotinus himself.

11, 13 *it is not legitimate (themiton) for us to attach anything to it*: *Ou themiton*: "not allowed by the laws of God and men" (LSJ); Sophocles, *Oedipus Tyrannus*, 993; Plato, *Apology* 30d.

11, 13–28: *Our thinking about the Good must be purified of all spatial representation.*

11, 13–28 *Generally, we who reflect upon this nature seem to approach this puzzle by inferring a space and place as some yawning gulf, and then, with a space already preexisting, we introduce this nature into an imagined or actual place, and, introducing it into this sort of place, just go on to seek, as it were, whence and how it has come there. Treating it as an interloper, we inquire of its presence and, as it were, its substantial being, as if it were thrown here from some depth or some height*: Note the emphasis: the phrase "we who reflect" could be directed against Peripatetics or any school that denies an originative principle beyond being (as Lavaud observes, 287n200), but the primary focus in this and the following chapter is much broader, namely, the problem *we* (immediate interlocutors, as among ourselves, or anyone at all) have in imagining or thinking about the Good, for we naturally tend to think about it as actually lying or seated "in" a preexisting space or as being thrown into it from above or below. This is, in the first instance, the way we have been conditioned to imagine it by poets such as Hesiod who imagine that everything emerges out of chaos: "First of all things came chaos into being, then broad-breasted earth" (*Theogony*, 116–117, cited in Aristotle, *Physics* 208b29–31). However, it is also a conditioning that comes from creation myths such as Genesis and Plato's *Timaeus*, that is, we imagine either God fashioning a pre-existing darkness or space (*chora, Timaeus* 52a–d) preexisting in an oscillating, chaotic state and the Demiurge introducing order into it (52d–53c). Equally, although the Aristotelian place or *topos* is defined as "the innermost motionless boundary of the container" (*Physics* 4, 212a20–21), it also "seems to be a surface, vessel and container" *in* which things appear (ibid. 212a28–29;

cf. *Timaeus* 52b–c). Hence, Plotinus emphasizes *chora* and *topos* at lines 15, 16, 17, and 18.

At the same time, terms like *bathos* and *hupsos* (depth and height) are common metaphors for imagining the divine in the *Chaldean Oracles* (as close as one can come to Scripture for the Neoplatonists)—for *bathos* see fragments 112, 1; 163, 2; 183, 1; 184, 1; and for *hypsos* see fr. 116, 2, Majercik. Place, and the rest of things (*ta alla*)—Plotinus thinks of the One versus "the others" from the second part of Plato's *Parmenides*, is later than the Good; and indeed place is later than everything (i.e., Intellect, Soul, and individual things in the physical world). If we imagine a void or chaos as primary and then ask ourselves how God created himself and the universe within that void, we will never arrive at a true understanding of the real Good, since the Good is the non-spatial space and measure for everything else. Yet, once we arrive at a vision of this absolute One, however incomplete this vision might be, we also come to realize the absolute necessity and reasonableness of its being itself and, thus, of all of its products (cf. Gleede, 2012, 289).

11, 22–23 *Therefore one must eliminate the cause of the puzzle by excluding from our immediate attention to it all place*: The word *epibolē*, whose root meaning is "casting" or "throwing upon," we translate here as "immediate attention." In Plotinus it is related to *prosbolē*, "casting toward or upon" (as in V.5.7, 8: *athroa prosbolē* or in III.8.9, 19–22: *epibolē athroa*, "immediate intuition or awareness") and to *paradochē* ("reception" in VI.7.35, 19–22: *epibolē tini kai paradochē*, "by an immediate awareness and reception"). It is a term used to specify a mode of immediate apprehension or intuition, that is beyond intellection and capable of attaining the Good/One (see Bussanich, 1988, 94; III.8.9, 19–22; VI.7.35, 19–22; and Emilsson, 2007, 92–95), but, as here, employed with a wider and more immediate application. Apparently *epibolē* is an Epicurean term (17A, 87); LS suggest that it is a process of visualization or mental assessment of imagining something external by apprehending its image (LS 77–78 and 90). Armstrong translates *epibolē* as "concentrated gaze," while Bussanich (on III.8.9, 19–22) translates it as "immediate intuition."

11, 28–38: *Neither quantity nor quality nor relation nor accidental happening can be attributed to the Good.*

11, 28–30 *So when we think as we do that this is placeless, and no longer circumscribe it with a circle, as it were, or can comprehend its extent, we will not at all attribute extent to it*: We therefore should not apply our definition of place to the Good, that is, Aristotle's definition of place as in some sense circumscribing a thing: "the innermost motionless boundary of the container" (*Physics* 212a20–21)—if this is what is in Plotinus' mind as he thinks about place. He may simultaneously have *Parmenides* 138a3–7 (and following) in mind: "If it were in another, it would be encompassed all round by that in which it is contained . . . " And for the circle image more generally in the *Enneads* see Commentary on VI.8.16.

11, 31–35 *and certainly not quality, for there could not be any shape—even intelligible—around it, nor attribute to it any relation to another, for it exists as self-dependent before anything else. So what further could the phrase "it happened to be this way" mean? Or how would we express this, since everything else said about this is said by abstraction of attributes?*: We must therefore deny quantity, quality, and relation of the Good (the Aristotelian categories, but also see *Parmenides* 137e–142a and Alcinous, *Didaskalikos* 165, 5–17)—even intelligible shape (for the phrase "shape" in relation to Intellect see VI.7.32, 35–39). *Aphairesis* is an Aristotelian term (see Bonitz, sv), but one that is shared by Middle Platonists such as Alcinous, *Didaskalikos*: "The first way of conceiving God is by abstraction of these attributes [quality, quantity, relation, etc.], just as we form the conception (*ennoēsamen*) of a point by abstraction from sensible phenomena, conceiving first a surface, then a line, and finally a point" (165, 17–19, trans. Dillon). Alcinous then outlines a second way by analogy and a third way by hyperbole of honor based on the Diotima-Socrates' ladder of ascent to the Beautiful in the *Symposium*. For Plotinus' understanding of these three ways, see VI.7.36, 6–10.

11, 35–37 *So that it is more true to say "it did not happen to be in this way" than to say "it happened to be in this way," when in fact it did not even "happen" at all*: The negation of the proposition that it happens to be in this way is truer than the affirmation, but the absolute negation is really correct.

Chapter 12

But we remain un-persuaded in soul, because our freedom is derivative and removed from full substantial being, yet real, nonetheless; and precisely because it is derived, through Intellect's substantial being, from the Good, we cannot logically deny freedom to the ultimate "freemaker." But the doubleness implied in the term self-mastery is incorrect, since the Good is one.

12, 1–3: But the soul remains un-persuaded and at a loss: isn't he master of what he is or of his being beyond being?

12, 1–2 *What then? Isn't he what he is? And is he himself master of his being what he is, or of his being beyond being?*: Here, again, Plotinus poses the riddle of a pure existence beyond substantial being. Surely the Good is what he is simply and master of his being or his being beyond being? The God of Exodus is the god "who is," and Plato for Numenius is an "atticizing Moses" [a Moses who speaks in Greek] (fr. 8, Des Places). Equally, for Aristotle in *Posterior Analytics* 73b7–8, substance/substantial being is just what it is: "substantial being, and as many things as signify definite individuals, is not something other than what it is." And, again, if the gods are not master of their own existence, as Alexander suggested (*De Fato*, 204, 12–16, Bruns), can the Good be said to be free?

12, 2–3 *For again the soul, not at all persuaded by what has been said, is puzzled*: So we fall into perplexity because we lack persuasion and have to make a leap to something that appears to be beyond our capability to understand and express (cf. Chapter 7, 16; 11, 1, 2, 13, 22 and also Chapter 13, line 5 below). For the need for persuasion mixed with necessity in Plotinus where other forms of conviction will not work, see VI.7.40, 4–5; V.3.6, 16–18.

12, 3–17: As bodily beings, we are far from substantial being in the full sense, but we are individual substantial beings, participate in such being on the level of soul, have experience of freedom ourselves, and so can understand the greater self-identical freedom of Intellect itself.

12, 3–11 *So one must reply to these issues that each of us is far from substantial being in respect of the body, but in respect of the soul and what we most are, we participate in substantial being and are a particular substantial being, and this is a compound, as it were, of difference and substantial being. So we are neither substantial being in the strict sense nor substantial being just in itself, and so we are not masters of our own substantial being. For somehow substantial being is one thing and we another, and we are not masters of our own substantial being; rather substantial being itself is master of us, since it is this also that adds the difference*: For substance/substantial being, see on 4, 24–28 and for different views, see Wurm, 1975; Corrigan, 1996; Chiaradonna,

2002 and 2015, 216–230. It is possible to make too much of the difference between Aristotle and Plotinus on the question of substantial being. Plotinus lives nearly six hundred years after Aristotle and Aristotle's thought and language are already his own, no matter how different a view Plotinus might have. Substantial being, for Plotinus, is really the whole world of Intellect's being where everything is subject thinking and object being thought simultaneously. We are obviously "far from" substantial being in this sense with reference to our bodies, but we are closer to it in our souls and "what we most are" (that is, our purified intellects in accordance with the Divine Intellect; for this notion in relation to Plato, see commentary on Chapter 13, 22–33). So for Aristotle, too, in *Metaphysics* 7, substance can signify the matter or the compound or the form and the form most of all—so much so that Aristotle calls soul "substance in the primary sense" four times (*Metaphysics* 7, 10, 1035b14–24; 11, 1036b28–32; 11, 1037a5; 28–30). Substantial being in the fullest sense, however, is the Divine Intellect, the Unmoved Mover, and all the Unmoved Movers that move the Celestial Spheres (47 or 55 depending upon how one counts them in *Metaphysics* 12, Chapter 8), though Aristotle never specifies how these Divine Intellects are interrelated or, again, how they are related to the Primary Unmoved Mover. So there is a continuum of the meanings of substantial being in Aristotle (and Plotinus) ranging from matter, through the compound entity of form and matter, and form and soul, to intellect and Intellects.

So, Plotinus continues, "we participate in substantial being and are a particular substantial being (*metechomen ousias kai esmen tis ousia*)." Participation is, of course, a Platonic term, but it is one that Aristotle uses implicitly of our intellectual powers becoming fully intellects/Intellect: "And intellect thinks itself *by participation* in the intelligible object. For it *becomes* intelligible in touching and thinking it, so that intellect and intelligible object are the same. For *what receives* the intelligible object and substantial being is intellect so that it acts in having it" (*Metaphysics* 12, 7, 1072b19–23). We italicize the words above to indicate that Aristotle appears to speak of our human experience as one of *participation* and *coming-to-be*. At this level, therefore, we are *tis ousia* in a special sense, for both Aristotle and Plotinus, that is, we are a particular substance. To be a substantial being is to be a definite individual, that is, a *tode ti*, as we saw above at 9, 39. For Aristotle, in the *Categories* 3b10: "every substance (*ousia*) seems to signify a definite thing (*tode ti*)." Plotinus even calls Intellect a *tode ti* at V.5 [32] 7, 5–7. And, of course, we as substantial beings in accordance with Intellect are much more free and masters of ourselves than we are as material or compound beings simply.

While Aristotelian scholars tend to emphasize Aristotelian primary substance in the compound sense (this dog, this human being, etc.), for Plotinus there is no real substantial being without all substantial beings, that is, without the whole of intelligible substantial being; so if you bracket intelligible substantial being, as Plotinus does in treatises VI.1–3 [42–44], "On the genera of being," then sensible substance on its own is just a shadow of being, a pale imitation and not really substance at all (see VI.3.8–9).

So, on the level of our compound existence (for this, too, see commentary on 2, 12–16), or even higher, "we are neither substantial being in the strict sense (*kuriōs ousia*) nor substantial being just in itself (*autoousia*)." *Autoousia* occurs only here in Plotinus and it intensifies and emphasizes Being-ness in itself. We are far from this, for "to be simply in itself" is evidently not identical with being me or you. We are not masters of our own substantial being, then, but rather the reverse. *Ousia* in the strict sense—all being-ness—is master of us, "*since it is this also that adds the difference* (*diaphoran prostithēsin*) . . ." What does Plotinus mean? Even seasoned Plotinian scholars find these statements hard to unravel.

Lavaud, for instance, cites IV.8.3, 23 as a parallel. The work of the rational soul, Plotinus argues, is intellection, but not only intellection, for otherwise what would make the soul different from Intellect? "For by adding to its being-intelligent something else (*proslabousa . . . kai allo*), it itself also has a work to do." Here, indeed, the addition of something else comes from Intellect/intellect, but Lavaud draws the following conclusions (290n214; 291n217 and 218): (1) "In Aristotelian ontology . . . the living creature as compound as well as the soul which is its principle can be designated by the term *ousia*. . . . For Plotinus, only the soul is truly *ousia*" (290n214); and this becomes even more sharply formulated two notes later: (2) "Consequently, when Plotinus maintains in this passage that "we are masters of ourselves, even here," he means that this is our capacity to live detached from every link with our body that makes us free" (291n 218).

Both of these statements are misleading, if not completely false. We saw in Chapter 6, in the definition of human freedom, that *actions* are included in what counts as free agency if they are referred not to themselves but to the source of agency, that is, the immaterial in us and in itself: "Everything therefore that comes from and because of this will is in our power—both everything external and everything self-dependent; what it wills and actualizes without hindrance, *this too is primarily in* our power" (6, 29–32). Mastery must in this focus include "actions" and "everything external;" it must therefore include the body.

And this can be confirmed if we ask ourselves what is the difference that *ousia* adds that makes us who we are. The answer is evidently that this must be *logos—a formative principle at work in us.* So if our *ousia* is primarily soul in relation to us, but soul in accordance with Intellect/intellect, then the *logos* that is added from our substantial being must include our compound nature, and even our matter, if there is a *logos* of matter—since our matter is organized by the formative principle to become a determinate nature. This is, in fact, precisely the way Plotinus defines the human being in the treatise before VI.8. In VI.7 [38] 4–5, he asks how we define the man "here" and he answers that this is "what it is that has made *this* human being, *indwelling, not separate*" (4, 28–30). This cannot simply be the rational soul (as Lavaud assumes in VI.8.12), he goes on to argue, and then concludes as follows: "What prevents man from being a compound, soul in this determinate formative principle, the formative principle being so to speak an activity of a determinate kind, and the activity not having power without the acting subject?" (VI.7.5, 2–5). Here in both VI.7 and VI.8, the difference added is the formative principle and it includes "seminal" *logoi* which Plotinus discusses briefly immediately following (VI.7.5, 5–6). But note how the intelligibility or definability of the structured being, that is, the determinate formative principle, depends upon the *active subject* as in the phrase "the activity not having power without the acting subject," exactly as we find in the definition of human free agency in VI.8.6.

In other words, if we take away intelligible substantial being, we have nothing to base anything on (as Plotinus will argue later in a critique of the Aristotelian categories in VI.1–3) and our substantial being is not worthy of the name, a shadow at best. By contrast here in VI.7.4–5 and VI.8.12, if substantial being adds the difference, we may be fairly low in the hierarchy of real being, and substantial being "in the strict sense" may be master of us, but we are still capable of being thoroughly real, since we are real to the tips of our toes, and capable too of being masters of ourselves and our actions *in this focus.*

Later in VI.2 [43], Chapter 21, Plotinus will confirm that everything that can be fitted to *logos* is in principle intelligible—so that even, as he puts it strikingly, "bodies were there too since matter and quality are there" (52–53). "For it was not at all legitimate for anything to be left out" (VI.2.21, 49–50).

12, 13–14 *But where substantial being*: We follow Theiler's conjecture *hou* adopted by HS_2 rather than the manuscript reading *ho.*

12, 14–18 *But where substantial being just itself is completely what it is, and its identity is not one thing and its substantial being another, it is also master of this and no longer related to something else insofar as it is and insofar as it is substantial being. For again it has been set free for self-mastery insofar as it is what is first in relation to substantial being*: Intellect, and substantial being in the strict sense, is *the* paradigm of mastery for everything else. Even if Intellect has an originative principle before it, this means that it "has been set free *for* self-mastery" as "first" for substantial being.

12, 18–31: How then can we deny freedom of the originative principle that makes Intellect and us free?

12, 18–19 *Now the One who has made substantial being free is clearly of a nature to make free and would be called freemaker*: If substantial being is free, it is free because of the

Good. The word "freemaker" (*eleutheropoion*) occurs only four times in extant Greek literature: three times in Philo (see refs in HBT; two occurrences, each time referring to God at *De sobrietate* 57, 5 and *Quis rerum divinarum heres sit*, 186, 4–5) and once in Epictetus, *Diss*. IV, 177, 1.

12, 19–31 *To what might he be a slave (if it is at all legitimate to speak thus)? To his own substantial being? But this freedom derives from him and is later than him, and it possesses no substantial being. So if there is some activity in him and we place him in the activity, he wouldn't therefore be other than himself and would not himself be his own master as author of the activity, since he himself is none other than activity. But if we will not at all grant that there is activity in him, but that other things possess their reality by being active around him, then we will refuse even more in this case to grant mastery or being mastered*: Of course, any notion of "slavery" is not legitimate (*themiton*), and the Good could not be bound by the necessity of its own nature or substantial being (cf. Alexander, *De Fato*, 204, 12–16); and its freedom is before substantial being and from itself. What then of an activity in the Good? And why should Plotinus even ask this question and then, implicitly, privilege activity over substantial being?

On the one hand, Plotinus denies any activity of the Good: III.9.9, 8–12; III.8.11, 8–10; VI.7.17, 10; V.3.12, 16; I.7.1, 19. Activity for him and for Aristotle is linked to *ousia* (*Metaphysics* 12, 7, 1072a 25).

On the other hand, Plotinus sometimes seems to allow—implicitly—that activity in the sense of pure unrestricted, generative activity is the closest that one can come to the Good, a first moment of thinking, for instance, that is "in" the product only because it is not "in" the One: see, for example, VI.7.40, 5–32; and compare two other passages where Plotinus seems to ascribe a non-thinking to *noēsis*: VI.9.6, 53–54: "thinking does not think but is cause of thinking for something else"; cf. V.6.6, 9–10. In addition, some passages seem to suggest that the One has some kind of *epistrophē*, conversion to itself, or some deeper understanding or thinking of itself (see, for example, V.4.2, 15–19; V.1.7, 1–26; and for comment both for and against, Bussanich, 1988, 7–54; Corrigan, 1986, 195–203; 1987, 975–993; Schroeder, 1986, 186–195; 1987, 677–699). These ambiguities may well help to explain Plotinus' train of thought above (and Plotinus allows for the possibility at lines 35–37 below: "But where there are not two as one, but just one—either *activity alone* or no activity at all . . ."): if activity is in the Good, it can only be perfect self-identity; if the activity is not in him, then it must be in those that are active around him. But we do not want any distinction between master and mastered, which is why we gave mastery to substantial being and placed the Good above such things.

12, 31–37: The term self-mastery is misleading because it implies two items, as if the essential self and the activity were separate, but in the case of the Good they are not "two as one," but simply "one."

12, 31–37 *So what would we place in more honor than what is its own master? It is because, since substantial being and activity are in this case somehow two items, and gave from the activity the notion of mastery, but this was the same as substantial being, for this reason what it means to be master came to be separate (from the activity) and was said to be master of itself. But where there are not two as one, but just one—either activity alone or no activity at all—the term "self-mastery" is inappropriate*: Here we can see that the irresolvable problem is the genesis of an ontological separation (*choris egeneto*) that inevitably enters into our language and thought about pure unity, so that we cannot use the term self-mastery without acknowledging what we are in fact doing. There remains an ambiguity about the Good even so: "either activity alone or no activity at all."

Why doesn't VI.8 stop at the end of Chapter 12? Why does Plotinus feel the need to go much further than he has ever done before or will do in the future? We suggest that it is because, in the milieux of his time, Plotinus has to show the dynamic and active side of Divine freedom and because he feels the need to convince his own colleagues/students and cognate schools, including Christian and Jewish Gnostics, that he can make better philosophical and theological sense of the ideas that, in his view, they either abuse or fail properly to understand (omnipresence, omnipotence, self-activation, self-making, self-loving, self-containing, self-waking up, etc.). Most important, however, Plotinus shows implicitly that the inner and outer activities whose organic unity make up the reality of human free agency have their source in the self-loving, self-productive dynamism of the Good. We shall see this confirmed in Chapters 13–21.

Chapters 13–21: Positive Discourse on the Freedom of the One

In Chapters 3–18, Plotinus introduces more clearly the concepts of the will, choice, and self-love as exercised by the One/Good. While these concepts are strictly speaking applied to the One as approximations, these chapters go beyond the instructions on silence and denial expressed in previous ones (especially 8–12), by now treating the One as the subject of his own being. The abundant use of reflexive pronouns combines to create a possible scenario of this Good as willing itself, a notion that, although it risks implying some duality in the Good, can nevertheless be used to refute the "rash" charge that the absolutely singular Good acts by chance or pure necessity, and thus is neither master nor cause of itself, and accordingly has no freedom or autonomy.

In his edition of VI.8, Émile Bréhier ("Notice" in Bréhier, 1924–1938, vol. 6, 129–132) suggested seeing in Chapters 13–18 a sequence of twelve arguments for the identity of the One with his free will. Although Plotinus uses several different starting points, their form of argument is always the same: "In the Intellect, the next lower reality from the

One, although one admits at least a logical distinction or duality between act and substantial being, the principle of the twelve arguments that follow is a kind of dialectic that poses this distinction in the One only in order suppress it" (129). He enumerates these twelve arguments as follows:

i) Since our customary distinction between act and substantial being cannot be allowed to stand in the case of One, we must identify its acting with substantial being, and since the One is master of his act, so also he is master of his substantial being (13, 5–11).

ii) Every being desiring the Good wishes to be that Good rather than what it (already) is; *a fortiori*, the Good wishes to be such as he is; in order to be himself, his will and being must be the same, so one could say that everything happens as if he had given being to himself (13, 49–50).

iii) It is necessary to distinguish the things that are what they are in themselves—such as humanity—from their individual instances—humans who merely participate in humanity; since the latter rank below things that are in themselves, the reality that is above them cannot be due to chance, if it has given itself existence (Chapter 14).

iv) As one moves away from sensible things toward their archetypes, beings, even sensible substances, have increasingly in themselves the source and unity of all their properties; this is true *a fortiori* of the One, who is quintessentially the originative principle of itself (Chapter 14).

v) Everything desires the Good; but in the Good, the lover is identical with that which is loved and the desirer is the same thing as the desired; now what is desired and loved is being, so his will is his being (Chapter 15).

vi) Among ourselves, the principle of freedom is isolation, the solitariness of inner contemplation apart from the multiplicity of things; *a fortiori*, since the Good is absolutely solitary; he has absolute freedom (15, 10–21).

vii) As we move from a life, subject to accident, toward rational life, one moves away more and more from chance; this distance is maximum when one is situated at the level of the Good (15, 21–36).

viii) If we say that the Good is everywhere, it means that everything is subject to him; therefore he is absolutely independent (16, 1–8).

ix) In Intellect, the thing thinking is identical to the thing thought; all the more reason that, for the Good, its existence is nothing but the gaze he casts on himself, and he does not exist prior to making himself (16, 8—29).

x) Any outward inclination contributes to the loss of an entity's being; while the life of Intellect generates being by always looking upon the Good, the Good is in an eternal wakefulness that is himself (16, 30–39).

xi) The sensible world has for its principle an intelligence, a certain rational coordination; such coordination can be due only to an absolute indivisible Unity, which only by itself can be what it is (17, 4–21).

xii) The Good is like the center of a circle whose circumference represents Intellect as its radiated image, which touches upon him in the way the radii asymptotically converge upon it, but are always distinct from, the center; just as chance cannot produce the stable and determinate being of Intellect, so too the Good as source of Intellect cannot be due to chance; indeed the Good wished only what it needs to be (18, 2–43).

As Bréhier, 131, remarks, these twelve arguments give not so much a description of the One as the motivation to ascend to a *vision* of the ineffable Good as described in Chapter 19 (1–12), which would constitute the decisive refutation of the "rash argument" of Chapter 7; this chapter concludes with the famous formula of *Republic* 6 509b that the Good is "beyond substantial being," which means that he is not a slave of substantial being (19, 12–30).

The self-reflexive language of Chapter 20 seems to posit a subject-object duality in the One, but positing it only to refute it by arguing that, if the One is not by chance and if it is not produced by another, it has produced itself. Now by distinguishing the product and the producer, one might imagine a point prior to this production in which the One would be prior to itself, but in the One, productive activity and producing subject are indistinguishable, and to isolate them from one another is to deny the unity of the One (20, 1–9). Moreover, this activity has no "before" or "after"; it is pure act, not subject to substantial being, since an act subjected to substantial being would not be the First; indeed, his act of will is himself (20, 9–27).

Chapter 21 deals with an argument (posited by some Gnostic thinkers): "Isn't it the same thing to say of your First One that he is free (to make himself, as to say that he "could have made himself something other than what he did make?" To this Plotinus responds that ability to be the contrary of what one is (or to choose between alternatives) is a sign of weakness, not of power; the One made himself with a superlative power that always remains with the best (21, 1–8). In Chapter 21, 19–26, by using an originally Stoic notion that "God contains himself," Plotinus risks applying another subject-object duality to the One, but he argues that this phrase actually means that God contains the things that come from and after him. Despite all these arguments, Plotinus concludes that one must ultimately return to the negative way of the previous Chapters 8–12 by abandoning all thought and speech in favor of silent contact or touching upon the very Highest, whose transcendence entails absolute freedom.

For other ways of structuring Chapters 13–21 and, indeed, the whole work, for purposes of comparison, see Horn, 2007, who isolates three major senses of freedom in VI.8.13–21: 1) a quasi-appetitive will (concerning the One's self-affirmation and self-constitution; 2) a quasi-providential will (regarding the One's structuring power); 3) a spontaneous or autonomous will (expressing the One's independence from anything else). Only 1) and 2), not 3), can be applied to the gods beneath the One (Horn, 2007, 177).

Westra, 1990, 54–74, basing herself on Cilento, 1973, 5–26 and 97–122, articulates 10 senses of freedom in VI.8 as a whole and in other *Enneads*. These are ranked in an ascending scale ranging from freedom as contemplation, salvation, ascent to interiority, daimon, explanatory principle, and goal of the ascent to freedom as the Good, Unity, root of existence, and finally, as creation.

Chapter 13

The need to persuade demands a certain deviation from expositional precision.

In Chapter 13, Plotinus introduces more clearly the concepts, not only of the will of the One, but also of choice and self-love, by applying the connection between human and divine *voluntary* activity he has previously developed to the free will of the Good/One, even though he must now risk applying language customarily reserved for human phenomena to the Good. Given the radical inability of all metaphysical language to express anything positive about God or gods, Plotinus admits that to speak of the free will of the One, he must speak of the One in an "incorrect" way, a way that appears to introduce a multiplicity of faculties and attributes—things that can be rigorously applied only to entities inferior to the One—into what should be the purest and absolutely simple Unity beyond any sort of determination. This forces Plotinus to make continual clarifications and corrections to his expositions in which any sort of predication can be applied only with an "as if" or "as it were" or "so to speak."

13, 1–5: The need to persuade demands a certain deviation from proper thought.

13, 1–5 *But if one must incorrectly introduce . . . for the sake of persuasion*: Compare this with Plotinus' similar point in Chapter 13, 47–50: "one necessarily uses for the sake of illustration terms that we don't precisely allow to be spoken." As O'Meara 1992, 348, notes, "The contrast between two methods, correct thinking and persuasive argument [for the confused soul], occurs elsewhere in Plotinus, for example in the treatise written just before VI 8, i.e., VI 7 [38], 40, 2–5 and a little later in V 3 [49], 6, 8–11. In the following chapters, this imprecise discourse will seem to allow for elements of duality and self-reflexivity, sometimes of necessity and even emotion in the nature of the One, (things) that are unusual for Plotinus." See also 8, 4–5; 13, 47–50; and 18, 52–53.

13, 5–11: The Good is as he wills, and is thus master of himself.

13, 5–11 *For if we were to ascribe activity . . . having his existence in his power*: As Sells, 1994, 24–25, remarks, Plotinus' "goal is to 'say' a union of act and being, an act so intense that the subject of the act and the act itself are one. The particular act in question is that of will, so that the willer and the willing are said to be the same. . . . He evokes an act so utterly complete and instantaneous that the subject is fused into the act to the point of no longer existing. At this point one is not aware of acting; indeed the One has completely merged into the act." Of course, Plotinus here speaks of not just one act, but a plurality of acts that also constitute both his will and his substantial being, even though he argues in

19, 12–20 that the Good is both absolutely simple and strictly beyond substantial being. Perhaps Plotinus uses the plural to indicate that the will of the One includes not just his own act of self-constitution, but also the acts of constituting what comes after him, such as Intellect and Soul. To say that the Good has his own existence (*einai*) in his power might imply a distinction and thus a duality between the one who has and what he has, yet the self-reflexive logic of the self-constitution of even a single entity cannot avoid such language.

13, 12–33: Everyone desires the Good and, once one has it, it becomes both one's will and one's voluntary substantial being.

13, 12–33 *Note this too: every being desiring the Good wishes to be that Good rather than what it is . . . he is neither one thing that happened to be nor another thing that he would have wanted to be*: The thesis that everything including people, plants, even rocks, desires what is good goes back indirectly to Aristotle, *Nicomachean Ethics* 1094a: "Every art and every investigation, and likewise every practical pursuit or undertaking, seems to aim at some good: hence it has been well said that the good is that at which all things aim"; see also in Plotinus III.8.1–7;.VI.7.1, 1; VI.5.1, 12; VI.7.16, 6. But since the Good already possesses the Good, it does not desire anything other than itself that is not itself already, while things other than the Good desire what they do not already have. This for the Good is its will in one with his so to speak "substantial being" (*ousia*). Here Plotinus echoes Plato, *Republic* 505d11–e2: "Now (this Good) which every soul pursues and is the goal of all that it does, (this Good) whose reality it intuits (*apomanteuomenē to einai*; Plotinus uses the same term in VI.7.29, 22), yet is perplexed and unable to apprehend its nature (*ti pot' estin*) adequately, or to attain to any stable belief about it as about other things." Just as the production of the cosmos occurs by a kind of free gift, so also all things have a desire for the Good (see VI.5.1, 11–13; V.6.5, 18–19; V.5.12; I.7.1, 9–13). Since for Plotinus all things derive from the Good, then all things desire the Good to whom they owe their existence.

Here we can also see Plotinus' application of two principles developed in Plato's *Republic*: first, the idea developed especially in Book 9, 585a–587b, that we are capable of degrees of reality, that is, of becoming *more* who we are, in our pursuit of the Good; and second, the idea that the pursuit of the Good itself is not a pursuit of something alien to ourselves but a pursuit of becoming ourselves in the highest degree: "what is best for each is that which most belongs to each" (*to beltiston hekastō . . . oikeiotaton*, *Republic* 9, 586e). So to desire the good is to desire not only what is best for us but also who we most are. For this idea see Chapter 12, 5 and compare I.1.7, 17; V.8.11, 31–34 (cf. I.2.4, 26). But this is by no means all that is at stake here—see immediately below on 13, 16–19.

The notion of the concurrence (*sundromos*) of the Good's willing to be himself and being what he wills in line 30, as well as of his own self with his self making at Chapter 20, 26, comes to be applied to the causal relationships among the persons of the Trinity in Cappadocian theology: See, for example, Gregory of Nyssa, *Apologia in Hexaemeron* 6, 9, 1; *Oratio Catachetica* 2, 33; 8, 150; *Contra Eunomium* 1, 1, 396, 2; 440, 3; 662, 7; 2, 1, 227, 3; 3, 7, 22, 9. For later Fathers, Lampe, PGL, sv. On this topic generally see Beierwaltes, 1965, 160, 162; 1972, 129–130; 1985; and Hadot, 1968, 1.1–30.

13, 16–19: Since the Good is singular, there is no good other than himself that he would want to choose, so to choose himself is to will himself.

13, 16–19 *the nature of the Good is for itself a much greater priority of choice, if whatever portion (moira) of the Good that is most to be chosen by another becomes its voluntary substantial being (ousia hekousios) supported by its will, and is one and the same with its will and is established through its will*: This is a remarkable sentence, part of a rapid flowing argument, but profoundly important for our understanding of freedom and choice. Choosing the Good itself and also choosing any portion (*moira*) of the Good which is most to be chosen in our daily lives becomes the voluntary or free stuff of which we are really made. Here choice is not between alternatives on a horizontal level (this house or that yacht, making this or that moral decision), but rather between alternatives on a depth level. Does this mean that real freedom avoids the nitty gritty ambiguous choices of ordinary life? Not at all, since this was precisely where we started in Chapter 1—powerlessness, being overwhelmed, out of which we needed to find a way to uncover the possible freedom dimly glimpsed and, in fact, implicitly presupposed by our apprehension of miserable powerlessness, addiction, compulsion.

What does Plotinus mean? He appears to mean that whatever we do—in any circumstance or in choosing anything—should be a choosing, even among relative goods, of what is best in and for itself. So even when I have to choose between proximate means and ends, I should have the deeper ends in mind—the deepest, in fact. How do we know these deeper or deepest ends, these ends that are most to be chosen?

Plotinus' choice of terms here shows what he means. Moira or portion is both that which we are allotted and that which we can freely choose. It is the moira we are allotted and choose—for better or worse—on the Plain of Truth in *Republic* 10. And we know from the entire argument of the *Republic* in Books 1–9, culminating in Book 9, that what is most choosable and most to be prized is the life of real wisdom over the honor-loving and the money-loving lives. Indeed, along the divided line with its cuts or portions, the "first portion" (*prōtē moira*) is explicitly said to be "science" (*epistēmē*, 533e8). But this first portion is already for Plato and Aristotle not simply a human attainment but more deeply a divine gift—or, rather, they are the meeting ground where the human being starts to have the chance of living a divine life. So, in Plato, the phrase "divine portion" or "divine chance" (a phrase also adopted by Aristotle; see *EN* 1099b10) signifies precisely this mysterious divine-human synapse. In *Republic* 6, for instance, Socrates argues that earthly philosophers will never ever become rulers if not for some divine chance (*theia tyche*, 492a-493a). There is, therefore, a decided emphasis here that the ability to share or participate in the divine life (in Plato's *Republic* and Aristotle's *Metaphysics* 12, 7–10, the life of the Good) is a gift of that Good itself. But for a human being this life as gift is also what is most choosable.

The Socratic paradox is the other side of this deepening and transformation of human life. "No one errs willingly—or wittingly (*hekōn*)" is a privative or limited formulation of Plotinus' fullest expression of Platonic/Aristotelian thought here. What is really voluntary, willed or choosable is in the very ground of our being, even if we for most of the time cannot see the forest for the trees. "*Sophia* and *phronēsis* are choosable in themselves," Aristotle asserts in the *Metaphysics* 1072a35. And this is also true for Plato in the whole argument of the *Republic*.

Therefore, if we ask what is most choosable in any "portion" of the Good, and in any of our actions, no matter how trivial or lowly, this is what we must aim for in everything we do: it is the Good which is the last to be seen but the most useful, fundamental and, therefore, choosable thing for itself in *Republic* 6, where the Good is first introduced (505aff.). It is *epistēmē*, the first portion (*moira*) at the top of the divided line (at the end of Book 6, 533e8). It is the immortal life of wisdom in *Republic* 9–10; it is philosophy as a divine portion in the 7th Letter 329b and goodness in the 7th Letter 337e, where *theia moira* and *tyche* occur together; and it is *sophia* and *phronesis* in *Metaphysics* 1072a35. These are just some of the options that lie behind Plotinus' use of moira.

Therefore, choosing the Good in anything that we do is the highest expression of our being and the deepest realization of our voluntary and freely willed being. This is where the divine and the human meet, where grace (see VI.7.22, 5–19: "the Good colors it, giving graces to them and passionate loves to the desirers") and agency coincide, and where in living and freely choosing a divine life, the divine lives in us in the most intimate way.

If the highest expression of substantial being is voluntary, therefore, this willed, voluntary being is the first gift of the Good, from which we are distinct, Plotinus says elsewhere, only by our otherness (cf. VI.9.8, 32–34; V.I.4, 37–38; VI.7.39, 1–9). While the Good, then, is of course beyond any voluntariness, it is nonetheless in voluntary substantial being activated and perfected by will that the first gift of the Good is to be found. This part of Porphyry's title for this work, then, is remarkably appropriate.

One question we might well ask at this point: does all of this only apply to human beings or is it a potential of all things? The "another" in the phrase "that is most to be chosen by another becomes its voluntary substantial being" surely refers to any other agent in the cosmos: visible and invisible gods, demons, heroes, human beings, other animals and plants—any agent, in fact, that has the appropriate freedom. Plotinus has focused on the human/divine connection in this work and ruled out free agency in children, mad people, etc. But could a case be made, one wonders, for the choosability of the Good by other animals and even plants? Plotinus will never write this work, but a fragment of a work by Proclus, *De Sacrificio et Magia* I 48, 1–10 (Bidez, trans. Copenhaver) seems to answer this question in a positive way: "What other reason can we give for the fact that the heliotrope follows in its movement the movement of the sun. . . . in truth, each thing prays according to its rank in nature . . . for the heliotrope moves to the extent that it is free to move . . . " (on this see Corrigan, 2014, 372–390).

13, 33–46: Since the Good is unique, there is no good other than himself that he would want to choose; therefore to choose himself is to will himself.

13, 33–46 *For what would he have wanted other than what he is? . . . such things are pleased with themselves either by participation in or imagination of the Good*: Every being desiring the Good wishes to be that Good rather than what it (already) is, but the Good would not want to become other than he is, but wishes to be such as he is and is indeed pleased to be so, a point Plotinus has already made in Chapter 7, 38–42. Since he is what he is by necessity, his will and being are identical with his being, and thus one can say that everything happens as if he had given being to himself. Other things, such as Intellect, Soul, and all the rest, achieve satisfaction only by contemplatively participating in or imagining the One. For an "imagination" of the Good see V.3.11, 4–8; and for the most conspicuous instance in later literature of a higher imgination, see the concluding lines of Dante, *Paradiso*, Canto XXXIII: "A *l'alta fantasia* qui mancò possa; ma già volgeva il mio disio e 'l velle, sì come rota ch'igualmente è mossa, l'amor che move il sole e l'altre stelle" ("Here vigor failed the lofty fantasy: But now was turning my desire and will, Even as a wheel that equally is moved, The Love which moves the sun and the other stars"). Hadot, 1989, 50, comments on the One's creativity as follows: "On peut dire qu'il s'invente lui-même, qu'il se pose lui-meme. Il est . . . de l'organisme vivant, 'une melodie qui se chante elle-même.'"

13, 47–50: Although normal discourse doesn't permit the use of such terms as "choosing," "willing," "wanting," etc., in reference to the Good, we use them only for illustrative purposes, always prefaced by an "as it were."

13, 47–50 *But one must consent to these terms if, in speaking of that Good, one necessarily uses for the sake of illustration terms that we don't precisely allow to be spoken. Let one take each such term with an "as it were"*: On the difficulty of speaking about the Good, see 13, 1–5 and 18, 52–53. In V.3.14, 1–14, Plotinus also ponders the question how one can speak of the One: we do not speak it, but speak *about* (*peri*) it from what comes after it.

"How then do we ourselves speak about it? We do indeed say something about it, but we certainly do not speak it, and we have neither knowledge or thought of it (cf. Plato, *Parmenides* 142a1–5). But if we do not have it in knowledge, do we not have it at all? But we have it in such a way that we speak about it, but do not speak it. For we say what it is not, but we do not say what it is: so that we speak about it from what comes after it. But we are not prevented from having it, even if we do not speak it. But just as those who have a god within them and are in the grip of divine possession may know this much, that they have something greater within them, even if they do not know what, and from the ways in which they are moved and the things they say get a certain awareness of the god who moves them, though these are not the same as the mover; so we seem to be disposed toward the One."

13, 51–59: Since the Good wills itself and its being is from itself, the Good didn't just happen to be, but made itself to be what he willed.

13, 51–59 *Given the reality of the Good . . . he is what he himself willed to be*: In lines 50 and 57 Plotinus uses the compounds *uphistēmi* (in both the perfect and aorist aspects) and the noun *hypostasis* to denote the eternally established "self-realized" (*hypostēsas an eiē auton*) reality of the Good, which "coexists" (*sunuphistēsin*) with his choice and will and which is the same (*tauton*) as his reality, similar to the notion of the "concurrence" (*syndromos*) of the Good's willing himself and being what he wills in 13, 30, and of his own self with his self-making in 20, 26. The assertion that the Good makes himself, already adumbrated in 7, 53, is repeated in 15, 8; 16, 4 and 30; 20, 2 and 21.

While here and in Chapter 9 Plotinus identifies the will (*boulēsis*) of the Good with its substantial being (*ousia*), the Valentinian *Tripartite Tractate* identifies the Father's will with his power (NHC I 54, 34–35) as well as his Spirit (72, 1; the "trace" by which he is known to his aeonic offspring). So also in the Valentinian *Gospel of Truth* (NHC I 27, 10–30), the determination of indeterminate, potential reality into the form of aeons is achieved directly by the Father's Will: "If he wills, what he wills appears." In the Valentinian theology of Ptolemy, the Father's ("Bythos, "Depth") will and thought are hypostasized as an entity separate from and generated by the Father. "But the followers of Ptolemy . . . say that Bythos has two consorts, which they call dispositions (*diatheseis*), Thought (*ennoia*) and Will (*thelēsis*), for he first thought what he wanted to produce and then he willed it. So when these two dispositions or powers (*dunameōn*), Thought and Willing, became united with one another, the production took place" (Irenaeus, *Against Heresies* 1.12.1).

Although Plotinus here says the Good is what he willed to be, earlier in Chapter 9, 44–48, he says that the Good is actually the power of total self-mastery and is greater than his willing, which he consigns to the beings that are after him: "but if it (the Good) is anything, it is total power of real self-mastery; it is this that it wills to be, and more so throwing off what it wills to be to the beings; itself greater than all willing, it sets willing after itself." In Valentinian theology, the Father's extroversive faculty of Will is the necessary projective Power without which any further instantiation of that which is conceived within his introversive faculty of self-directed Thought would be impossible. The longer version of the Sethian *Apocryphon of John* (NHC II 4, 19–29), adds the instrumentality of the supreme deity's "will" or "desire" (Coptic *ouōše*) to the shorter version's (BG 26,15–27,1) account of the emanation of the second principle from the first. So also the *Chaldaean Oracles* 37.1–5 [Majercik] attribute the generation of the Ideas to the "Will" and "Fire" (i.e., the power) of the Paternal Intellect: "The Intellect of the Father, while thinking with its vigorous Will, shot forth the multiform Ideas. All these leapt forth from one Source, for from the Father comes both Will and perfection." In line 53, HS_2 delete *kai to thelein* as a probable dittography with *to de thelein* that begins the next sentence.

On the self-making of the supreme principle, compare the *Tripartite Tractate* (NHC I 56, 1–4): "For it is truly his ineffable self (the Son) that he engenders. It is self-generation, where he conceives of himself and knows himself as he is. He brings forth something worthy of the admiration, glory, praise, and honor that belong to himself, through his boundless greatness, his inscrutable wisdom, his immeasurable power, and his sweetness that is beyond tasting. It is he himself whom he puts forth in this manner of generation"; cf. VI.8.21, 7. Lavaud, 298 (following Krämer, 1964, 402), refers to Neopythagorean characterizations of the Monad that produces itself (Iamblichus, *Theology of Arithmetic* 21, 4; 3, 17 [de Falco], and Hippolytus, *Refutations* IV,43, 4–5 [Markovich]: *autēn heautēn gennōsan*), and to Hippolytus' testimony on the Naasene first principle (*Refutations* V, 7, 25, 3 [Markovich]), "I become what I will" as well as to *Corpus Hermeticum* IV, 10, 3–5: "The monad, because it is the principle and root of all things, is in them as root and principle (*archē kai riza*). Without a principle there is nothing, and a principle comes from nothing except itself (*archē de ex' oudenos all' ex autēs*) if it is the principle of everything" (trans. Copenhaver); the *Asclepius* 26 (Latin, 331, 12–14 [Nock-Festugière]): "For the will of God has no beginning, since it is the same and is eternally as it is. For the nature of God is the deliberation of his will," and in the Coptic abridgement (*Excerpt from the Perfect Discourse*, NHC VI 74, 12–16): "For the will of God has no beginning, even as his nature, which is his will (has no beginning). For the nature of God is will. And his will is the Good." Lavaud also refers to the expression *autopatōr*, "self-father," as the Valentinian first principle in Epiphanius (*Panarion* I.1.390, 10 [Holl]), to which one might add the non-Valentinian *Eugnostos the Blessed* (NHC III 75, 6, *autogenetōr*; 77, 15); *Sophia of Jesus Christ* (NHC III 102, 2; BG 8502 95, 10), not to mention *Orphic Hymn* 10 and later Neoplatonizing authors like Synesius, *Hymn* I, 145–147 (*Pater ōn pantōn, pater autopatōr, propatōr, apatōr*); Porphyry, *Historia Philosophiae*, frg. 18, 11 (*autogennētos ōn kai autopatōr*); and Iamblichus, *De Mysteriis* VIII, 2, 7–10: God is "first and source of all and basic root of all the first objects of intellection, i.e., the Forms. From this One the self-sufficient (*autarkēs*) god has autonomously shone forth, for which reason he is termed 'father of himself' (*autopatōr*) and 'principle of himself' (*autarchēs*). For this one is originative principle and god of gods, a monad from the One, pre-substantial being and originative principle of substantial being" (*archē gar houtos kai theos theōn, monas ek tou henos, proousios kai archē tēs ousias*). See Whittaker, 1980, 176–193.

Chapter 14

Just as there is no contingency in the intelligible realm, there is no contingency in the Good who transcends Intellect; as self-determined, he is "cause of himself."

14, 1–16: One must distinguish the realm of true being, the things that are what they are in themselves, such as humanity, from the individuals of the sensible realm, such as individual humans who merely participate in ideal humanity; since the latter rank below the things that are in themselves, things that cannot be random, the reality that is above them also cannot be due to chance, if it has given itself existence.

14, 1–16 *And furthermore, one must see it also in this way: each of the things said to exist is either the same as its existence or different, as for instance this particular human being is one thing and being human another; of course, the human being participates in what it is to be a human being. <And soul and what it is to be soul> are the same thing if soul is simple and not a thing predicated of something else, and a human as such is also the same as what it is to be a human being. Now one might chance to become a human being insofar as it is different from essential humanity, but essential humanity could not come to be by chance: and this means "humanity as such is self-derived." So if essential humanity comes from itself and this is not by chance or contingency,* *how could what is above humanity itself and is the generator of humanity itself and source of all real beings be said to be by chance, a nature simpler than essential humanity and all being in general? Besides, as one approaches the simple, chance is not brought along, so it is impossible that chance ascend to the simplest of all*: The idea that composite things such as sensible things are different from their essential existence (*einai*) (and occur as individuals separate from their prototypical Forms) is due to matter, while immaterial, non-sensible things, like soul are separate from matter and thus the same as their existence, is Aristotelian: see Aristotle, *Metaphysics* 8 1043b2–4: "Soul and essence of soul are the same, but man and essence of man are not, unless the soul is also to be called man; and although this is so in one sense, it is not so in another." However, Plotinus is a Platonist who holds that the existence or essence of a thing resides, in the first instance, not in itself, but in its Form (*eidos*) which is entirely separate from the thing, which merely participates in its Form as an instance of it, a position rejected by Aristotle, who locates the Form within its particular instance: cf. *Metaphysics* Z 6 1031a28–b3: "But in *per se* expressions (*ta kath' auta*), is the thing necessarily the same (*tauto* as its essence), e.g., if there are substances which have no other substances or entities prior to them, such as some (Plato) hold the Ideas to be? For if the Ideal Good is to be different from the essence of good, and the Ideal Animal from the essence of animal and Ideal Being from the essence of being, there will be other substances and entities and Ideas besides the ones which they describe; and prior to them, if essence is substance" (*ei to ti ēn einai ousia estin*).

For Plotinus, "the human as such is also what it means to be a human being" (*anthrōpos auto kai to anthrōpōi einai*), while a "particular human being is one thing and being human another." Since the Form of essential humanity is separate from and transcends its image, that is, the individual human, who may be subject to chance, the Form is not subject to chance. Essential being belongs to the intelligible realm of Intellect which is certainly not subject to chance; so much the more, the Good, who not only generates (*to gennētikon* in line 12) but also transcends all intelligible Forms of which he is the source, clearly cannot be subject to chance. We should remember, however, that there is also a secondary, extended sense of substantial being, from the perspective of which Plotinus thinks of the essence as a formative principle (*logos*) actually at work in the sensible individual, that is, as "something indwelling, not separate" that actually makes the sensible individual what it is (VI.7.4–5; see especially 4, 28: *to einai anthrōpōi* and commentary on 12, 3–11). This secondary sense is also relevant for what follows in Chapter 14.

14, 16–35 *Moreover, it is appropriate to remember what has already been said somewhere . . . that from which they derive . . . is better than they are*: As Leroux, 337, points out, in lines 16–20, Plotinus is referring to his previous treatise VI.7 [38] 2, 6–27 (in part): "But in reality there in the intelligible there is man and the reason why there is man, if the man there must also himself be an intellectual reality, and eye and the reason why there is eye; or they would not be there at all, if the reason why was not. But here below, just as each of the parts is separate, so also is the reason why. But there all are in one, so that the thing and the reason why of the thing are the same. . . . For what a thing is *is* the reason why it is. But I do not mean that the Form is cause of existence for each thing—this is of course true—but that, if also you open each individual form itself back upon itself, you will find the reason why in it. . . . But Intellect in this way has each and every reason why of the things in it; but it is itself individually all the things in it, so that none of them has come to be in need of a reason why, but it has come to be along with it and has in itself the cause of its existence."

In lines 19–23 (as in VI.7.18–19), Plotinus makes the important point that the form or essence of a thing is also the cause of that thing. In his *Posterior Analytics* 90a15 ("In all these cases it is clear that what it is and why it is are the same"), Aristotle agrees on the identity of essence and cause, but for a Platonist like Plotinus, one may think that the essence of a thing is transcendent of the thing, to be traced, not to the thing as such, but to its transcendent Form. At the same time, however, as we noted above (commentary to 12, 3–11) one has to keep in mind that this essence is a productive essential nature that, as Plotinus argues in VI.7.4, is also "that which makes *this human being* (i.e., the sensible human being), indwelling, not separate" (VI.7.4, 28–30). Essential being is *both* the Form in Intellect *and* the productive cause in each individual thing that makes each thing what it is. On essence, existence, and substantial being, see Gerson, 1994, 42–108; Corrigan, 1996c, 105–129; 1996b, 28–42; Chiaradonna, 2002 and 2014, 216–230; and for more references see commentary to 12, 3–11.

In lines 25–35, the immediate "cause co-originating each part (of the body) belongs to each and causes the parts to exist because of one another" would seem, to be the soul, which is present in all the parts it co-originates, as we can see, for instance, in VI.9.1, 39–44: "The soul is many and one, even if it is not composed of parts; for there are a great many powers in her, reasoning, desiring, apprehending, which are held together by the one as by a bond. The soul then brings the one to others being herself also one by virtue of something else" and VI.4.4, 32–33: "The soul hasn't been divided among the parts of the body, but is present throughout in its entirety."

But the more direct point that Plotinus is making here, in summarizing his argument from VI.7, Chapters 1–5, is that things in this world are parts of a mutual interlacing system of causality springing from the intelligible multiple unity of Intellect, but present dynamically and creatively in each part of physical reality too. That is why causes can be seen at work in their mutual implication even though at first we see the fact and the cause as different. Causality is an inherent fact of this sensible world, even though it is grounded in the intelligible world where everything exists in an intense togetherness in the sense that each individual Form involves and, in some sense, *is* every other Form; and where reasoning—even scientific reasoning—is unnecessary, because reasoning only comes afterward (when we are trying to explain or to unfold the fullness of Being). In the physical world, we have to reason out the cause from the event or chain of events we experience sequentially, but, in fact, this causality is grounded in the total simultaneity of Intellect, in which everything is simultaneously thinking subject and object thought. Both this total simultaneity or mutual implication in Intellect and the more attenuated, or unfolded mutual causality that we find in our experience of a physical world, have to be mapped onto the broader progression from body and soul through intellect/Intellect to the Good. For Plotinus' extended treatment of this see especially VI.7.1–11 and V.8.4–7.

Of course, the ultimate cause and "single source" (*ek mia pēgēs*, line 30) of every existence and cause and symphony is Intellect and the Good who, unlike our souls or even the Demiurge of the *Timaeus* (e.g., 32c8, 39e9), provide these without reasoning (*dianoia*) or deliberation (*ou lelogismenēs*, line 31) (Cf. VI.7.1–2) or—for that matter, in the case of the Good—without even any form of thought.

14, 35–42: The Good is not only Father of cause, causative principle and causative being, but also cause of himself.

14, 35–42 *So if there is nothing random . . . he is primarily and transcendently himself*: Since, as Plotinus will go on to state, the One is cause of himself (*aition heautou*, 14, 49; cf. "self-constituted," *upostēsas auton* in 16, 29), the One is transcendently the source, originative principle and paradigm—none of which can be contaminated by the chance and contingency that affect sensible realities—of everything.

The notion of being Father of the cause (to which Plotinus adds the unparalleled "*logos* of the cause") is derived from Plato, Letter 6, 323d4 "swearing by the Lord and Father of the Ruler and cause" (*tou hēgemonos kai aitiou patera kurion epomnuntas*), perhaps in reference to the Demiurge of the *Timaeus*. Lavaud, 301n271, refers to Hippolytus' account of Valentinian theology in *Refutations* VI, 29, 5: "There was a time when there was nothing whatsoever created, and beyond the unbegotten Father who alone existed, without place, chose counselors, without time, without counselor, and without any other entity capable of being thought of in any way. He was alone, solitary, as they say, and reposing in isolation within himself. But since he was productive, he decided once to generate and bring forth the fairest and most perfect that he had in himself, for he was not fond of solitariness. Indeed, he was all love, but love is not love if there is nothing which is beloved." Compare the *Tripartite Tractate* NHC I 51, 6–52, 6: "Of him it may be said that he is a true father, incomparable and immutable, because he is truly singular and God. . . . The only Father and God in the true sense, therefore, <is> the one who has been born by no one, but who, on the contrary, has given birth to the All and has brought it into being." The same treatise also scorns those who do not recognize the Father as cause of "the things that exist":

"Because of that, they have put forward different explanations. Some say that the existing things exist by providence (*pronoia*); these are the ones who observe the regularity of the movement of the creation, and its reliability. Others say that it is something alien (*allotrion*); these are the ones who observe the <diversity> and the lawlessness of the powers and its evil character. Others again say that the existing things are what are destined to be; these are the ones who have occupied themselves with this matter. Others yet again say that it is in accordance with nature (*kata physin*); and still others say that it is self-existent (i.e., spontaneous, accidental). The great majority, however, have only reached as far as the visible elements and know of nothing more than these (*Tripartite Tractate* NHC I 109, 5–23, trans. Thomassen).

The first three theories listed above are those of the Stoics, the Epicureans, and the astrologers. Of the last two theories, the second ("accidental" or "spontaneous") is an Epicurean position, whereas the first (*kata phusin*, "according to nature") simply indicates the opposite view, though it corresponds to an opinion held by both Stoics and Platonists.

A similar doxography of false opinions is found in *Eugnostos the Blessed* (NHC III 70) and the *Sophia of Jesus Christ* (NHC III 92–93). The term "father of himself" is used also by Iamblichus (*De Mysteriis* VIII, 2, 7–10, cited above in the comment on 13, 51–59).

On the notion of the Good as cause of himself and being himself by himself in line 42, see "by him/itself" (*par' autou*) in 2, 21; 9, 13; 12, 21; 13, 54–56; 14, 9–10; 15, 2; and especially 16, 37; 19, 4–6; and 20, 19. Plotinus' notion that the Good is "himself from and through himself" his own cause is very similar to the phraseology of the Hermetic *Asclepius* 30 338, 18–29 [Nock-Festugière]: "god alone . . . is whole, full and perfect in himself and by himself" (*in se est et a se est*). On self-causation, see Pierre Hadot, 1971, "Causa sui" in J. Ritter, K. Gründer, and G. Gabriel, *Historisches Wörterbuch der Philosophie* (Darmstadt: Wissenschaftliche Buchgesellschaft, 1971, Vol. 1) cols. 976–977; Narbonne, 2007, 179–198; and Whittaker, 1975, 193–237, who distinguishes between the notions of self-causation and self-generation, and notes that Plotinus' argument that the Good is self-caused because in him will and being coincide is found also in the Hermetic *Asclepius* 14 [Nock-Festugière II, 313, 12–19]: "The everlasting God, god eternal, neither can nor could have come to be—that which is, which was, which will always be. This is the nature of god, then, which is wholly from itself" and 26 [Nock-Festugière II, 331, 12–14] = *Perfect Discourse* (NHC VI) 74, 12–15: "For the will of God has no beginning; not even his nature, which is his will; for the nature of God is his will, and his will is the good." Likewise, in Neopythagorean thought, the Monad produces himself (*autēn gennōsa*, pseudo-Iamblichus, *Theology of Arithmetic* 21, 4 and 3, 17 [de Falco]). Leroux, 342, notes that Plotinus emphasizes the "hyper-essential" attributes: that of originary causality, which removes from the One any trace of chance or contingency, and that of primacy, which establishes his supremacy to any sort of determinate being.

For the importance of this in later thought, see Beierwaltes, 2001, 123–159; cf. Hadot, 1971, 1.976–977; Narbonne, 1993, 177–195; Lavaud, 195–196. Plotinus' *causa sui* model developed in these chapters can be traced through Iamblichus' implicit critique in the *De Mysteriis* and Eunomius' espousal of the *agennētos/agenētos* formula (Eunomius tends to confuse the two forms—see Vaggione, 1997, 29), to Basil and especially Gregory of Nyssa's Trinitarian thinking; see Corrigan, 2008, 114–34.

The notion of higher principles being causes of lower entities occurs in Gnostic literature also. In Sethian literature, the supreme principle through his Triple Power is cause of true being and indeed everything: in *Allogenes* NHC XI 48, 19–21, "a Unity subsisting as a [true cause] and source of [Being]"; in *Allogenes* 49, 16–17, "a (determining) cause of truly existing things (*ontōs onta*); *Allogenes* 52, 33 "cause of everything"; in *Zostrianos* NHC VIII 128, 22–24, the Triple Powered Invisible Spirit "exists for itself, [even the cause] for them all [and of] those that truly exist" (*ontōs onta*). So also the second principle, Barbelo, is cause of multiplicity (*Three Steles of Seth* NHC VII 122, 2–10); and in *Zostrianos* 91, 15–18 an "all-perfect [receptacle and a foundation] of them all and a cause of [them] all."

Chapter 15

The Good as self-desire or self-love, cause of beings, cause of himself, and Father of every formative principle and cause.

15, 1–10: For the Good who desires himself, the desiring agent and the object loved are one and the same and constitute his very being.

15, 1–10 *And he himself is loveable and love and love of himself insofar as he is beautiful only from and in himself. For even his communion with himself could not be otherwise than if the conjoiner and the conjoined were one and the same. And if conjoiner is one with the conjoined, and what so to speak desires is one with the desired, and what is desired is in accord with existence and a sort of substrate, it again appears to us that desire and being are the same. But if so, it is again he himself who makes himself and is master of himself and hasn't come to be as something else willed, but as he himself wills*: The motif of the supreme principle's self-love also occurs in Valentinian Gnostic sources. Although Plotinus here expresses the self-love of the Good using forms of the Greek verb *eran, erasthai* (to "love, desire, yearn for"), see 16, 12–15, where Plotinus uses the apparently Christian terms "loving," "loved," and "most beloved" (*agapēsas*, ēgapēse and *agapētotaton*), as in pseudo-Hippolytus' summary of the western Valentinian theologian Ptolemy's account of the supreme Father's generation of all further reality in *Refutations* VI.29.5–6: "He (the unbegotten Father) was alone, solitary, they say, existing in isolation within himself. But since he was productive, he decided to generate and bring forth the fairest and most perfect that he had in himself, for he was not fond of solitariness. Indeed he was all love, but love is not love if there is nothing that is beloved (*agapē gar, phēsin, ēn holos, hē de agapē ouk estin agapē, ean mē ēi to agapōmenon*). Thus the Father himself, since he was alone, brought forth Intellect and Truth." So also in the eastern Valentinian treatise, the *Tripartite Tractate* (NHC I 58, 8–12) we find: "It is he (the Father) himself whom he puts forth (in the form of the Son in this manner of generation, and who receives glory and praise, admiration and love (*agapē*), and it is also he who gives himself glory, admiration, praise, and love (*agapē*)." These uses of *agapē* and *agapaō* rather than forms of *erōs* and *erasthai* raise the question of a possible Christian, specifically Valentinian Gnostic, affiliation for Plotinus' interlocutors and of their influence on Plotinus' own thought (but for a more nuanced view, see commentary on 16, 8–15). In the area of Sethian Gnostic thought, the idea of self-love is also applied to its second principle Barbelo, the "First Thought" of the supreme principle, who exclaims "I am androgynous. [I am Mother (and) I am] Father since [I mate] with myself. I [mate] with myself [since it is] myself that [I] love, [and] it is through me alone that the All [stands firm]" (*Trimorphic Protennoia*, NHC XIII 45, 2–6).

15, 10–21: The experience of seeing in ourselves a nature that seems completely independent of ourselves and our everyday experience is not just an accident, but is due to illumination from the omnipresent Good whose own existence is not by chance but from himself.

15, 10–21 *Moreover, when we say that he doesn't receive anything into himself nor does another thing receive him, even by this we would put such a thing outside chance existence, not only by making him alone and pure of all things, but because, if sometimes we too see in ourselves such a nature that has nothing in common with other things connected to us, so as to experience whatever might happen by chance—for all other things that pertain to us are enslaved to and at the mercy of fortune and approach us as by chance—it is only by this that one has self-mastery and self-determination, through an activity of a <well-formed> and good light even superior to that of Intellect, whose superiority to Intellect is not extraneous*: Despite his pronouncement in Chapter 7, 25–26 that "it is impossible for something to make itself and bring itself into existence," Plotinus here quite openly says that the Good makes himself and has come to be as he himself wills. Such a claim closely resembles that of Naasene Gnostics concerning their first principle according to Hippolytus, *Refutations* V.7.25.3: "I become what I wish and I am what I am" (*ginomai ho thelō kai eimi ho eimi*). That the supreme principle neither receives or is received is a notion also applied to the supreme Unknowable One of *Allogenes* (NHC XI) 62,

3–6: "he is not left over in any way, as if he yields something that is assayed or purified [or] as if he receives or gives"; 63, 24–25: "nor does he receive anything from anything else."

Plotinus denied implicitly in Chapters 8–12 that the Good in any sense has a nature. Here he carefully points to a certain nature *in us* which is not to be coordinated with everything else in the intelligible and sensible worlds. Instead, it appears to be a kind of singularity we share in some way with the Good. Is this a good-formed (*agathoeides*) nature we receive from the Good (see below)? Or is this equivalent to what Plotinus calls in Chapter 18, 27 an "intellect-in-unity," and as he explains in 18, 32–33: "For in that One, there is so to speak something like what is in Intellect"? Or again is this the experience of pure light, "itself in itself" that Plotinus describes elsewhere, for example, at the end of V.5.7? Or finally, is it the experience of unrestricted, infinitival activity that Plotinus sometimes contrasts with determinate, participial being (*to on*)?

At the end of his commentary on the First Hypothesis of Plato's *Parmenides*, preserved in William of Moerbeke's translation of Proclus' *In Parmenidem* (*IP*), Proclus argues (commenting on *Parmenides* 142a2–3) that, while no description or knowledge can apply to the One, we call it "one" by virtue of the understanding of unity which is in ourselves. For since everything that exists naturally longs for the first cause, this striving cannot come from knowledge, for otherwise "what has no share in knowledge could not seek it"

(*IP* 54, 3–10): "What else is the One except the operation and energy of this 'birth pang' in us (*odinos huius operatio et adiectio*)? It is therefore this interior (*intrinsecam*) understanding of unity, which is a projection (*provolem*) and, as it were, an expression of the One in ourselves, that we call 'the One.' So the One itself is not nameable, but the One in ourselves" (*IP* 54, 11–14).

On the self-generation or self-constitution of the Good, in addition to 15, 8 see also 7, 53; 13, 55; 16, 14 and 30; 20, 2 and 21. In line 19, the term *agathoeidou* ("well-formed," literally "of the form of the Good") derives from Plato, *Republic* 6, 509a.

The fact that we sometimes see in ourselves a nature that seems completely independent of ourselves and our everyday experience is not just an accident, but is due to illumination from the omnipresent Good; the Good one that dwells in us is in fact our own inmost good.

15, 21–36: Our soul's freedom allows us to reascend to the Good, certainly not by chance, and not even by reasoning or formative principle (*logos*), but because of the transcendent beauty of the Good, who is the tree from whose root all formative principles derive.

15, 21–36 *Indeed, when we ascend to and become this alone, abandoning the rest, what can we say of it except that we are more than free and more than self-determining? Who would then constrain us by chances or randomness or happenstance when we have become, or have come to be in, the true life itself, which has nothing else, but is itself alone? For the other things, when isolated, do not have the autonomy to exist, but this One is what it is even while isolated. But the first existence is not in a condition of soullessness or of irrational life, for such an existence is too weak to exist, a dispersion of formative principle and an indefiniteness. But so far as it advances toward formative principle, it leaves chance behind, for what is in accord with a formative principle isn't by chance. But for us, as we ascend, That is not formative principle but more beautiful than formative principle, so distant is it from happening by chance. For it is from itself the root of formative principle and all things terminate in it, like the origin and basis of a very great tree living according to formative principle, itself remaining self-dependent but granting existence to the tree according to the formative principle it has received*: This is one of the most remarkable passages in the *Enneads*. What does it mean to become the Good? What does it mean to "abandon the rest"? The famous final lines of VI.9 [9] 11, 49–51 have come to characterize Plotinus' thought for many readers: "This is the life of gods and of god-like and blessed human beings, deliverance from things of this world, a life which takes no delight in the things of this world, a flight in aloneness to the alone" (trans. Armstrong, adapted). Does becoming the One involve a kind of solitary confinement in which everything is obliterated or is it the deepest form of intimacy in which everything is left behind, but in some sense also transformed? Plotinus' insistence that the Good is not soulless, irrational, pure indefiniteness, or a dispersion, that is, an annihilation, is evidence for some version of the latter alternative. For the "alone to the alone" formula in earlier thought, see Peterson, 1933, 30–41; Theiler, 1930, 134; Cilento, 1973, 108–110; Atkinson, 1983, 130; and Corrigan, 1996b, 28–42.

Lavaud, 305, notes that the term dispersion (*skedasis*) in line 29 ordinarily denotes the scattering of sensible reality as opposed to the unity and simplicity of intelligible reality: compare IV.7 [2] 1, 2; IV.2 [4] 1, 12; IV.8 [6] 2, 9; V.5 [32] 9, 10–11. It can also denote the loss, not only of reason or formative principle, but also of the stability and inactiveness of contemplative concentration upon the supreme principle as in *Allogenes* NHC XI 60, 2–8; 61, 25–28; 67, 33–35.

Plotinus uses the image of the One as the root of a great plant, giving and yet self-standing (III.6 [26] 4, 33–44; VI.6 [34] 9, 38–39; III.8 [30] 10, 2–14 and VI.8 [39] 15, 33–36). The same image occurs in the *Tripartite Tractate* NHC I 74, 5–18: "Or, to use other similes, it (the supreme Father) is like a spring that remains what it is even if it flows into rivers, lakes, streams, and canals; or like a root that spreads out into trees with branches and fruits; or like a human body that is indivisibly divided into limbs and limbs—main limbs and extremities, large ones and small." Cf. also *Tripartite Tractate* NHC I 51, 17–19: "That singular one who is the only Father is in fact like a tree that has a trunk, branches, and fruit." See Zandee, 1961, 11; and Corrigan and Turner, 2015, 91–124.

Chapter 16

Especially in Chapters 7 and 16, Plotinus reluctantly speaks in a highly metaphorical or analogical fashion, frequently applying terms that ordinarily refer to sensible or substantial realities or are suggestive of a subject-object duality, but which he nevertheless applies to the One-beyond-being and must qualify with phrases such as "as it were," "so to speak," and so on, as he explains in 13, 47–50: "But one must consent to these terms if, in speaking of that Good, one necessarily uses for the sake of illustration (*endeiexeōs heneka*) terms that we don't precisely allow to be spoken. Let one take each such term with an 'as it were' (*hoion*)," an expression he uses sixty-seven times in VI.8, and no less than ten times in this chapter. That is, we cannot predicate anything of the One nor can we speak about it in the proper sense. We transfer "what is less from lesser things because of incapacity to find what we ought to say about it" (8, 1–7). In his determination to persuade his interlocutors (cf. 7, 11–19) that the Good, in analogy with human beings, is indeed free and has the power of self-determination, in 13, 1–5 Plotinus says quite openly: "But if one must inappropriately introduce these terms for the One we seek, let it be repeated that it is correct to say that it is not to be made into a duality even conceptually, although for the time being there must be in our discourse a certain departure from precision (*ti paranoēteon*) for the sake of persuasion (*peithous charin*)," a problem he also addresses in VI.7.40, 2–5 and V.3.6, 8–11. As we note in the Introduction: "What is remarkable (about *Ennead* VI.8) is the extent to which Plotinus, after denying things of the One in Chapters 7–12, is prepared for the sake of "persuasion" to develop modes of expression in Chapters 13–21 that appear to contradict his entire metaphysics: The One makes itself (7, 53; 13, 55); it is exactly what it wishes to be (9, 44–45); the One is ruler of himself (7, 13; 35; 9, 44, etc.); it didn't "happen to be" by chance or randomness; it is not by necessity the sort of thing it is, but because "being what it is" is the best (10, 25–26); its will is identical with its existence (13, 55–56); it is cause of itself, exists by itself, and for itself (14, 41–42); it brought itself into being (16, 15); it is as it woke itself up to be (16, 33); it is entire will (21, 14)." As Bussanich, 206, puts it, in Chapter 16, 12–13, Plotinus "begins the astonishing exploration of the inner life of the Good."

16, 1–8: The everywhere and nowhere pervaded by the Good is actually the Good himself.

16, 1–8 *But since we say—and so it seems—this is everywhere and again nowhere, we must reflect upon this and, looking from this point of view, think out what one must posit about the subjects of our inquiry. For if he is nowhere, he hasn't happened to be anywhere, and if everywhere, he is as much as he is at every point, so that he is the "everywhere" and the "in every way," not that he is in that everywhere, but that he is this himself, and in this "everywhere" he gives existence to the others lying alongside him*: The divine omnipresence is a widespread theme, not only for Plotinus, especially in VI.4–5 (*On the presence of being, one and the same, everywhere as a whole,* and also in III.9.4, 3; V.5.8–9; VI.4.3, 18) but also his predecessors like Philo (*On the Confusion of Languages* 136) and the Stoics, for whom the universe is God's self-expression. On the "placelessness" and omnipresence of the One, see III.9.4, 1–9; III.8.9, 24–28; V.5.9, and of intelligible reality generally, VI.4.2, 46–49. Similarly for Porphyry, *Sententiae* 31, God, Intellect and Soul are both everywhere and nowhere, probably in the sense that the nature of a productive source is everywhere present to its products, but is also nowhere, since they are all completely "other" than their source. The same notion occurs in the Nag Hammadi Sethian Platonizing treatises, for example *Zostrianos* (NHC VIII) 74, 17–24: "It is everywhere and nowhere that he (the supreme One) [empowers] and activates them all. The ineffable, unnamable one—it is from himself that he [truly] exists, resting himself [in] his perfection" (cf. Victorinus, *Adversus Arium* I, 50, 9–11). While Plotinus and perhaps *Zostrianos* apply this notion mainly to the supreme principle, *Allogenes* (NHC XI) 57, 17–24 applies it to all the incorporeals because they lack magnitude: "for the incorporeal natures have not associated with any magnitude; thus endowed, they are everywhere and they are nowhere, since they are greater than every magnitude and less than every exiguity." Lavaud, 306, traces this notion to the first hypothesis of Plato's *Parmenides* 138a2–3: "Moreover, being of such a nature, it (the One that is not) cannot be anywhere, for it could not be either in anything else or in itself"; the question of the location of intelligible reality (the Forms) generally ("Do you think the whole idea [*eidos*], being one, is in each of the many participants, or what?") is discussed in 131a–c. For commentary on Chapter 16, see also Bussanich, 1988, 202–220.

Plotinus' notion that the Good is both everywhere and nowhere is most radically expressed in V.5.9, 21–26: "The things, therefore, which are in something are there where they are; but everything which is not somewhere has nowhere where it is not. For if it is not here, it is clear that another place contains it, and it is here in something else, so that the 'not somewhere' is false. If therefore the 'not somewhere' is true and the 'somewhere' is false (so that it may not be in something else), it will not be absent from anything. But if it is not absent from anything and is not anywhere, it is everywhere independent. And one part of it is not here and another there: it is not even here as a whole; so that it is everywhere as a whole; nothing possesses it or does not possess it; that is, everything is possessed by it." Because the Good is before everything and thus differs from everything, nothing contains it, so it has no "place" (Aristotle, *Physics* 4 4, 212a6); it is present in everything by its absence: "But the Good, since it was there long before to arouse an innate desire, is present even to those asleep and does not astonish those who at any time see it, because it is always there and there is never recollection of it; but people do not see it, because it is present to them in their sleep" (V.5.9, 18–23).

The phrase "lying alongside" (*parakeisthai*), and "in this 'everywhere' he gives existence to the others lying alongside him," we suggest is a reminiscence of Plato's *Symposium*, where the participants lie alongside one another. This suggests a sort of philosophical intimacy in which Alcibiades and Socrates lie alongside Agathon (i.e., a pun on the Good).

16, 8–15: Self-determination of the Good includes self-directed love, activity, vision, inclination, and awakening.

16, 8–15 *But since he has the highest rank—or rather doesn't have it but is himself the highest—he has all things as slaves; he is not contingent for them, but they are for him, or rather they surround him who does not look to them but they to him. But he as it were tends toward his interior, loving himself so to speak—the "pure radiance"—being himself what he loves, and this is his self-constitution, if indeed he is enduring activity and the supremely beloved, rather like Intellect*: Being precedes having; one must exist before one can have anything. Therefore the Good *is* the highest and does not *have* the highest rank.

The omnipresence of the Good is confirmed by its primacy in the hierarchy of all realities. Unlike the Judaeo-Christian God and even Plato's Demiurge who exercise provident care and even love for the created order, the Good looks only inward, loving only himself. In his previous treatise, Plotinus had already anticipated the question of such self-reflexive love in connection with the Stoic concept of *oikeiōsis*, the innate sense of kinship, being in accord with "what is one's own": "Accordingly those that are pure and more good have a closer kinship with themselves. It is therefore absurd to inquire why a thing which is good is good for itself, as if it would have to get out of its own nature and not love itself as good. But in the case of a simple reality in which there is never one part, then another, one must consider whether kinship with itself is what is good for itself" (VI.7.27, 18–24). The idea that what is good or best for anything is also what most belongs (*oikeios*) to it is fundamental to Plato's *Republic*, in the first instance, that we should do "our own work" (*ta hautou*) for which we are best fitted rather than meddle in others' business (*Republic* 2, 369e–370c) and, in the final instance, that "what is best for each is that which most belongs to each" (*to beltiston hekastōi . . . oikeiotaton*) (*Republic* 9, 586e). On this see also commentary on 13, 22–33.

Rather than using lexemes connoting desire and yearning for what one needs such as *erasmios*, *erōs*, *ephesis*, *ephetos*, and *ephiemenos* in 15, 1–8, Plotinus here uses terms dominant in Christian sources, such as *agapēsas*, ēgapēse, and *agapētotaton*, which connote outgoing concern for what is other than oneself. Like Aristotle's Unmoved Mover who by thinking itself becomes the supremely desirable object of attraction to which everything else instinctually moves

(*Metaphysics* 1072b3; 1074b34), Plotinus' Good is not an intellectual or intelligible entity that thinks itself, an activity he restricts to the second hypostasis Intellect. Although the Good cannot be considered as a self-thinking intellect, Plotinus goes on to ascribe to it the same sorts of self-reflexive activity he elsewhere attributes to Intellect. In fact the lines of Plotinus' ensuing argument seem to draw on this doctrine of Aristotle, to the extent that Lavaud, 308–309, infers from them an Aristotelian intellectual provenance for Plotinus' presumed interlocutors. To better understand Plotinus's argument, consider the following excerpts from Aristotle's *Metaphysics* 12, 7, 1072 a24–b30 on the First Mover who loves and thinks only itself:

"There is something which moves without being moved; something eternal which is both substance and actuality (*ou kinoumenon kinei, aidion kai ousia kai energeia ousa. kinei de hōde to orekton kai to noēton; kinei ou kinoumena*). The object of desire and the object of thought move without being moved. The primary objects of desire and thought are the same. . . . [1072a34] But the Good, and that which is in itself desirable (*to kalon kai to di hauto haireto*), are also in the same series; [1072b] and that which is first in a class is always best or analogous to the best and it causes motion as being an object of love, whereas all other things cause motion because they are themselves in motion. Such, then, is the first principle (*archēs*) upon which depend the sensible universe and the world of nature. . . . [1072b18] Now thinking in itself is concerned with that which is in itself best (*tou kath hauto aristou*), and thinking in the highest sense with that which is in the highest sense best. And thought thinks itself (*hauton de noei ho nous*) through participation in the object of thought; for it becomes an object of thought by the act of apprehension and thinking (*thinganōn kai noōn*), so that thought and the object of thought are the same (*tauton nous kai noēton*), because that which is receptive of the object of thought, i.e., essence, is thought. And it actually functions when it possesses this object. Hence it is actuality rather than potentiality that is held to be the divine possession of rational thought, and its active contemplation is that which is most pleasant and best. . . . [1072b27] For the actuality of thought is life, and God is that actuality (*hē gar nou energeia zōē, ekeinos de hē energeia*); and the essential actuality of God is life most good and eternal. We hold, then, that God is a living being, eternal, most good; and therefore life and a continuous eternal existence belong to God; for that is what God is."

In line 13, the phrase "the pure radiance" is from Plato, *Phaedrus* 250c4: *en augēi katharai*, referring to the souls' pre-incarnate vision of the intelligible world. We should note that here *agapē* is equivalent, if not identical to *erōs*, as we can also see in VI.7.31, 5–18; V.3.8, 30–31. The Good is *agapētotaton* in VI.7.30, 35 (cf. 31, 5) and Intellect is a loving intellect (*nous erōn*) at VI.7.35, 24. On this see Rist, 1964, 98–99; Beierwaltes. 1965, 311n37; Bussanich, 1988, 208–209;

and for equivalence between these terms already in Plato, see Corrigan/Glazov-Corrigan, 2004b, 44–46.

16, 12–15: The good as *eros*: an assessment.

How are we to assess the Good's self-love that Plotinus expresses in terms that would have been familiar and acceptable to traditional Platonists (including Peripatetics) and other schools, as well as to Gnostic Christians and Jews? The Beautiful and the Good are the supreme object and goal of desire, as we can see in the *Symposium* and *Republic*; and for Aristotle, the Unmoved Mover is the ultimate beloved, for it moves "as being loved" (*hōs erōmenon*). Here, for Plotinus, the Good itself is pure love. Is there any way that this self-love might be said to pre-contain the desire and love of everything else?

At first sight, this might seem farfetched since one cannot imagine a Form, much less the Form of the Good, actually loving anything, any more than we can imagine Zeus or Aristotle's Unmoved Mover having any active loving relation to other things.

Nonetheless, the broader context in both Plato and Aristotle, shows that the notion of care or love is not entirely foreign. In Plato, particularly, there is a care of the higher for the lower not only at every level of ascent (*Symposium* 210c1–6; d5–6; 212a3–6), just as in the *Phaedrus* all-soul cares for that which is without soul (*Phaedrus* 246b–c) but also in so far as immortality and god-belovedness are *gifts* of the Beautiful (*Symposium* 212a). Nothing of this appears in Aristotle, but there is something equally significant that should not be overlooked. While a loving Unmoved Mover might be entirely beyond the pale, the question of how the Unmoved Mover is related to itself and how it is related to the world is very much a part of Aristotle's treatment (*Metaphysics* 12, 9–10), which itself, we might suggest—although in a different mode—picks up Aristotle's treatment of friendship in the *Ethics*: that is, the quality of one's relation to oneself is an integral precondition of how one is related to one's friend or of what one gives to another (*Nicomachean Ethics* Books 8–9, especially Book 8, 10 and Book 9, 4 and 8–9).

In Aristotle, too, it should be emphasized, there are different views on the complex question of friendship: on the one hand, friendship requires human exchange of affection; indeed, "it would be strange if one were to say that one loved Zeus" (*EN* 1159a5–8; *MM* 1208b26–31). On the other hand, a pre-eminent friendship of human beings to gods and of god to the human being, as of father to son, also appears in *EN* 1162a4–5; 1160b25–26; *EE* 1242a31–35; cf. *EE* 1239a17–19). Moreover, the wise person who acts in accordance with intellect is, on Aristotle's view, "most god-beloved" (*theophilestatos*, *EN* 1179a22–24), because he shares most in the unity of God's activity.

And so even in the case of the Unmoved Mover, it does not follow that, in thinking itself, the Unmoved Mover bears no relation to the world or that its thinking is empty or non-creative. It makes more sense to suppose that in thinking itself it includes the whole world, not, as we experience it, piecemeal and extended in time and space, but rather as indivisibly *whole*: "intellect does not have the good in this bit or in that bit, but *the best is in a certain whole, being something different*" (*Metaphysics* 12 9, 1075a7–9). In other words, God's self-thinking is richer than the contemplation of the universe because God's life is both himself and all the energy of the world but in a divine mode. And if this is so, then God's self-relatedness must pre-include not only our own, but also the best-relatedness of everything to Him (see also commentary on 13, 16–19).

In this light, when Plotinus argues that the Good is infinite and formless and that there is therefore correspondingly an infinite love in the soul for the One, "so great a degree of happiness has it reached" (in VI.7.34, 35–38; cf. VI.9.9, 44–45); or when in VI.7.35, 3–28 he can speak of a drunken intellect that, by virtue of the continuity of its contemplation, no longer sees a sight, but *mingles its seeing with what it contemplates*; or again when in VI.8—probably because of the questions of his colleagues and his students and the influence of the Valentinian Gnostic *Tripartite Tractate*—he speaks of the Good's *love of itself*, there is more than a suggestion that such dynamic love of itself must include or pre-include everything that is valuable or loveable even in the intelligible and sensible worlds. If this seems to be a stretch, then at least, if the soul or intellect can be "mingled" with the Good, and the Good loves itself, then anything "mingled" with the Good *must love and be loved by the Good.*

This is not an explicit step that Plotinus himself will make, but it will be taken later by Proclus and Pseudo-Dionysius. On these later developments, see Corrigan, 2014, 82–115. And, indeed, the double—internal-external—activity that constitutes human free agency in VI.8.6, can now be traced to and intensified by the Good who loves itself.

Rist, 1970, 168, points out that the soul's power to love is given, along with its existence, by the One itself. And in the act of loving, that power is actualized by the direct inspiration of the One. In a very real sense our eros is caused by God's nature. As Bussanich, 1988, 209, observes: "This reading is fully justified when we juxtapose the present passage [VI.8.16, 13–14] with the claim made at VI 7, 31, 17–18 that the soul loves the Good since it is moved by it to love from the beginning. Fundamentally, therefore, the Good's undiminished giving, its power to generate, is a direct manifestation of its eros."

Rist, 1964, 82, had argued that as eros, the Good "must love not only 'itself in itself' but 'itself as present with its effects.' Furthermore, in the mystic union, at the time the soul is restored to unity with the One, it must itself be the object of the One's love, since the One loves itself, and the elevated soul is the One's self . . . In the mystic union, then, the One loves the soul since the soul is no longer soul." A little further on, however, he argues that in such union the soul "still remains numerically distinct" from the One (1964, 104; 1967, 224, 227–228, 230). Bussanich, 1988, 210, by contrast, wants to argue that in mystical union the soul "ceases to exist as an individually distinct entity. . . . In short, the soul loses itself but gains the absolute reality of the Good. The ultimate state, on this reading, is not non-existence, but an absolute existence which is fully erotic, as well as visionary and actual . . . "

How would we be able to determine which of these alternatives—persistence or annihilation of the self/soul—is more likely? Perhaps it is more judicious to leave the question open, since we cannot determine beyond any ambiguity whether in mystical union the self/soul/intellect is annihilated, remains numerically distinct, or is transformed erotically into the Good, or is, again, eternally and hyper-eternally drawn ever toward and into the Divine, as Gregory of Nyssa argued later in his doctrine of *epektasis*, namely, the doctrine that the soul is continually drawn out into God (on which see Daniélou, 1953, 309–326). One might also argue, on the basis of Plato's conclusion, shared by Plotinus, that what is best for each is that which most belongs to each, that if, to be most oneself at the level of Intellect is to be everything else through and through, then at the level of the Good to be Love at its most intense is both to be utterly transformed and yet to be most oneself. In other words, one is most oneself when one is beyond oneself. However this may be, this debate about the

Good as eros is important, and it is prompted by Plotinus' development of a new theology that can unite or at least link some of the best pagan, Christian, and Jewish insights without stepping over the limits of each, however porous these limits may be in thought if not in everyday practice.

16, 30–39: The self-directed activity of the Good stems not from chance but from his own self-directed will.

16, 16–23 *And Intellect is an actualization . . . it is not random*: We translate *energeia* here as actualization, instead of activity, to emphasize the dynamism at the heart of Plotinus' notion of power. Intellect is the actualization of a non-temporal potentiality as an unrestricted power that lies at the heart of intelligible activity. By contrast, the Good is the actualization of pure unrestricted power in itself. Here may be discerned the roots of the distinction between existence and essence; see Cilento, 1973, 101; Westra, 67–68n27, who views Plotinian freedom and the primacy of existence over essence as foreshadowing Heidegger; and for the existence/essence distinction broadly, see Corrigan 1996c, 105–129.

Just as Intellect is an actualization of the power of the Good, so too the Good, who constitutes himself (*upostēsas auton;* cf. "cause of himself," *aition heautou,* 14, 49) "is his own actualization"; he is both enduring causative activity (*energeia menousa*) and its resulting actualization (*energēma*). Of course such a distinction implies a partitioning of the Good into both producer and product, a difficulty of which

Plotinus is surely aware, since in Chapter 20, 1–27 he deals with the similar distinction between the Good as both the maker (*poiounta*) and himself as the product (*poioumenon*) he makes: "What then? Might one say. 'Doesn't he happen to be before he came to be? For if he makes himself, in respect to himself, he does not yet exist, but in respect to the making, he is already prior to himself since what is made is he himself.'" In response to such linguistic (agent versus patient), temporal (antecedent versus consequent) or logical (premise versus conclusion) distinctions, Plotinus argues that in the case of the Good, self-constitution is a pure, eternal activity that is entirely without substantial being (*aneu ousias* 20, 10) and has no result distinguishable from the act itself.

In Chapter 7, 46 Plotinus states that the existence of the Good is identical with its act (as also in the case of Intellect, cf. 18, 21); compare 20, 9–15: "For one must not be afraid of positing that the first activity is without being; rather he must posit this lack of being as itself his so-to-speak existence. And if one posited an existence without activity, the most perfect principle of all would be defective and imperfect. And if one adds activity, unity is not preserved. So if activity is more perfect than being, and the most perfect is the first, the first would be activity." Lavaud 308–309 infers from these lines an Aristotelian intellectual provenance for Plotinus' interlocutor, given their multiple allusions to the divine Intellect treated by Aristotle in *Metaphysics* 12, 7, 1072 a24–b30, cited in commentary on 16, 8–15.

The act of "looking" toward oneself in lines 20–21 is used by Plotinus to describe the manner in which the spontaneous efflux of a generated product becomes instantiated by turning about in an act of contemplating its source, the prefiguration of itself in the hypostasis immediately above it:

"It is because there is nothing in it (the One) that all things come from it: in order that Being may exist, the One is not being, but the generator of being. This, we may say, is the first act of generation: the One, perfect because it seeks nothing, has nothing, and needs nothing, overflows, as it were, and its superabundance makes something other than itself. This, when it has come into being, turns back upon the One and is filled, and becomes Intellect by looking toward it. Its halt and turning toward the One constitutes Being; its gaze upon the One, Intellect. Since it halts and turns towards the One that it may see, it becomes at once Intellect and Being" (V.2[11].1.8–13).

But this act of generation can only be applied to a product that is different than its source, while Plotinus' point here in VI.8.16 is that the Good has no other source than itself; it contains no prefiguration of itself, since it already and always is what it is, as it is.

This reflexive act of self-looking or inclination toward itself rather than away from or outside itself turns out to be an instance of Plotinus' notion of the double activity endemic to any real entity, one internal to itself by which it maintains and even makes itself as it is, and the other an external or exteriorizing activity by which it gives rise to something other than itself as an extension of its internal activity which it necessarily accompanies ("his [external] activity was brought along with himself"). For a striking example of this double activity developed from Plato's definition of justice in *Republic* 4, in relation to Aristotle's notion of activity/*energeia*, see Chapter 6, 19–31. On double act theory generally, see Rutten, 1956, 1100–1106; Lloyd, 1990, 98–105; Emilsson, 2007, 22–68.

16, 24–30: The Good as omnipresent, supreme, immobile, eternal act; The Good's power is his act.

16, 24–30 *But that such an inclination of himself to himself. . . . Therefore he brought himself into existence, his activity having been linked with himself*: While here Plotinus asserts that the Good "is his own actualization," already in 7, 46, Plotinus has stated that the existence of the Good is identical with his activity (as is true also in the case of Intellect, cf. 18, 21). And further on in 20, 9–15 Plotinus says: "For one must not be afraid of positing that the first activity is without being; rather one must posit this lack of being as itself his so to-speak reality (*hypostasis*). And if one posited an existence without activity, the most perfect principle of all would be defective and imperfect. And if one adds activity, unity is not preserved. So if activity is more perfect than being, and the most perfect is the first, the first would be activity." By this self-directed activity, the Good brings himself into existence, literally "hypostasizing" (*hypestēsen*) himself.

The term "inclination" in lines 24 and 26 is normally applied by Plotinus to the descent of the soul away from its proper ontological level (I.1.12, 23–25; VI.5.4, 9; II.1.3, 22; II.9.4, 6–7; 10, 19–25; 11, 13; 12, 40–43; IV.4.8, 54), while any such inclination in the Good is directed to itself, as in line 12 ("he as it were tends toward his interior"), a completely internal self-directed activity. For this linking language (*synexenechtheisēs*) see Plato, *Republic* 6, 508a and the anonymous *Parmenides Commentary* 12, 32–35 [Hadot].

16, 30–39: The self-awakening of the Good is not a conscious act, but an eternal state of wakefulness beyond any sort of intelligizing.

16, 30–39 *So if he didn't come into being . . . he is not as he happened to be, but as he himself willed to be*: The self-awakening of the Good is not a conscious act, as if the Good were aware of a previous state in which he was not awake; it is rather an eternal state of awakening that can be described as a kind of hyper-intelligizing beyond the pure being of Intellect *per se*, whose act of thought is its life. Here and in V.5 [32] 1, 33–38; 10, 13 and VI.7 [38] 8, 25–27, Plotinus probably draws upon Plato's *Sophist* 248e6–249a2, to the effect that ultimate reality (*to pantelōs on*, for Plotinus, Intellect in union with the intelligibles) must be possessed of life and intelligence and upon Aristotle's similar notion that life is the actuality of thought (*Metaphysics* 12 1072 a24–b30, cited in part in commentary on 16, 8–15); he concludes that Being, Intelligence, and Life form the triad of essential characteristics of his second hypostasis Intellect, a triad later formalized by Neoplatonists as the "noetic" or intelligible triad of Being, Life, and Mind, where Mind (*nous*) denotes the thinking subject; Being (*to on* or *ousia*) denotes the object of its thinking; and Life (*zōē*) denotes the activity of thinking itself. In 1072b16–18, Aristotle also uses the concept of "awakening," in the sense that the actuality of the first principle is also its "pleasure," in particular its "awakening, sensation and thinking (*egrēgorsis, aisthēsis, noēsis*)." As Leroux, 364, notes, this awakening is a self-actuated "intelligizing transcending thought (*hypernoēsis*) that is eternal," as in line 32. Of course for Plotinus, intelligizing normally denotes a subject thinking the intelligibles (or Forms) as its object of thought, which is identical with the thinking of Intellect.

Because thinking always implies a certain duality of or distinction between thought and object of thought, Plotinus rejects any identity between the One and Intellect, and often insists that the One does not think (see V.4.2, 6–8; VI.9.6, 43–57; III.9.9, 1; V.6.5, 11–12; VI.7.35, 44–45; V.3.13, 6–8), and that it is even "before thought" (*pro tou noēsai*; *pro noēseōs* as in V.3.10, 14; V.9.6, 43–44). Nevertheless, in the early treatise V.4 [11] 2, 15–19 he does seem to credit the One with a kind of thinking beyond that of Intellect, namely, the *prefiguration* of (the) Intellect-to-be as an internal activity of the One that he calls the "intelligible": "The intelligible (*noēton*) . . . is not like something senseless; all things belong to it and are in it and with it, it being completely able to discern itself. It contains life in itself and all things in itself, and its comprehension of itself is itself in a kind of self-consciousness (*synaisthēsis*) in everlasting rest and in a manner of thinking (*noēsis*) different from the thinking (*noēsis*) of Intellect." On this "intelligible," see Corrigan, 1986, 195–203. For *synaisthēsis* see V.4.2, 18; V.I.7, 11–13; III.8.4, 19–20; IV.3.26, 44–46; VI.7.16, 19–22; V.3.13, 13ff. and for *synesis* VI.9.4, 1–3, 17–18; VI.7.33, 27–28. And see Schwyzer, 1960, 343–390; Szlezák, 1979, 164n539; Schroeder, 1987, 677–699; Bussanich, 1988, 23–25, 116; and in relation to the Stoics, Graeser, 1972, 126–137. For further references SP, 1980.

For Plotinus, the will of the One/Good is not a determinate faculty or attribute of the Good—which would imply its multiplicity—but is rather the pure, indeterminate activity of the Good, an act of willing that completely transcends the activities of intelligizing, thinking and living—and being as well—and has no source other than itself.

Probably even before Plotinus, Sethian Gnostic sources (*Zostrianos*, *Allogenes*, the *Three Steles of Seth*) make use of an abstract version of this triad, namely Existence, Vitality, and Mentality (*hyparxis* or *ontotēs, zōotēs, nootēs*) as a triad of interhypostatic powers between the supreme Unknowable One or Invisible Spirit and the intellectual Aeon of Barbelo. In the Platonizing Sethian treatises, the boundless Vitality overflowing from the supreme One (itself coincident with Existence) results in the generation of the Barbelo Aeon as the power of Mentality that turns back upon its source to take on the determinate being of a divine intellect. A similar idea is found in VI.7.7, 13–26: "Life, not the life of the One, but a trace of it, looking toward the One was boundless, but once having looked was bounded (without bounding its source). Life looks toward the One and, determined by it, takes on boundary, limit and form . . . it must then have been determined as (the life of) a Unity including multiplicity. Each element of multiplicity is determined multiplicity because of Life, but is also a Unity because of limit . . . so Intellect is bounded Life." Here Plotinus refers to both a primary and secondary life or vitality as virtual synonyms for his doctrine of double activities (*energeiai*), an "internal" primary activity by which an entity is what it is, and an "external" or secondary activity that it emits as an image or trace of its primary internal activity. Indeed, *Allogenes* NHC XI 48, 29–49, 1 characterizes this "primary Vitality" as "the indivisible activity" of the supreme One, which is said to be "an hypostasis of the primary (activity) of the One that truly exists," which apparently gives rise to "a secondary activity" as its consequence or efflux, which in all probability is the "Mentality" that by contemplative reversion upon its prefiguration ("Existence") in the One takes on the determinate being of the Barbelo Aeon. All this raises the possibility that this noetic triad was of Gnostic origin; see Rasimus, 2010, 37–63.

Only in an ontology like Aristotle's, where to be real is to be a being, can *energeia* signify the reality of every existent thing and thus most truly signify the first reality which for Aristotle is the first Intelligence, the Unmoved Mover, while Plotinus prefers to signify the first reality by the concepts of unity and power (*dynamis*), and to refer terms like *energeia* and *ousia* to his second hypostasis Intellect (e.g., V.4 [7] 2, 3–33). In fact, in V.6 [24] 6, 2–3 he says "the Good would certainly not have any place for thinking, since the Good for the thinking principle must be something different than itself. So the Good is without activity (*anergēton oun*)." Once again, one must bear in mind Plotinus' caveat in 13, 47–50: "But one must consent to these terms if, in speaking of that Good, one necessarily uses for the sake of illustration terms that we don't precisely allow to be spoken. Let one take each such term with an 'as it were.'"

On the phrase "his existence then comes by and from himself" in line 37, compare 19, 14–20. As this existence is an eternal state of affairs willed by the Good, and not an event, nothing can "happen" to the Good; all contingency whatsoever is excluded.

Chapter 17

Providence assures that neither Intelligibles not Sensibles exist by accident.

17, 1–11: The Good as turned toward itself and interior to itself.

17, 1–11 *And still another viewpoint . . . then let him realize that Intellect stands before this All, this All which is from and according to Intellect*: Here, as in III.2.2, 20–27, Plotinus rejects the idea that the universe is made and governed "according to providence" (*kata pronoian*) by an intelligence that makes use of deliberative or calculative reasoning (*logismos*) to make a choice (*proairesis*) between better or worse options (compare III.2.14, 1–5; VI.2.21, 32–38; VI.7.1, 28). Clearly he has in mind the demiurge in Plato's *Timaeus* 30b4—c1: "Because of this reflection (*logismos*) he (the Demiurge) constructed reason within soul and soul within body as he fashioned the All, that so the work he was executing might be of its nature most fair and most good. Thus, then, in accordance with the likely account, we must declare that this cosmos has truly come into existence as a Living Creature endowed with soul and reason owing to the providence (*pronoia*) of God." Significantly, Plotinus expresses the key common terms "deliberations," "according to providence," and "fashioned" (*logismois, kata pronoian, eirgasato*) in unreal conditionals ("as if," "would have") rather than in the indicative statements in order to indicate that these concepts apply to lower orders of reality, but not to the Good, who transcends the providence exercised by Intellect and the deliberation and fashioning typically engaged in by soul. Although he left no detailed exegesis of *Timaeus* 29e–30c, Plotinus in fact denies that almost every trait that Plato ascribes to his Demiurge can be applied to his conception of a creative Intellect, namely, that the Demiurge proceeds from the wish—resulting from his goodness and his lack of envy toward anything and anybody—for all other things to be like himself, that he reasons and finds order to be preferable to chaos and intellectuality preferable to non-intellectuality, and finally decides to make up a soul as the only means to endow the ordered universe with intellect. He does of course believe in providence, just not in a deficient, calculating kind (see III.2–3 [47–48]).

Rather than something dependent upon choices or upon sequential, discursive reasoning from premise to conclusion—things characteristic of souls but not Intellect—Plotinus defines Providence as an eternal and unchanging expression of the permanent and stable being of Intellect in which all the Forms coexist simultaneously and forever. In V.5.1, 37–39 and V.8.5, 19–6, 12 Plotinus argues that the gods do not think in propositions or linguistic representations of reality but by means of non-discursive images (*agalmata*), like those of Egyptian ideographs, that embrace all things at once (*athroon*), against those like the Stoics who conceive

Intellect's knowledge as a form of discursive reasoning involving premises (*protaseis*), propositions (*axiōmata*) and sayable expressions (*lekta*); intelligizing is a direct intuitive grasp of the intelligibles themselves rather than something mediated through their linguistic representations. On this transformative movement of thought, see Beierwaltes, 2002, 19–33, and for the relation between providence and freedom, see Westra, 1990, 147–174.

17, 11–18: Since Intellect is an ordered "one-in-many," it cannot be subject to irrational chance.

17,11–18 *So if Intellect is before all things . . . then let him realize that Intellect stands before this All, this All . . . chance, embedded in irrationality, is contrary to reason*: Even though Intellect is an ordered "multiplicity" (*plēthos syntetagmenon*, the term *plēthos* perhaps going back to Speusippus' primal principles of the One and Multiplicity according to Aristotle, *Metaphysics* 13 9 1028b18–24; 7 2 1085b5), it is nonetheless organized into a unity (*eis hen syntetagmenos*), since its complex unity is dependent on the absolute and simple unity of the Good. As Plotinus says in V.3.15, 18–21: "For that (Intellect) which comes immediately after it (the One) shows clearly that it is immediately after it because its multiplicity is a one-everywhere (*hen pantachou*); for although it is a multiplicity it is at the same time identical with itself and there is no way in which you could divide it, because in it 'all things are together'" (*homou panta*, Anaxagoras frg. B1 Diels). Such an organized whole cannot derive from irrational happenstance.

The notion of Intellect as a "one-in-many" stems from the second hypothesis or deduction of Plato's *Parmenides* 143a5–6: "Do we say that the one partakes of being, and hence is?"—"Yes."—"And for this reason the one that is was shown to be many." Since this implies the unity of Intellect's multiplicity that makes orderly reason possible, Intellect cannot be subject to irrational chance.

17, 18–27: The Good is a single originative principle unrelated to anything but itself alone.

17, 18–27 *But if what is prior to such a thing (Intellect) is an originative principle, it clearly borders on this that has been rationally formed. . . . He is thus by himself what he is, related and directed to himself so as not to be related to anything external or to anything else, but totally self-related*: As Leroux, 369, notes, Intellect's immediate proximity to the One as its principle probably originated in the notion of the juxtaposition of the One and the indefinite Dyad in Plato's so-called "unwritten" teaching, or of the One and Multiplicity in the thought of Speusippus. Plotinus understands these entities, not as two interacting and coeval primal principles, but in a vertical hierarchy of power and logical priority originating in the Good as the superior principle of absolute unity above and beyond, although immediately proximate to its consequent, the multiple unity of Intellect. Since the Intellect is "made rational" and is the expression of the Good's power according to the will of the Good, Plotinus goes so far as to speak of the Good as its source in terms perhaps more appropriate to the Intellect rather than to the Good, which he here calls the dimensionless "one rational principle for all things" (*heis <eis> panta logos*), probably in the sense that the Good is cause, father, and root (*rhiza*) of the Logos (14, 37; 15, 33; cf. 18, 5).

Normally Plotinus holds that Intellect's contemplation of the One produces the plurality of the Intelligible Forms from which, in turn, will spring the formative principles (*logoi*) and seminal formative principles (*logoi spermatikoi*) (on which see Graeser, 1972, 41–43) that will serve as the productive power or essence in the Soul, which in turn is the active or generative principle within the lower realms (V.9 [5] 6–7). But as he indicates in 16, 33–37, the Good is entirely hyper-intelligence (*hypernoēsis*), "beyond intellect and thought and life," and thus clearly transcends any sort of reasoning or *logos*; thus the phrase "one rational principle <for: Cilento> all things (*heis <eis> panta logos*)" is not to be taken as defining the Good, but as emphasizing the solitary unity and power—without which there would be nothing—of the Good as opposed to the multiplicity of *logoi* generated by Intellect. As Lavaud, 313, notes, throughout Chapters 15, 16, and 17, Plotinus attributes numerous determinations and activities to the Good: in Chapter 15, he is self-love, self-producer, master of himself, light and love; in Chapter 16, he is both everywhere and nowhere, pure radiance, both activity and its result, will, awakening, and hyper-intelligence; in Chapter 17, he is one *logos,* number one, and entirely self-related (he is himself by himself, in relation to himself, directed toward himself). This language stands in strong contrast to the frequent apophatic language of earlier chapters and especially to the statement in Chapter 8, 13–15: "But we must say he is altogether unrelated to anything, for he is what he is even before them, since we take away even the 'he is' and so too any relation whatsoever to real beings."

Chapter 18

Seek the Good from its interior as container and measure of all things.

18, 1–2 *And as you seek, seek nothing outside him, but seek within him all things that come after him, but let him be*: On approaching the Good through the things that come after him, see V.3.14, 1–14 (cited above in comments on 13, 47–50, VI.5.4, 17–24 (cited below in comments on 18, 2–31) and VI.7.36, 3–26 (cited in comments on 19, 1–12). To seek within is to seek the unity that underlies everything including the seeker. Plotinus underscores this interiority in VI.5.1, 25–27 ("We have not departed from being, but are in it, nor has it departed from us; so all things are one") and VI.9.8, 19–22 ("we lift ourselves up by the part [of ourselves] that is not submerged in the body and by this join ourselves at our own centers to something like the center of all things, just as the centers of the greatest circles join the center of the encompassing sphere, and we are at rest"). Compare *Allogenes* NHC XI 56, 15–20: "If you [seek with perfect] seeking, [then] you shall know the [Good that is] in you; then [you shall know yourself] as well, (as) one who [derives from] the God who truly [pre-exists]."

The phrase "but let him be" (*auton de ea*) is almost exactly what the Good does: it makes "thinking things think and the living things live, breathing in to them intellect, breathing in soul, and, if something cannot live, (breathing in) to be (*einai*) (VI.7.23, 22–24). The phrase "let him be," we suggest, is from Aristodemus's reply to Agathon who has insisted on rousing Socrates from his contemplative reverie early in the *Symposium*. Aristodemus replies: "No way; just let him be" (175b1: *mēdamōs, all'eāte auton*).

18, 2–31: The Good is like the center and radii of a circle whose circumference is tangent to Intellect.

18, 2–31 *For he is himself the outside, the comprehension and measure of all things. In depth, he is inside, while his outside, touching and stretched around him like a circle, is all formative principle and Intellect, or rather would be Intellect insofar as it touches him and in the way it touches and depends on him insofar as it has from him its being Intellect. Thus just as a circle <that> would touch its center round about might be agreed to have its power from the center and be as it were centriform insofar as the radii in the circle, converging into a single center, direct their extremity toward the center to which they are so to speak led and from which they, as it were, sprout forth. The center is superior to the radii and to their extremities—the circumferential points of the radii themselves—and they are so to speak that (center), but they are also dim traces of that (center) which enables them by enabling the radii that impinge upon it at every point. And what that (center) is, is revealed through the radii, unfolded as it were without being unfolded.... What chance concurrence—or spontaneity or* *happenstance!—could approach such an intelligence-creating and truly creative power?*:

Given that the Good is everywhere present, he is both inside and outside all other realities, yet as the supreme principle, he embraces everything else, much as Plato (*Timaeus* 30c7–d1) conceived the supreme paradigm of all else: "For that Living Creature embraces and contains within itself all the intelligible living creatures, just as this universe contains us and all the other visible living creatures that have been fashioned." The Good is not only the exterior, container (*perilēpsis*, a *hapax legomenon* noun in the Plotinian corpus) and measure of all things, but also their innermost "depth" (*bathos*), a term close to the term "depth" (*bythos*) applied to the supreme principle in both the *Chaldaean Oracles* (fr. 18 [des Places]) and Valentinian theology (Irenaeus, *Against Heresies* 1.11.1; Hippolytus, *Refutations* 6.29.22; *Tripartite Tractate* NHC I 54, 21; 60, 16–28; *Valentinian Exposition* NHC XI 28, 25–36; 28, 20).

The innermost depth of the Good is compared to the center of a circle. Throughout this passage, Lavaud, 214n330, calls attention to the dynamism of the terminology—to "converge" (*suniousai*, lines 10–11), be "developed" or "unwound" (*exelichthen*, line 18), be "led" (ēnechthēsan, line 12), and to "sprout forth" (*exephysan*, line 13)—that Plotinus applies to the relation between the center and periphery of the circle as a way of signifying the active power of the One in metaphorical terms, as is indicated by Plotinus' initial use of the optative mood (*homologoito*, "might be agreed to have its power") and the fifteen-fold repetition of *hoion* ("as it were") throughout this chapter.

Plotinus often expresses the principle that posteriors are always included in their priors by describing the One as the center of a circle (or sphere) along whose radii there emerges a series of concentric circles symbolizing spheres of lower degrees of power and reality: Intellect, Soul, and onward to sensible things; cf. IV.2 [4] 1, 24; VI.9 [9] 8, 23; V.1 [10] 7, 5–10; 11, 10–13; VI.5 [23] 5, 11. Just as the center of this circle, the Good, timeless and eternal, so too all the circles or concentric spheres radiating from it exist simultaneously with the center and are likewise timeless and eternal; in this connection Leroux, 372, cites VI.5.4, 17–24:

"Or even if we may be talking about something else after the One itself, this again will be together with the One itself and what is after it will be around that One and directed to that One and like something generated from it in close touch with it, so that what participates in what comes after it has also participated in that One. For, since there are many things in the intelligible, firsts and seconds and thirds, and they are linked like one sphere to its one center, not separated by distances, but all existing together with themselves, wherever the thirds are present, the seconds and firsts are present as well."

As the very first of these radiating circles or spheres, Intellect is the innermost, nearest to and most tangent to the

Good, even to the point of "touching" (*ephaptetai*), a term Plotinus frequently uses to express the contact between the contemplative aspirant and the One with whom he wishes to unite (cf. VI.5.10, 41 and VI.9.4, 27). In his treatment of the Prime Mover, Aristotle too uses the metaphor of touching (*thigganein*), but goes a bit further than the mere tangency of thinker and object of thought by identifying one with the other: "And thought thinks itself by participation in the object of thought; for it becomes an object of thought in touching (*thigganōn*) and thinking its object, so that thought and object of thought are the same" (*Metaphysics* 12 7, 1072b19–21). Ross (vol. 2, 1975, 277 on 1051b24) comments on the metaphor of touch: "The metaphor of contact in the description of simple apprehension recurs [at] 1072b21. Its implications are (1) the absence of any possibility of error . . . (2) The apparent . . . absence of a medium in the case of touch. [It] means an apprehension which is infallible and direct." In fact, Plotinus uses both *thigein* and *ephaptesthai* together in VI.9.4, 27 and V.3.10, 43. Lavaud, 314, goes so far as to detect an analogy between the radii as the forms in Intellect and the circumference as the realm of individual souls. Leroux, 375, points out that a similar image of center and periphery is applied in VI.9.8, 5–22 to the soul's acquisition of true self-knowledge and god-likeness by centering itself on its true Source, the "center of all things."

However, an alternative picture is presented in V.5.9, 20–26, where the One is said to be the container of all, as if *it* were the circumference of a circle that circumscribes all else; there is nothing that is not within it. The notion of a circle as embracing both unity and multiplicity may derive from Alexander of Aphrodisias, *Questions and Answers* 96, 13–18 [Bruns], speaking of the center of a circle, which "is able to be simultaneously one and many (*hama men hen einai, hama de polla*); this is like the point, when it receives the terminus (*peras*) of many radii, for these all lead directly from the periphery of the circle to its center (*kentron*) having as a terminus the center of the circle, one unique point, which is both a unitary point (*hen sēmeion*) and somehow also many, when each of the radii drawn to it receives a terminus."

In lines 20–21, "poured out and unfolded and suspended from its own intelligent nature attesting that there is a sort of intellect-in-unity" (*ekchythen kai exelichthen kai exērtēmenon, ek tēs autou noeras physeōs martyrein ton hoion en heni noun ou noun onta*). HS_2 displace the comma from line 21 (*phuseōs, marturein*) to line 20 (*exērtēmenon, ek*), thus reading "Intellect and Being, originating from that One, as it were poured out and unfolded and suspended, from its own intelligent nature (i.e., of the generated Intellect) attesting that there is a sort of intellect-in-unity" rather than "Intellect and Being, originating from that Good, as it were poured out and unfolded and suspended from its own (i.e., the Good's) intelligent nature, attesting that there is a sort of intellect-in-unity." That is, the "intelligent nature" here more likely refers to the nascent Intellect and Being originating from the Good than to the Good itself. Nevertheless, the phrase "intellect-in-unity that is not Intellect" certainly implies a kind of quasi-intellect in the Good (who must be beyond Intellect and Being), as does the rather audacious attribution to the Good of a kind of super-thinking (*hypernoēsis*) in 16, 30–35: "if he didn't come into being, but his activity always was and was as it were an awakening when the awakener was not something else—an eternal awakening and an intelligizing transcending thought (*hypernoēsis*)—then he is as he awakened himself to be. But his awakening is <beyond Being> and Intellect and <intelligent Life>, yet these things are he himself."

The "intellect-in-unity" of line 21 (*ton hoion en heni noun*, a phrase which HBT would suppress, yet compare *en heni noun* as the Good's image in line 27) cannot be Intellect proper—which is both one and many—but rather the as-yet-unified prefiguration of Intellect still somehow resident in the Good, perhaps as an internal activity. Compare V.4.2, 12–19: But how does that Intellect (*nous*) come from the Intelligible (*to noēton*)? The intelligible (*noēton*) . . . is not like something senseless; all things belong to it and are in it and with it, it being completely able to discern itself. It contains life in itself and all things in itself, and its comprehension (*katanoēsis*) of itself is itself in a kind of self-consciousness (*sunaisthēsis*) in everlasting rest and in a manner of thinking (*noēsis*) different from the thinking (*noēsis*) of Intellect." In V.1.7, 1–6 Plotinus calls this prefiguration of Intellect an image of the Good: “But we say that Intellect is an image (*eikōn*; in 18, 27 Plotinus uses *indalma*) of that Good; for we must speak more plainly; first of all we must say that what has come into being must be in a way that Good, and retain much of it and be a likeness (*homoiotēs*) of it, as light is of the sun. But Intellect is not that Good. How then does it generate Intellect? Because by its return to it, it sees; and this seeing is Intellect.”

Although HS_2 follow Igal in reading lines 29–30 (<*ek*> *tēs dynameōs autou noun gennēsantos*) as if *nous* (intellect) were in the nominative case, some manuscripts along with Ficino’s marginal annotation read *noun* as the accusative object of *gennēsantos* (whose antecedent is the Good) as the only reading that makes sense.

As center of the circle, the Good is its Father; for the One as Father of Intellect, cf. V.1 [10] 8, 4; II.9 [33] 2, 1–4; VI.7 [38] 29, 28; earlier in Chapter 14, line 1, the Good is Father of the cause.

In Chapter 18, Plotinus twice uses the term “trace” (*ichnos*) to denote the intersection of the radii radiating from the center of the circle with its peripheral circumference. Emilsson, 2007, 44, remarks, “the *Enneads* abound in uses of this word (*ichnos*) to describe the external acts of the hypostases. Thus, Intellect is or contains a trace of the One (III, 8, 11, 19; V.5, 5, 13–14; VI.7.17, 13–14; VI.8.18, 15), Soul is a trace of Intellect (V.1.7, 44; VI.7.20, 12), the sensible form is a trace of the intelligible form (I.6.8, 7; II.6.3, 18), and so forth. This is of course an instance of the feature mentioned above that the external act is some kind of image of the internal one, *ichnos* being one of several words used to convey the Platonic notion of image."

On geometrical analogies for the generation of Intellect from the One, Lavaud, 316, compares III.8 [30] 8, 32–38: "But beginning as one it did not stay as it began, but, without noticing it, became many, as if heavy [with drunken sleep], and unrolled itself because it wanted to possess everything—how much better it would have been for it not to want this, for it became the second!—for it became like a circle unrolling itself, shape and surface and circumference and center and radii, some parts above and some below."

The main point of Chapter 18 seems to be that, if the Good has the power to create Intellect, then how could anyone attribute randomness or mere chance activity to it? As Leroux, 377, observes, even though Plotinus seems to consider this geometrical analogy for the relation between the One and all that proceeds from his power as an argument against their accidental generation, he does so on the grounds of a logico-mathematical necessity rather than as a consequence of the One's exercise of free will. However, from a Platonic/Pythagorean perspective, mathematics and geometry are forms of free growth and generation, not subject to rigid necessity.

18, 32–43: Intellect is a plurality of formative principles that are the dispersed image of the Good—the cause of causes—and thus not a mere happenstance.

18, 32–43 *For in that One there is so to speak something like what is in Intellect, although in many ways greater, like a light dispersed from some single entity translucent in itself. . . . And his will is not irrational or random or as it "turned out" for him, but as it had to be, since nothing There is random*: In this chapter Plotinus calls the supreme principle the "One" rather than the "Good" only here, perhaps because, as Lavaud, 316–317, suggests, he is stressing its absolute unity. The light dispersed from the Good is clearly the prefigurative intellect or the inchoate, as yet indeterminate intellect-to-be, something like what is in Intellect, probably the "intelligible" (*noēton*) of which Plotinus speaks in V.4.2, 12–19 (cited in commentary on 18, 7–31).

Plotinus' notion that this "something like what is in Intellect" is also "translucent in itself" is probably derived from Plato's analogy between the sun and its light and the relation between the Good and the other Forms in *Republic* 6 509b. Although what is dispersed from the Good is an image, it remains the same as its source, and is not an "alien form." The metaphors of radiation and aqueous flowing are explicitly combined in the *Apocryphon of John*, which offers a somewhat similar depiction of how the supreme principle emanates its "first thought" as Barbelo—the image of the Invisible Spirit and equivalent of Plotinus' Intellect—as a dispersion of light: BG 26, 15–27,7: "It is he who contemplates himself alone in his own Light that surrounds him, namely the Fount of living water, the *Light* that is full of purity. The fount of the Spirit flowed from the luminous living water, and he supplied every aeon and worlds. In every direction he contemplated his *image*, beholding it in the pure luminous water surrounding him. And his thought became actual and appeared and stood at rest before him in the radiance of the light."

On the notion of the presence of a radiant or burgeoning, as-yet-indeterminate prefiguration of a product within and its spontaneous emission from its source, see Corrigan, 1986, 195–203; Schroeder, 1986, 186–195. On the relation of such prefiguration and internal and external activity of the One, see Emilsson, 2007, 24–34. The inchoate intellect's awareness or consciousness of the possibility contained in the One's power enables the self-constitution or self-determination of Intellect proper.

Of course, the fact that Intellect as the dispersed image of the Good is "not an alien form" (*alloeides*, literally "another form," a *hapax legomenon* in Plotinus' corpus) should not be taken to imply that the formless Good as its source also has a form.

As the cause of all causes, what the Good generates cannot originate from chance, but from his own will. Here Plotinus emphasizes the unbroken continuity between all levels in the hierarchy of degrees of reality by regarding the prime cause—the Good—as in a superior way not only pre-containing or prefiguring what is contained in its product but also generating it by will. This of course implies that the freedom and self-determination that Plotinus ascribes to the human soul originates in and necessarily presupposes the absolute freedom and self-determination of the Good as its ultimate source. Yet in Chapter 19, 16–20 Plotinus will also conceive the prime cause as generating a product—in this case substantial being (*ousia*)—which is entirely absent from and has no counterpart in the producer. Lavaud, 317, traces the phrase "as it 'turned out' for him" in line 42 to Plato's *Philebus* 28d6–7: "Shall we say, Protarchus, that all things and this which is called the universe are governed by an irrational and fortuitous power and mere chance (*tēn tou alogou kai eikēi kai to hopēi etuchen*) . . ." For an overview of the relation between roles of will, chance, contingency and necessity throughout VI.8, see Gleede, 2012, 289.

18, 43–51: Platonic Metaphors: The Good is that which needed to be in a timely fashion.

18, 43–51 *Whence Plato spoke* of <*"what needs to be and the timely moment"*>, . . . *And needful is not like a substrate, but is like a primary activity manifesting itself as what it needed to be*: Plotinus here opposes being timely (*kairon*) and appropriate or needful (*deon*) to what is merely random or accidental by alluding to Plato, *Statesman* 284e2–8: "We should evidently divide the science of measurement into two parts in accordance with what has been said. One part comprises all the arts which measure number, length, depth, breadth, and thickness in relation to their opposites; the other comprises those which measure them in relation to the moderate, the fitting, the opportune (*ton kairon kai to deon*), the needful, and all the other standards that are situated in the mean between the extremes." For Plotinus, such measures insure that things do not happen by chance or accident. Lavaud, 317–318, and Leroux, 382, trace the phrase "appropriate and timely" to Plato's *Philebus* 28d6–7: "Shall we say, Protarchus, that all things and this which is called the universe are governed by an irrational and fortuitous power and mere chance (*tēn tou alogou kai eikēi kai to hopēi etuchen*)," and remark that Plotinus ascribes to the Good an activity which is necessary, timely, and intentional, and above all unified and focused, an activity that can hardly be the result of chance, and, somewhat paradoxically, which he nevertheless thinks is free and voluntary.

Need or necessity is not an unstructured, persistent and passive substrate (*hypokeimenon*) that can only be acted upon, but is itself a structuring activity, and indeed a "primary" activity. For Plotinus, everything has both an internal (intrinsic or primary) and an external (extrinsic or secondary) activity, a first, "internal" activity constituting a thing's own substance or essence (*ousia*), and a second, "external" activity that departs from its substance and appears as an "image" (*eikōn*) or "trace" (*ichnos*) of the prior internal activity. Even if the Good is strictly speaking not a thing or a substance, it is plausible that the structure of primary and secondary activities found in lower things applies also in its case and that the absolutely simple activity which it is gives rise to a secondary activity which is somehow different from it. As V.4.2, 21–37 puts it:

"When, therefore, the Intelligible (*noēton*) abides 'in its own proper way of life' (i.e., the demiurge's retirement in *Tim.* 42e5–6), that which comes into being does come into being from it, but from it as it abides unchanged. Since therefore it abides as Intelligible, what comes into being does so as thinking (*noēsis*), and since it is thinking and thinks that from which it came—for it has nothing else—it becomes Intellect, like another Intelligible and as it were that principle, a representation and image (*mimēma kai eidōlon*) of it. But how, when that abides unchanged, does Intellect come into being? In each and every thing there is an activity which belongs to the Being (*ousia*) and one which goes out from the Being; and that which belongs to Being is the activity which is each particular thing, and the other activity derives from that first one, and necessarily follows it in every respect, being different from the thing itself: as in fire there is a heat which constitutes its Being, and another which comes into being from that primary heat when fire exercises the activity which is native to its Being in abiding unchanged as fire. So it is also in the intelligible; and much more so, since while it [the first principle] abides 'in its proper way of life,' the (external, other-directed) activity generated from its perfection and its coexistent activity (*sunousēs energeias*, i.e., its internal, inner-directed activity by which it is what it is) acquires substantial existence (*hypostasin*), since it comes from a great power, the greatest of all, and arrives at being and Being (*eis to einai kai ousian*): for that other is beyond Being (*epekeina ousias*, cf. *Rep.* 509b)."

The internal activity is thus pure "active" power (*dunamis*) that remains unchanged rather than passive possibility or potential (*en dunamei*). As such, it is indeterminate or better, infinitival, as suggested by the priority of *to einai* ("to be") over *ousia* ("being") in Plotinus' phrase *eis to einai kai ousian*, while the external activity is its direct and necessary consequence—for Plotinus its "image" (*eikōn*) or "trace" (*ichnos*)–and represents an outer-directed movement, even though in both activities it is the same agent that is acting. On the internal and external activity of the One, see V.9.8, 1–22; IV.8.6.1–2; V.4.2.21–37; V.1.6.28–35; IV.5.7.13–23; II.9.8.11–19; and VI.2.22.26–29. All this suggests that the inchoate or prefigurative Intellect's awareness or consciousness of the possibility contained in the One's power enables its self-constitution or self-determination as Intellect proper. In Plotinus' hierarchy of hypostases, the One has a totally self-contained internal activity as well as an inchoate Intellect as an external activity, which is an image of the One itself; this inchoate Intellect reverts to its source, whereby it becomes determined Intellect whose internal activity is identical with Intellect's substance, and whose internal activity in turn has Soul as its external act. While the inner activity is the real thing itself, its outer act is its image or representation. On the prefigurative or inchoate nous, see Schroeder, 1986, 186–195.

18, 52–53 *For one must speak of him in this way since one is unable to speak of him as one would wish*: On such inability to speak of the Good, see 8, 4–5 and 11, 2–3. From Chapter 13 onward Plotinus attempts a series of persuasive arguments falling short of what is correct (cf. 13, 1–5 and 47–50), yet, as he says in 19, 1–3, they serve to raise the soul up to a better view of things. As O'Meara 1992, 348, remarks: "We could describe these arguments as conceptual exercises, a philosophical therapy for the confused soul which is scarcely satisfactory as a discourse about the One." These chapters, therefore, serve, however imperfectly, as an ascent to and a sustained attempt to dwell in the Good.

Chapter 19

Contemplation of the Good is superior to all speech about him.

19, 1–12 *Roused up from what has been said toward That, let one accept that That Itself, and he too shall see, . . . and wherever one directs one's gaze, he sees That, unless, abandoning the god, he should gaze elsewhere, no longer thinking about him*: Chapter 19 moves toward the conclusion of this treatise by recapitulating some of the points made in Chapters 13 to 18 in the light of Plotinus' fundamental declaration, based upon Plato's *Republic* 6 509b7–10, that the Good is utterly beyond being and thus all definition and description. Ultimately these arguments are not intended to describe the Good or appeal to cognition, so much as they are designed to motivate the auditor to ascend into union with him.

The ascent to the Good begins from discourse (*tōn eirēmenōn*) and reason (*logos*) from which one is carried (*lambanetō*) into a vision (*theasetai*) of the Good *within* the visionary himself (*idōn de ekeino en hautōi*—reading *hautōi*, "onself" for *autōi*, i.e., "in the Good"; cf. 18, 3: "seek nothing outside him, but seek within him"). Compare VI.7.36, 3–26.

Having abandoned discourse and reasoning, one necessarily enters into the realm of unknowing. Similarly in *Allogenes* NHC XI 60, 1–61,22, which narrates an actual mystical ascent, we have an ascending sequence of mental states which is nearly the exact reverse of the sequence of the ontogenetic phases or modalities by which the Aeon of Barbelo, the equivalent of Plotinus' Intellect, emanates from the Triple Power of the supreme Unknowable One. This Triple Power is comprised of three powers: Existence, Vitality, and Mentality or Blessedness. Originating as a purely infinitival Existence (*hyparxis* or Coptic *petšoop* translating either *hyparxis, einai,* or *ontotēs*) latent within and identical with the supreme One, this power proceeds from the One as an indeterminate Vitality (*zōotēs*) or "primary activity" which—in its final phase as a "secondary activity" or Mentality (*nootēs*)—contemplatively reverts upon its prefiguration in the One and takes on the character of determinate being (*to on*) as the intellectual Aeon of Barbelo.

Once Allogenes has contemplatively ascended through the various intelligible levels of the Barbelo Aeon, his ascent through the three powers of the Triple Power is described as a centrifugal sequence of self-withdrawals from determinate self-knowledge, to a complete loss of determination, ending in union with the original prefiguration of his own self still resident in the supreme One. First perceiving the quiet Blessedness that conveys self-knowledge, Allogenes next seeks himself by withdrawing to and joining with the more indeterminate and unstable level of Vitality. His third and final withdrawal is made toward the completely stable level of Existence, where he is "filled" by this manifestation of unity, stability, and silence; see *Allogenes* NHC XI 60, 1–61, 22.

In *Allogenes*, these withdrawals constitute a series of reflexive reversions toward the interior self, as if the entire triad comes to abide within the mystical subject; they are essentially acts of diminishing self-cognition ending in complete incognizance or "unknowing" as one's self retreats into its pre-existent prefiguration—its "originary manifestation (*prōtophan*[*e*]*ia*)—still latent in the source from which it originally emanated.

For Plotinus, once one has seen the Good within oneself, one realizes that the Good so transcends being that whatever being one might attribute to him (line 5, *eiper eichein ousian*) cannot be his own being (line 4, *touto on*) but only his slave and product, since as lines 16–17 below state, he is not being, as if he had any (line 6, "as if derived from him"), but is instead the principle (*archē*) of being. Given this, to attribute anything to the Good, let alone randomness or chance occurrence, would be not only to compromise the simplicity of the Good, but would be unthinkably audacious; see the "rash account" (*tolmēros logos*) earlier cited by Plotinus in Chapter 7, 11. In positive terms, the soul who should know the Good would be "astonished" or "struck dumb" (I.6.7, 14; VI.7.31, 7).

The Good, whom Plotinus here calls "the god," is omnipresent, appearing everywhere, no matter where one looks; see 16, 1–8 and commentary thereon. Referring to Hadot, 1963, 81–85, Leroux, 386, notes that Plotinus follows Plato (*Timaeus* 45b–46a) in distinguishing the exterior illumination of objects of sight and the interior illumination stemming from the soul, as in V.5.7, 22–35: "Just so Intellect, veiling itself from other things and drawing itself inward, when it is not looking at anything will see a light, not a distinct light in something different from itself, but suddenly appearing, alone by itself in independent purity, so that Intellect is at a loss to know whence it has appeared, whether it has come from outside or within, and after it has gone away will say 'It was within, and yet it was not within.'" The phrase "eyes of the soul" in line 10 probably comes from Plato, *Republic* 7 533d2; cf. *Phaedo* 66d8–e2: "It really has been shown to us that, if we are ever to have pure knowledge, we must escape from the body and observe things in themselves with the soul by itself (*autē tē psychē theateon auta ta pragmata*)" and Ovid, *Metamorphoses* XV, 63: "what nature denied to human vision he (Pythagoras) drew out with the eyes of his soul" (*oculis ea pectoris*).

19, 12–20: The Good is Beyond Being.

19, 12–20 *And likewise one ought to know that it was in this way that the phrase "beyond substantial being" was mentioned by the ancients, in the form of a riddle . . . nor again does he make the "it is" in accord with his existence*: The idea that the Good is beyond being (*epekeina ontos*) is based on Plato, *Republic* 6 509b7–10: "you are to say that the objects of knowledge not only receive from the presence of the Good their being known, but their very existence and essence is derived to them from it, though the Good itself is not being but still transcends being in dignity and surpassing power."

Here Plotinus apparently contradicts or at least corrects his earlier statement in 16, 37 "his existence then comes by and from himself" (*par' autou ara autō kai ex autou to einai*). Compare *Allogenes* NHC XI 61, 32–39: "Now he (the Unknowable One) is an entity insofar as he exists, in that he either exists and becomes, or lives or knows, although he acts without Mind or Life or Existence—or Nonexistence—incomprehensibly." Cf. Sells, 1994, 27: "Self-making refers then to *nous* (noetic self-reflexivity) and to the one (fusion identity) at the same time. The propositions 'it is as it willed/made/thought it(self) to be' not only split the reference, but the infinite regress implied in them continues to split the reference as long as the gaze (*theoria*) is maintained. The split reference of self-causality, the "projection" of being outside the self, the process of dis-ontology [in order for 'being' to be, the source of being, the One, cannot be being], the breakdown of the self/other dichotomy are all aspects of emanation."

While in Chapter 18, 39–40, Plotinus regards the prime cause—the Good—as in a superior way pre-containing what is contained in its product, here in 19, 16–20 he conceives the prime cause as producing a product entirely outside and different from itself, in this case producing being or substantial being (*ousia*)—something that it neither has nor pre-contains—and which has no correspondence to its own existence (its "isness," *to esti*). As Plotinus says in Chapter

8, 13–21: "But we must say he is altogether unrelated to anything, for he is what he is even before them, since we remove even the 'he is' and so any relation to real beings; nor is there any 'as he naturally is,' for this too is later. . . . One must not even say 'it is not from itself,' since we have taken away the 'to be,' and 'not from itself' would imply the (generative) agency of another."

Chapter 20

If the Good is self-produced, does He then precede Himself?

20, 1–9 *What then?... there are not two but one*: If the Good is not by chance and if it is not produced by another, it has produced itself, and so it would be prior to itself. The force of this objection comes from distinguishing the product and the producer, but in the case of the Good's self-production this is an absolutely simple act; it is he himself. To isolate the producing subject from the act of producing is to deny the Good.

On the grounds that the Good transcends being, Chapter 20 shifts from an object-oriented discourse about persistent entities—such as being—to discourse about dynamic processes and activities, thus privileging act or activity over essence, substantial being, or nature; activity not in the normal Aristotelian sense, which may or may not involve motion (*De anima* 3, 7, 432a6–7: "for movement is an activity of what is imperfect, while activity in the absolute sense, the act of what has been perfected, is different from movement"), but more in the Stoic sense of activity as opposed to the passivity of substance; cf. Pierre Hadot, 1968, 1.375. Of course, the concept of "act" is very close to that of "happening," which can come very close to the notion of "happenstance" or accident. Therefore, for Plotinus, activity or action, particularly as regards the Good's activity must be understood as hyperintentional or willed activity, undirected toward and unproductive of any object; it is thus not a purely random activity, which is the very accusation he is concerned to refute.

On the notion of self-making (*ei gar poei heauton*), often expressed by such terms as *autogenēs, autogennētos, autogenetōr,* "self-generated," "self-generator," which Plotinus may here avoid because of its prominent use in Gnostic thought, see the thorough study of Whittaker, 1980, 176–193. Perhaps for this reason, Plotinus' use of this concept in VI.8 is exceptional not only in his oeuvre, but also in other contemporary metaphysical systems. Given the paradox that the product of a maker cannot exist prior to the productive act ("Might one say 'Doesn't he happen to be before he came to be?'" *Ou symbainei, eipoi tis an, prin ē genesthai gegonenai*?), although the productive act must precede the product even if the product is the producer, there can be no sense in characterizing the Good's self-production as accidental; if there is nothing other than the making, there is nothing else to "fall together" (*sumbainei,* literally to "come together" in line 1, normally denotes a chance occurrence) with it. Any sort of production normally implies a subject who produces and an object that the subject produces, but in this case producer and product are the same, which is why Plotinus calls this making (*poiēsis*) absolute (*apoluton*), an activity (*energeia*) that is entirely himself, since at the origin of everything, there can be nothing other (*allo, allou* in lines 6–7) than the originating producer itself.

While Plotinus here applies the concept of self-making to the supreme principle, in Gnostic thought, the concept of self-generation is applied, not to the supreme first principle, but to its immediate product. This concept, though dating from at least the fifth century BCE, is frequent in Gnostic texts. Thus in the Nag Hammadi treatise (NHC III 3; V 1) *Eugnostos the Blessed*, the second principle is self-generated from the first; III,3 74.21–75.12 (cf. also: "The Lord of the Universe is not rightly called Father but Forefather; cf. *propatoros* in V.4.3, 23). For the Father is the principle of what is visible. For he is the beginningless Forefather. He sees himself within himself, like a mirror, having appeared in his likeness as Self-Father, that is, Self-generator, and as confronter, since he confronted the ungenerated First Existent. He is indeed of equal age with the one who is before him, but he is not equal to him in power." Cf. also the *Sophia Jesus Christ* (NHC III 4) 98.24–99.13. In the *Apocryphon of John*, the name of the third member of its supreme Father-Mother-Child trinity is the Self-generated one (*autogenēs*), and in other Nag Hammadi Sethian treatises, the reflexive language of self-generation, self-knowledge, self-seeing, self-love, self-mating, and self-existence is frequent, for example, the *Three Steles of Seth* (VII 126, 3–4); *Zostrianos* (VIII 20, 4–15; 74, 20–24; 124, 17–19); *Allogenes* (XI 56, 13–14; 65, 22–27); the *Trimorphic Protennoia* (XIII 45, 2–8). The Sethian *Gospel of the Egyptians*

(NHC III 41, 6–7) seems to form an exception, since *both* the supreme Invisible Spirit and his child the Autogenes Logos are said to be self-generated; the supreme Invisible Spirit is said to be "self-generated, self-begotten, successor, another kind" (*autogenēs, autogenios, epigennios, allogenios*). In this respect, the Nag Hammadi Valentinian treatise *Tripartite Tractate* (NHC I 5) 56, 1–57, 3 is ambiguous; even though the narrative presupposes the Father's existence, the generation of the Father's Son seems to be regarded as the Father's own self-generation:

"For it is truly his ineffable self (the Father or Son?) that he engenders. It is self-generation, where he conceives of himself and knows himself as he is. He brings forth something worthy of the admiration, glory, praise, and honor that belong to himself, through his boundless greatness, his inscrutable wisdom, his immeasurable power, and his sweetness that is beyond tasting. It is he himself whom he puts forth in this manner of generation, and who receives glory and praise, admiration and love, and it is also he who gives himself glory, admiration, praise, and love. This he has as a Son dwelling in him, keeping silent about him, and this is the ineffable within the ineffable, the invisible, the ungraspable, the inconceivable within the inconceivable. This is how he exists eternally within himself. As we have explained, by knowing himself in himself the Father bore him without generation, so that he exists by the Father having him as a thought—that is, his thought about himself, his sensation of himself and . . . of his eternal self-standing."

Such ambiguities also occur in Plotinus' account of the generation of the Intellect from the One through an act of self-contemplation. Here the ambiguity of antecedents is necessary, since the object of the self-perception of both the first and second principle is one and the same, that is, the second principle is always prefiguratively present in the first. For example, in *Ennead* V.1.7, a parallel to the *Tripartite Tractate* here, the subject of self-perception can be properly called neither the Good nor Intellect, but is rather a subject that starts out as the Good, but by perceiving itself, ends up as Intellect:

"But we say that Intellect is an image (*eikōn*) of that Good; for we must speak more plainly; first of all we must say that what has come into being must be in a way that is Good, and retain much of it and be a likeness (*homoiotēs*) of it, as light is of the sun. But Intellect is not that Good. How then does it generate Intellect? Because, by its return to it, it sees: and this seeing is Intellect" (V.1.7, 1–6).

By contrast, in Chapter 20 Plotinus is unambiguously clear that the subject of self-generation is the supreme Good itself; it is an act that has no product other than the producer.

In lines 2–4 of Chapter 20, Lavaud, 320, suggests abandoning the dative of respect *tōi* by adopting the reading of manuscript x: "For if he makes himself, on the one hand, *this* 'himself' does not yet exist, but on the other hand, *the* (act of) *producing* exists already, since he exists prior to himself as being what is made" (*Ei gar poiei heauton, to men "heauton" oupō esti, to d' au poiein estin ēdē pro heautou tou poioumenou ontos autou*) instead of HS_2: "For if he makes himself, *in respect to* himself, he does not yet exist, but *in respect to* the *making*, he *is* already prior to himself since what is made is he himself" (*Ei gar poiei heauton, tōi men "heauton" oupō esti, tōi d' au poiein estin ēdē pro heautou tou poioumenou ontos autou*).

The idea that the act of making precedes the product of the making is ancient; cf. Melissus *apud* Simplicius, *Commentary on Aristotle's Physics* 9.162, 22–26: "What was was forever, and ever shall be (*aei ēn ho ti ēn kai aei estai*). For, if it had come into being, it must have been nothing before it came into being. Now, if it happened to be nothing, in no way could anything have arisen out of nothing." This notion prevails long after Plotinus, as in Philoponus, *Commentary on Aristotle's Physics* 6, 51, 20–25: "For if he generated being, he generated either from being or from not being, so, if from being, being will be before generation . . . and if from not being, being would be from that which in no way is (*ek tou mēdamēi mēdamōs ontos*). For if absolute being (*to haplōs on*) comes to be, it would arise from absolute non-being (*ek tou haplōs mē ontos*)"; also 16, 169, 23–26: "So nothing comes from that which in no way is." A similar notion is expressed by Plotinus also in VI.7 [38] 40, 30–34: "For it (the One) did not act before it generated activity, for then activity would have been there before it generated thought; for then it would have thought before thought came to be."

Plotinus' point is that in self-production, the product and producer are one and the same, with no distinction between subject and object or agent and patient. The Good's self-making is its self-contained internal activity (see 4, 28; 7, 49; 12, 36; 13, 7; 16, 17 ("he is his own actualization"); 18, 15 and the commentary on 16, 30–35) which is absolute and independent (line 6, *apolytos*, literally "set free,") of anything other than itself. Even if there is an external activity that may incidentally accompany it, this does not imply an external object acted upon. In the case of self-making, external activity is identical with internal activity. The activity *of* the Good is self-creative freedom, while the activity *from* the Good follows necessarily from the first, but is a necessity *sui generis*, that is, a necessity that follows from an act of freedom.

As Michael Sells, 1994, 26, remarks, there is here: "an oscillation and continual shifting of referents . . . not only in the object (it makes it[self]) but throughout the proposition, in the subject and predicate. What is it that makes itself? It must be *nous* since *nous* is defined as reflexive act. But then it would have had to make itself in order to exist in order to make itself. *Nous* as self-making devolves in infinite regress. On the other hand, if we say that the one makes itself, then we must withdraw not only the 'itself,' but also the division between maker and making by posing a making without a maker or a maker without a making. Insofar as 'it makes,' it cannot be the one because the one cannot be referred to in a subject-predicate delimitation. *Nous* both is and is not the one. The double dialectic of self-causality and self-transcendence brings to life the underlying apophatic logic."

20, 9–27: Since the Good's self-making is an eternal activity or process and not caused by some substantial reality other than himself, there can be no "before" or "after" in his self-making.

20, 9–27 *For we must not be afraid of positing that the first activity is without substantial being . . . let this phrase "he has made himself" be understood to mean the concurrence of the "having made" with his own self, for the being is one with the making and is as it were an eternal generation*: In lines 9–11, Plotinus posits that the Good is an activity (*energeia*) whose "reality," a kind of quasi-hypostasis (*tēn hoion hypostasin*), is without being (*ousia*). Yet in I.7.1, 17–20 and V.3.12, 22–34 Plotinus maintains that the Good is beyond activity; because the Good is beyond being, it would also transcend activity on the assumption that activity implies being. In any case, Plotinus evidently believed that the Good has an internal "character" that can be likened to activity and which is responsible for the external act of the Good. See Bussanich, 1988 on V.6.6, 1ff. and VI.8.16, 15–18, and Gerson, 1994, 26 and 235n28. On the relation between activity and being in Plotinus, Bussanich, 1996, 48 observes:

"Plotinus describes the One's "essence" or "substance" as activity (*energeia*) and what proceeds from this activity as both "activity from the substance" and as power or active potentiality (*dunamis*). In itself the One's existence (*hupostasis*) is one with its activity (VI.8.7.47), with its will (V.8.13.56–57), and with its "essence" (VI.8.12.14–17). Insofar as it is efficient cause the One's operational attributes are activity and power. Do *energeia* and *dunamis,* which figure in Aristotelian causal connections between sensible substances, substantialize the One? Plotinus answers this objection by insisting that "the first activity (*energeia*) is without substance (*ousia*)" and that this fact is "his, so to speak, existence (*hupostasis*). But if one posited an existence without activity, the principle would be defective and the most perfect of all imperfect" (VI.8.20.9–13; cf. V.6.6.8–11). To rule out any duality, VI.8.7.46–54 *identifies* activity, existence, and being, often invoking the qualifier "as if" (*hoion*); cf. also VI.8.16.15–18, 25. Typically, Plotinus asserts that the One is beyond actuality (1.7.1.17–20, V.3.12.16–28, VI.7.17.9–11), especially when he wants to distinguish it from Aristotle's first principle, the divine Intellect."

For Aristotle, only pure activity entails perfection: "for movement is an activity of what is imperfect, while activity in the absolute sense, the act of what has been perfected, is different from movement" (*De anima* 3 7 432a6–7).

A similar insistence that the supreme One is pure activity without being occurs in the anonymous Turin *Commentary on Plato's Parmenides* 12.22–35 (on *Parmenides* 142b–c): "It has not been said that Being participates in the One, but that the One participates in Being (*to on*), not because the first was Being (*to on*), but because an otherness from the One has turned the One towards this whole One-Being (*to hen einai*). For from the fact of being engendered somehow at the second level, being-One (*to hen einai*) is added. . . . the One, which is beyond substance and being, is neither being nor substance nor act, but rather *acts and is itself pure act, such that it is itself being before determinate being* (*to hen to epekeina ousias kai ontos on men ouk estin oude ousia oude energeia, energei de mallon kai auto to energein katharon, hōste kai auto to einai to pro tou ontos*). By participating this being (the *einai* of the first One; cf. *Parmenides* 137c–142a), the One (scil. the "One who is" of *Parmenides* 142b–144e) possesses another being (*einai*) declined from it (the *einai* of the Supreme One), which is (what is meant by) participating in determinate being (*to on*; cf. *ousia* in *Parmenides* 142b). Thus, being (*einai*) is double: the one preexists determinate being (*to on*), while the other (*on*) is derived from the One who transcends determinate being (*to on*), who is absolute being (*einai*) and as it were the idea (*idea*) of determinate being (*to on*) by participation in which (the *einai* of the first) some other One has come to be to which is linked the being (*einai*) carried over from it."

To be compared is the following passage from the Sethian Platonizing treatise *Allogenes* which, although it is in an epistemological context, nevertheless speaks of a double activity in the Unknowable One, a primary activity considered as the reality or *hypostasis* of the One, and a secondary activity called the hidden or latent aspect of pure existence (*hyparxis*), which is identified as a "pre-vitality" emitted from the Unknowable One that becomes the equivalent of Intellect by contemplatively reverting upon its source: *Allogenes* NHC XI 48, 8–49, 1: "If they come together—since it is impossible that the Individuals (actively) comprehend the All [situated in the] place that is higher than perfect—they thereby (passively) apprehend through a preconception (*tšorp nennoia* = *proennoia*), not, as it were, of Being—[rather] he (the Unknowable One) provides Being along with [the] latency of Existence (*hyparxis*), [providing] for [it in] every way—since this is what [shall] come into being when he intelligizes himself. . . . But when they (passively) apprehend (i.e., through a preconception), they participate in the pre-vitality (*tšorp mmntōnh* = *prōtē zōotēs*; cf. *zoē prōtē* in III.8.9, 33), even an indivisible activity (*energeia*), a reality (*hypostasis*) of the primary (activity) of the One that truly exists. And a second activity (*energeia*) [. . .] however, is the [. . .] . . . "

Since *Allogenes*—and quite possibly the anonymous *Commentary*—was known to Plotinus and members of his seminar, it may have been among those sources that contributed to Plotinus' notions about the One's activity. In any case Plotinus emphasizes that activity is not something added to the one—which would violate its utter simplicity—but is innate to, or rather, *is* the Good.

As Lavaud, 321, points out, lines 13–15 constitute a classic syllogism: "So if activity is more perfect than being, and the most perfect is the first, the first would be activity." Here HS_1 read *prōton an energeia eiē* "the first (*prōton*) would be activity," while HS_2 read *prōtē an energeia eiē*, "it (the first one) would be the first (*prōtē*) activity."

As pure activity, the Good has no before and after, and this activity since it is devoid of and beyond being, is absolutely (*katharōs*, "purely") free of any being to which it might be subservient; he is himself by himself. Moreover, as stated in Chapter 21, 19–21 and also in V.5.9, the Good contains all and is contained by nothing. The notion of the supreme principle as containing all but contained by none is a virtual *topos* found in authors extending from Melissus (fr. 5) and Philo (*De aeternitate mundi* 106) through Justin (*Dialogue with Trypho* 127.2) and Theophilos (*Ad Autolycum* 2.3) and beyond among the Stoics, for whom the divine Pneuma contains and unifies everything in the universe (*SVF* II, 441, 2 = Alexander of Aphrodisias, *De mixtione* 223, 26–27).

The notion that the Good's self expression coincides or is concurrent with himself (*to syndromon einai to pepoiēkenai*) seems almost a corollary of Plotinus' earlier statement in 13, 29–30 that "his willing to be himself by his own agency is concurrent with his being what he wills" (*kai syndromos autos heautō thelōn autos einai kai touto ōn, hoper thelei*).

That the Good's making is "like" (*hoion*) an eternal generation excludes the possibility that there is a time before or after in which this generation or making takes place—it is continual and coincident with the Good itself.

20, 28–39: "Ruling himself" cannot entail any distinction between ruler and ruled; the Good is entirely self-determined.

20, 28–39 *Whence there is also the notion of "ruling himself." . . . For were there anything in him not his work, he would be neither purely autonomous nor omnipotent, neither master of that nor omnipotent, that is, he would have no power over that of whose making he is not master*: Although the concept of ruling implies the duality of an object ruled by a subject, in ruling himself, the utter simplicity of the Good—compare the unhindered uniqueness (*monachon*) of the Good in 7, 38—excludes any object on which the Good might act; since the Good is first with nothing before him, such objectless ruling implies his absolute sovereignty and power over everything. Absolute sovereignty implies total autonomy and self-determination (*autoexousiōs*). Leroux, 395, observes that, the phrases "Then what is there of him that is not himself?" and "What is there that does not act, that isn't his work?" imply an identity between the One and his product, and thus a monistic pantheism, but this is not the case, since the One is not every other thing (cf. Corrigan, 2004a, 185–186).

Chapter 21

The Good cannot produce himself as other than he is.

21, 1–8 *So could he have been able to make himself other than what he did make? . . . But his making of which we speak must be once for all, for it is beautiful*: Compare Plotinus' notion of the Good's own self-making with the *Tripartite Tractate*'s account of the Father's generation of himself as the Son cited in the commentary on 20, 1–9.

21, 4–5 *For There, the ability to make isn't to make contraries but to make with unshakeable and immoveable power*: True freedom is not the power to choose or waver between opposites but to choose the good for its own sake from a power that is unshakeable (*astemphei*) and immoveable (*ametakinētōi*). Plotinus' choice of words emphasizes simultaneously the One's supreme freedom and the possibility of true human freedom. The unusual adjective *astemphēs* echoes Helen's description to Agamemnon of the unshakeable hold of Odysseus upon his staff in Iliad 3, 219: "he clutches it stiff and still like a mindless man" (or in Homer's language, "like a mindless light" (*aidrei phōto eoikōs*), but the power of his words is irresistible. Compare *astemphēs* at Odyssey 4, 419 and 459. In this context, Plotinus' use of this adjective therefore implicitly stresses a continuity between human and divine freedom. Even in war (as in VI. 8. 5) such unshakeability is in our power. The adjective *ametakinētos* also reinforces this continuity since it echoes Plotinus' earlier discussion of voluntary and involuntary action and refers the reader implicitly to Aristotle's definition of the virtuous person who must act with knowledge, deliberately choose the action and for its own sake [i.e., not as a choice between opposites], and whose action must result from a fixed (*bebaiōs*) and immoveable (*ametakinētōs*) character (*EN* 1105a29–33). For a discussion of Plotinus' use of rhetorical and literary flourishes in the service of philosophy, see J. Dillon, "Plotinus Orator."

21, 8–19: A Perfect identity between the will and reality of the Good.

21, 8–19 *And who would alter something . . . all this he already was*: At the center of what one might conceive as Plotinus' positive henology lies the notion of will, which VI.8 considers as completely detached from thought. *Boulēsis* is not *noēsis*, since thought has an intelligible content at least logically different than itself. One might say that thought is always representation and difference, while will in its initial manifestation is self-will, pure self-affirmation. Will is what allows Plotinus to propose that the Good constitutes itself in the pure and free dimension of will. In the nine lines (8–16), the term "will" (*boulēsis*) occurs sixteen times; the vocabulary and argumentation are at the very limits of what is sayable, and this repetition forms part of the originality of henological discourse. Since it is impossible to speak and think of the Good directly, it is up to the philosopher to attempt to understand what the unique nature of the Good might be. If the term "*ousia*" (substantial being), denoting what can be known by our intellect, is somehow appropriate for the Good, we must understand that its *ousia* would be pure and simple will, a will that Plotinus is careful to distinguish from activity (*energeia*); it is a will that is in a sense empty of any determinate content, or a will simply willing itself without engaging in any activity such as that of Aristotle's Prime Mover. The Good is not pure act, but pure willing.

Lavaud, 324, attributes to Plotinus' interlocutor the hypothesis that the Good is "without will in his very existence," in the sense that if the Good is pure existence, one cannot explain why any free will could emerge from him, raising the conflicting possibilities that either his will would precede his existence, which is impossible, or else that he is a pure existence deprived of activity from which the emergence of will cannot be explained.

In the *Tripartite Tractate*, once the Father's self-knowledge has exteriorized his very self as the Son (56,1–5), the multiplicity of all subsequent reality is generated through his own free will, which is identical with his power ("He possesses power, which is his will" NHC I 55, 34–35) and with his Spirit which is the "trace" by which he is known to his aeonic offspring: "For the Father, the exalted one, they know by his Will, which [is] the Spirit that breathes through the members of the All and gives them a thought to search for the unknown" (NHC I 71, 36–72, 5). Moreover, it is the Father's will that establishes the boundary separating the intelligible Pleroma from the created cosmos (NHC I 76, 31–77, 1). So also in the Valentinian *Gospel of Truth* (NHC I 27, 10–30), the determination of indeterminate, potential reality into the form of distinct aeons is achieved, not by cognitive reversion of a product upon its source, but directly by the Father's Will: "All the realms (Coptic *maeit* 'paths,' 'spaces,' i.e., aeons) are from him. . . . If he wills, what he wills appears when he gives it form and a name—and he does give it a name." Yet in distinction from VI.8, these two Valentinian treatises do not disassociate the supreme principle's will and thought; instead, the Father's extroversive faculty of will is the necessary projective Power without which any further instantiation of that which is conceived within his introversive faculty of self-directed thought would be impossible. Somewhat similarly, in the *Chaldaean Oracles* (fr. 37.1–5), the "Will" and "Fire" (that is the power) of the first self-generated Paternal Intellect externalize its content in the form of multiform Ideas.

This concept of the emergence of will has often been neglected by historians of philosophy anxious to make will appear as a properly human faculty, perhaps precisely because the history of philosophy has privileged the negative and apophatic aspects of Plotinus' henology.

In lines 18–19, with Ficino, Armstrong, and Lavaud, "it (his will) generated nothing further *in himself*," we read *autōi* ("in himself") rather than the *autois* ("in them") of the manuscripts, which would signify the products of his generation, while the intent is to deny any plurality in the Good.

21, 19–25: The meaning of containing Himself.

21, 19–25 *And his containing himself is to be understood, if one were to express it rightly, such that all else that exists is contained by him, since they exist by a certain participation in him and they all lead back to him. And from himself he has no need of containing or participation, but he is all things by himself, or rather none of them, since he doesn't need all things to be himself*: Here and previously in 20, 21, the Good is said to contain itself, indeed everything, as in II.1.1, 35 and 4.18. In V.5 [32] 9, 7–15, perhaps because the priority of the One means that it has nothing else to be in, the One is said to be the container of all as if it were a circle that circumscribes all else; there is nothing in which it is not, while all other things are contained in it. On the notion that the supreme principle contains all but is contained by none, see comment on 20, 9–27. While the One is nowhere, everything else has its place "in" the One; thus the sensible world is in Soul, Soul in Intellect, and Intellect in the One. On the question of the participation of other entities in the Good, cf. V.5.4, 1–2: "the ascent must be made to a One, and this means truly One, but not one like all other things which are multiple and one by participation in a one," but it is difficult to understand what sort of participation this might be, since things normally participate in a Form, and the One has no Form. On God's self-causation, Leroux, 400, refers to Candidus; *Epistle to Marius Victorinus* I, 3, 7–17 [Hadot] which associates this notion with those of self-causation and divine unity: "What indeed is it 'to be' God—what kind of cause or what is its cause? This: the very fact 'to be' God. Truly the first cause is cause of itself also, not so that it is cause as something other than itself, but the selfsame God is cause that he is. He is for himself his own habitation and his own inhabitant without any appearance of duality (cf. *Zostrianos* NHC VIII 66, 21–22: "He is his own place and its inhabitant"). He himself is the single one. For he is solely 'to be'" (*Quid vero esse Deum? qualis? aut qua causa ipsum Deum esse? Etenim prima causa est: et sibi causa; non quae sit altera alterius: sed ipsum hoc quod ipsum est, ad id ut sit, causa est: ipse sibi locus, ipse habitator. Non sic ut imaginatio duorum fiat, ipse est unum et solum. Est enim esse solum*).

On the notion that all things lead back to the One, see III.8.10, 20 (cf. also V.4.1, 2 and the passage just cited from V.5.4): "Everything leads back to some prior unity—not immediately to the absolute One—until it comes to the absolute One, which leads to no other (unity than itself)"; also VI.9 (*On the Good or the One*) in its entirety. In line 23, with Ficino, BHT, Armstrong, and Lavaud, we read *autos* instead of *autois* as does Leroux, who follows HS_1 and most manuscripts, although it is also true that all entities are contained in the One.

On the One's being all things yet none of them, compare V.2 [11] 1, 1–2: "The one is all things and not a single one of them" (*to hen panta kai oude hen*), and Plato's *Parmenides* 160b2–3: "Therefore if One exists, the one is all things and nothing at all in relation both to itself and to all others."

21, 25–33: To attain to the Good, one must abandon all things.

21, 25–33 *But when you speak or think of him, abandon all other things . . . only this that is truly free lies far above, since it is not enslaved to itself but is only itself and really itself, while each of the others is both itself and something else*: On the exhortation to "abandon all things" (*aphelōn panta*), see V.3.17, 38; 13, 11, and for the exhortation to cease further seeking, see especially VI.5.12. To abandon all things and leave them behind is essentially a rephrasing of the method of negative theology, one of the three approaches to the knowledge of God as classically expressed by Alcinous, *Didaskalikos* X 165, 17–33: "The first way to achieve intellection of God is abstraction (*noēsis kata aphairesin*) of these attributes (i.e., bad-good-indifferent, qualified-unqualified, part-whole, same-different, mover-moved), just as we get the conception of a point by abstraction from what is sensible, conceiving first a surface, then a line, and finally a point. A second way of obtaining an idea of God is that of analogy (*hē kata analogian*), as follows: the sun—not itself sight but enabling sight to see and visible things to be seen—is to sight and to visible things as the first mind is to the mind of the (world) soul and its intelligible objects—it is not itself intellection but provides intellection to it as well as intelligibility to its objects, illuminating the truth concerning them (cf. Plato, *Republic* 508b). The third way of achieving an idea of God is this: one contemplates (*theōrōn*) the beauty of physical objects; after this one passes on to the beauty of the soul, from there to the beauty of customs and laws, and so on to the vast ocean of the beautiful. After this one intuits the good and the lovable and the desirable like a shining light which, as it were, illumines the soul which is thus ascending. And together with this, one intuits God because of his pre-eminent excellence (*theon sunepinoei dia tēn en tōi timōi hyperochēn*; cf. *Symposium* 208e; *Epistle* 7 341C–D).

The *via analogiae* (*kata analogian*) or way by approximation from effects to cause, inferring the source from its products or inferiors, was based on the parable of the sun in Plato's *Republic* 6 508–9. The *via negationis* (*kata aphairesin / apophasin / analusin*), or way by abstraction or negation of all affirmative predicates, was regarded as the only logically self-sufficient path to the divine, and was perhaps based on the first hypothesis of the *Parmenides* (137c–142a). This method figures prominently, not only in Plotinus (e.g., V.9.3, 40–45: "Thus the One is neither something nor a quality, nor a quantity nor an intellect nor a soul; neither is it moving nor even standing, it is not in place, not in time, but one of a kind by itself; rather it is formless before all form, before movement and before stability, since these relate to being and would make it many"), but also in the negative theologies at the beginning of the *Apocryphon of John* (BG 8502, 24, 6–25,7; NHC II 3, 18–33) and in the revelation by the Luminaries in *Allogenes* (NHC XI 62, 36–63, 25; cf. *Zostrianos* NHC VIII 64, 13–75, 21): "For he is not perfect, but he is another thing that is superior. He is neither boundless nor is he bounded by another. Rather he is something superior. He is not corporeal; he is not incorporeal. He is not Great; [he is not] Small. He is not a <quantity>; he is not a [<quality>]. Nor is he something that exists, that one can know. Rather he is something else that is superior, which one cannot know. He is primary revelation and self-knowledge, since it is he alone who knows himself. Since he is not one of those things that exist, but is another thing, he is superior to all superlatives, even in comparison to his character and what is not his character. He neither participates in eternity nor does he participate in time. He does not receive anything from anything else" (*Allogenes* NHC XI 62, 36–63, 25).

The way of negation often involves two steps, a radical affirmation of the supreme principle's transcendence in terms of its priority to any notion whatsoever, often by simultaneous negation of two opposed predicates (it is neither X nor non-X), or the affirmation that it surpasses simultaneously affirmed contraries (neither X nor non-X but superior). Here the *via negativa* becomes in effect a *via oppositionis*, or way by paradoxical or oxymoronic predication of opposites: the supreme deity is neither this nor its opposite, but superior to these. The *via eminentiae* (*dia tēn en tōi timōi hyperochēn*) or way by ascending degrees (*anabasmoi*), based on Plato's *Symposium*, corresponds to the stage by stage withdrawal (*anachōrēsis*) to the highest level of the Triple-Powered One in *Allogenes*. This method usually builds on the others: synthesis of instances or negation of all alternatives on one level of thought launches the mind upward to a new, more eminent level of insight. The outcome of these methods ultimately comes to an end in a condition of total unknowing, as expressed in the anonymous *Parmenides Commentary* (II 4–27 [Hadot 2.68–70]): "It is necessary therefore to subtract everything and add nothing: to subtract everything, not by falling into absolute non-being, but by thought attending to everything that comes to and through him, considering that he is the cause of both the multitude and the being of all things, while himself being neither one nor multiple, but beyond being in regard to all the things that exist on his account. Thus he transcends not only multiplicity, but even the concept of the One, for it is on his account that both the One and Monad exist. And thus one will be able neither to fall into the void, nor dare to attribute anything to him, but to remain in a non-comprehending comprehension and in an intellection that intuits nothing. Through such means, it will occur to you at some point, having stood apart from the intellection of the things constituted by him, to stand upon the ineffable preconception of him which represents him through silence, a preconception that is unaware of being silent and not conscious that it represents him and is cognizant of nothing at all, but which is only an image of the ineffable and is ineffably identical with the ineffable, but not as if knowing him, if you can follow me—even though imaginatively—as I venture to speak."

A similar result also occurs in *Allogenes* This Unknowable One is so unknowable that it is in some sense its own unknowable knowledge, and forms a unity with the nescience that sees it. In fact it seems to be equated with the state of mental vacancy itself: "But he is self-comprehending, like something so unknowable, that he exceeds those who excel in unknowability. . . . And thus he is unknowable to all of them in every respect, and through them all he is in them all, not only as the unknowable knowledge that is proper to him; he is also joined/united through the unknowing that sees him" (*Allogenes* NHC XI 63, 28–64, 14).

The "nescience that sees" is identical with both the self-apprehension of the aspiring visionary *and* the unknowable deity's own incognizant self-apprehension that gives rise to the ontogenetic process itself. In this way, both the Unknowable One and the visionary aspirant are united by a common nescience and originary manifestation. For unknowing (*agnoein*) as mystical technique in Plotinus, see VI.9.7, 17–21: "withdrawing from all external things, she [the soul] must turn completely to the within, and not be inclined to any of the external things, but 'un–knowing' (*agnoēsanta*) all things (both as he had at first, in the sensible realm, then also, in that of the forms) and even 'un–knowing' (*agnoēsanta*) himself, come to be in the contemplation of that One" (cf. also VI.9.6, 50–52; VI.7.39; V.3.12, 48–53).

A similar sentiment on the cessation of all seeking occurs in *Allogenes* NHC XI 67, 21–31: "And concerning all these matters, you have heard certainly. And do not seek anything more, but go. We do not know whether the Unknowable One has angels or gods, or whether the One who is at rest contains anything within himself except that very stillness which he is."

Despite the inability of thought or language to comprehend the One, it can nevertheless be "touched" (*ephaptesthai*), in the moment of mystical union, an experience best described by physical rather than cognitive terminology. Plotinus is fond of expressing mystical apprehension as an *epiballein* or *epibolē*, as a "touching," "grasping" or "thrusting upon" the object. One must "as it were, grasp and touch" the One (*hoion ephapsasthai kai thigein*, VI.9.4, 27), much as Intellect is said to touch the Good in the metaphor of the circle and its center in the opening lines of Chapter 18; apprehension of the One occurs through an "inchoate (or: sudden) thrusting" (*epibolē athroai*, III.8.9, 21; cf. VI.7.35, 22 and 39, 2), or "only a touching and, as it were, a grasping" (*thixis kai hoion epaphē monon*, V.3.10, 43–45; cf. also V.1.11, 13; V.3.17, 25–26; V.6.6, 35; VI.9.7, 25).

In lines 29–30, the exhortation "For even you can touch upon something else about which it is no longer possible to speak or apprehend" is, we suggest, intentionally reminiscent of Diotima's invitation to Socrates in the *Symposium*

209e5–210a4: "Even you, Socrates, could probably come to be initiated into these rites of love. But as for the purpose of these rites when they are done correctly—that is the final and highest mystery, and I don't know if you are capable of it. I myself will tell you, and I won't stint any effort. And you must try to follow if you can." Diotima concludes by saying "when one looks at Beauty in the only way that Beauty can be seen—only then will it become possible for him to give birth, not to images of virtue, but to true virtue, because he is in touch, not with an image, but with the true Beauty. The love of the gods belongs to *anyone* who has given birth to true virtue and nourished it, and if any human being could become immortal, it would be he." As this conclusion shows, and as Plotinus is fully aware, the "even you" is meant to include *anyone*. For the distinction between the Beautiful and the Good in Plato and Plotinus, see Corrigan, 2014, 90–92.

In the final analysis, the freedom and the sovereignty of the Good are based on his utter simplicity, guaranteeing the absence of any otherness that might somehow constrain it or suggest anything random or adventitious. All that can be said is that it is *only itself and really itself, while each of the others is both itself and something else*. We end, then, with the contrast of the latter part of Plato's *Parmenides*, between what can be said of the "One" and what can be said of "the others."

Glossary

A list of some of the principal terms in our translation and their Greek equivalents for easy reference:

accident: *symbebēkos*. Aristotelian-Peripatetic term for non-essential attributes of sensible substances or substantial beings. For Plotinus, there are, strictly speaking, no accidental attributes in the intelligible world, for everything there is Form and substantial being.

act, actualization: *energēma*. Used to refer to the result or product of an activity or actuality.

act, activity: *energeia*; also, actuality; actualization. Aristotelian-Peripatetic term referring primarily to intellection and implying no imperfection—as in Plotinus' two-act theory, the act *of* a substantial being and the act *from* a substantial being. Contrasted with power, potency (*dynamis*) and potentiality (*dynamei* in the dative), which relate, in the first instance, to sensible compounds and the changes they experience, but also, in the second instance, may be applied to our intellect and Intellect itself insofar as there is something like a distinction between activity and potency in their dynamic unfolding. Unlike Aristotle, however, Plotinus applies power ("the power of all") to the One primarily and Intellect derivatively.

chance: *tyche*; also, luck, fortune. Used broadly for that which occurs without the guidance of reason. Occasionally, spontaneous (*automaton*) is used synonymously, but the two are distinct: chance and spontaneity, for Aristole, are cases of apparent purposiveness, but chance events are restricted to human activities, whereas spontaneous events are not so restricted. For example, a stone falling off a cliff could have been thrown for a purpose but was not. "Randomly" (*eikēi*) is an adverb Plotinus frequently uses in VI.8, more related to spontaneity than chance insofar as it does not involve agency.

choice: *proairesis*; also, *hairesis*, as in VI.8.5, 13. Aristotelian-Peripatetic term used for deliberate desire or the culmination of a deliberative process; related to **what is in our power** (*to eph' hēmin*), but used in VI.8 only of Intellect and implicitly the One—see also **self-determination**.

desire: *epithymia, orexis. Epithymia* or *epithymetikon* is a term used in Plato's tripartite division of the soul (together with *thymos*—translated here as "high spirit"—and *logistikon, logismos*—translated here as "reasoning" or the reasoning power/part of the soul); *orexis* is one Aristotelian and post-Aristotelian term for desire.

form: *eidos*. Distinguished from shape—*morphe*—the word can be applied to enmattered or immaterial forms that, at different levels, constitute all physical individuals, and it can also refer to Intelligible Forms in Intellect—or even characterize matter (V.8 [30] 7, 22–23).

formative principle: *logos*. But sometimes—especially in the early chapters of VI.8—reason, discourse, reasoning, definition.

free: *eleutheros*. Also related to "what is in our power," "what is voluntary," "self-determination," "will," "free will"—see **self-determination**.

free will: *thelēsis*. And intimately related to *boulēsis*, which we translate as "will" (see **self-determination**).

exist: *hyparchein*. Often with the sense of belonging to or found in something, and always with the sense of being concretely real.

existence: *einai* (to be); *to einai* (the "to be").

immaterial: *aulon*. That which is separate from matter in contrast to that which is enmattered (*enulon*).

impulse: *hormē*. A Stoic term, also used by Alexander of Aphrodisias, for the source of psychical motion and roughly synonymous with **desire**.

Intellect: *nous*; also, intellect (lower case). Intellect is the second great reality or hypostasis after the One or the Good. It is also the true identity of all rational living beings and everything that exists—from horses to rocks. Our intellects are undescended, even if we do not recognize this or actualize this intimate connection, and they engage or can engage in the same activity that Intellect does. The mode of cognition of Intellect and of all intellects is non-discursive, namely, pure understanding without having to work things out laboriously by reasoning and study. Each intellect is, so to speak, both itself and a window on all intellects, a holographic part, as it were, of the great Intellect.

notion/concept: *ennoia*. A Stoic (and Platonic) term used by Plotinus for a notion or intellectual state derived (in Stoicism) ultimately from sense-perception. Closely related to *epinoia*, translated here as "reflection," that is, a kind of natural urge to reflect on or to examine one's notions more closely.

One, the: *to hen*, or **the Good**: *to agathon*. The first originative principle of everything, beyond Intellect and substantial being, and yet a property of everything that exists in any way, because everything is, in its own way, one. Nonetheless, the Good is a Unity beyond the normal comprehension of anyone, vaster than Intellect, Soul, or the physical universe, yet present from the beginning of our experience and intimately present, without intermediary, to everyone. The Good, according to Plato in the *Republic*, Book 6, is something we only vaguely intuit at first, if we recognize it at all, but it is is the principle by which we are able to conceive the best state of anything, a principle disclosed in the acts of seeing or thinking themselves, just as in seeing we see the light of the sun, according to Socrates' analogy in *Republic*, Books 6 and 7, and in thinking objects of thought we think of them as "good-form" or "good-like" (*Republic* 6, 508d–509b).

originative principle: *arche*. Sometimes simply "origin" where the usage is non-philosophical.

random/ly: *eikēi*. See **chance**.

reflection: *epinoia*. Closely related to *ennoia*—notion, concept or "in-thought"—and other cognate words such as *synnoia*, with-thought, *dianoia*, through-thought or discursive reasoning, and *pronoia*, fore-thought, by contrast with *noēsis*—intellection, thinking or understanding—used primarily of Intellect.

reality: *hypostasis*. At any level, from soul to the One.

reason/reasoning: *logos/logismos*. See also **formative principle**.

self-determination: *to autexousion*. Related to what is voluntary, but distinct and a stronger volitional term. In VI.8, Plotinus uses several terms to express the notion of what we might call will or free will, many of them deriving from Plato and especially Aristotle's Ethics, the Stoics, etc.: *to eph' hēmin* (what depends on us or what is in our power), *hekousion/akousion* (voluntary/involuntary), *to autexousion* (self-determination), *exousia* (freedom), *boulēsis* (wish, will), *thelēsis* (will), *to eleutheron* (freedom), *proairesis* (choice). While *boulēsis* and *thelēsis* seem synonymous, *hekousion* and *to autexousion*, the voluntary and the self-determining, are different, since an action can be voluntary but not truly self-determined. Freedom is therefore closer to self-determination than to what is voluntary.

shape: *morphe*. Primarily shape in the sensible world by contrast with ***eidos***, form.

Soul: *psyche*; also, soul (lower case). The third great reality or hypostasis after Intellect and the One. Also, soul is the principle of motion and life in any living being. Soul or All Soul is the hypostasis that includes many different perspectives that contribute to the complex beings that living creatures are: the World Soul that prepares bodies for us to articulate in our own lives, Nature that is its lowest part, the Soul of the Earth because everything in the cosmos is ensouled or, in the case of the elements, has a relation to soul, and our souls, with their complex range of relation to Intellect and the Good, and every other soul of plant and other animals, wherein in different configurations, all these cosmic and hypercosmic perspectives meet.

spontaneous: *automaton*. See **chance**.

substantial being: *ousia*. A word that in Greek is not equivalent to its Latin counterpart, *substantia*, that is, "standing-under"; *ousia* means real stuff: in compound things, it can mean the matter, the compound of matter and form, the form that makes the particular thing what it is, or soul simply, or, above all, intellect—in us, and the Divine Intellect. In VI.8, it can be applied, incorrectly, to the Good.

virtue, moral excellence: *aretē*. We translate as "virtue" because of its predominant contemporary usage, but it really means for Socrates, Plato, and Aristotle the good or best functioning of anything—from a table to a hand, a human being, and a mind. Virtue and moral excellence in the best sense, for Plotinus, is the measure and organization of mind, soul, and body in accordance with Intellect and the Good.

voluntary/involuntary: *hekousion/akousion.*

what is in our power: *to eph' hemin.* Related to "what is voluntary" but not identical with it.

will/wish: *boulēsis.* The power in virtue of which something can be **in our power**. In practice what is **in our power** is usually equivalent to **voluntary**, but they are not identical in definition. Rational will or wish, and in VI.8 since it is applied pre-eminently to the Good, it is therefore both rational and hyper-rational will.

will (free)/wishing: *thelēsis.* It is used mainly for the Good to indicate its perfectly unimpeded or unmediated activity, and therefore it includes both rational and hyper-rational **will** (*boulēsis*).

Select Bibliography

I. Ancient Authors

ALCINOUS: *The Handbook of Platonism*, translated by J. Dillon. Oxford: Clarendon Press, 1993.

———: *Alcinoos: Enseignement des Doctrines de Platon*, edited by J. Whittaker. Paris: Les Belles Lettres, 1990.

ANONYMOUS COMMENTARY ON THE *PARMENIDES*: *Porphyre et Victorinus* II, P. Hadot. Paris: Études augustiniennes, 1968.

———: *The Anonymous Commentary on Plato's "Parmenides,"* edited by G. Bechtle. Berner Reihe philosophischer Studien 22. Bern/Stuttgart/Wien: Paul Haupt, 1999.

———: *'Ein neuplatonischer Parmenidescommentar in einem Turiner Palimpsest,'* edited by W. Kroll. *Rheinisches Museum* 47 (1892): 599–627.

ALEXANDER OF APHRODISIAS: *De Anima Liber cum Mantissa*, edited by I. Bruns. Berlin: Reimer Verlag, 1887.

———: *On Fate: Text, Translation, and Commentary*, R. W. Sharples. London: Duckworth, 1983.

———: *On the Soul, Part I*, translated by V. Caston. Ancient Commentators on Aristotle Series. Bristol: Bristol Classical Press, 2012.

———: *Supplement to* On the Soul (Mantissa), translated by R. W. Sharples. Ancient Commentators on Aristotle Series. London: Duckworth, 2004.

———: *Quaestiones 2.16–3.15*, translated by R. W. Sharples. London: Duckworth, 1994.

Aristotle: *La Métaphysique*, edited by J. Tricot. 2 vols. Paris: Vrin, 1986.

———: *Aristotle's Metaphysics*, edited by W. D. Ross. 2 vols. Oxford: Clarendon Press, 1975.

———: *L'*Éthique *a Nicomaque*, edited by R. A. Gauthier and J. Y. Jolif. 4 vols. Paris: Louvain, 1970.

———: *Aristotelis Ethica Nicomachea*, Recog. L. Bywater. Oxford Classical Texts. Oxford: Clarendon Press, 1894.

———: *Aristotle's Physics*, edited by W. D. Ross. Oxford: Clarendon Press, 1960.

———: *Aristotelis Analytica Priora et Posteriora*, edited by W. D. Ross. Preface and appendix by L. Minio-Paluello. Oxford Classical Texts. Oxford: Clarendon Press, 1964.

———: *Aristotle De Anima: Introduction and Commentary*, edited by W. D. Ross. Oxford: Clarendon Press, 1961.

CHALDAEAN *ORACLES*: *Oracles Chaldaïques*, edited by E. des Places. Paris: Les Belles Lettres, 1971.

———: *The Chaldean Oracles*, edited by R. Majercik. Leiden: Brill, 1989.

CORPUS HERMETICUM: *Corpus Hermeticum*, edited by A. D. Nock and A. J. Festugière. Collection des Universités de France. Paris: Les Belles Lettres, 1945–1954.

DIOGENES LAERTIUS: *Diogenes Laertius: Lives of Eminent Philosophers*, with an English translation by R. D. Hicks. 2 vols. Cambridge, MA: Harvard University Press, 2005.

———: *Diogenes Laertius*, edited by H. S. Long. 2 vols. Oxford: Clarendon Press, 1964.

———: *Die Fragmente der Vorsokratiker*, edited by H. Diels and W. Kranz. 6th ed. 3 vols. Berlin: Weidmann, 1951–1952.

HIPPOLYTUS: *Hippolytus, Refutatio omnium haeresium*, edited by M. Markovich. Patristische Texte und Studien 25. Berlin/New York: De Gruyter, 1988.

IAMBLICHUS: *On the Mysteries (Writings from the Greco-Roman World, V. 4.)*: Text and translation, E. C. Clarke,

J. M. Dillon, and J. P. Hershbell. Atlanta: Society of Biblical Literature, 2003.

———: *In Platonis Dialogos Commentariorum Fragmenta,* edited by J. M. Dillon. Leiden: Brill, 1973.

The Nag Hammadi Scriptures, edited by M. Meyer. New York: HarperCollins, 2007.

NUMENIUS: *Fragments,* edited by É. Des Places. Paris: Les Belles Lettres, 1973.

———: *The Fragments of Numenius of Apamea: Text, translation and commentary,* R. Petty. Westbury, Wiltshire: Prometheus Trust, 2012.

PHILO JUDAEUS: *Philonis Alexandrini Opera quae supersunt,* edited by L. Cohn, P. Wendland, and S. Reiter. 6 vols. Berlin: Reimer, 1896–1915.

———: *Philo,* with an English translation in 10 volumes, edited by F. H. Colson and G. H. Whitaker. London: Heinemann, 1929–1962.

PLATO: *Platonis Opera,* edited by J. Burnet. 5 vols. Oxford: Clarendon Press, 1900–1907.

PLUTARCH: *Plutarch, Moralia,* Loeb Classical Library in 15 volumes by various translators. Cambridge, MA: Harvard University Press, 1987.

PORPHYRY: *Porphyre: Sentences.* Études *d'introduction, texte grec et traduction française, commentaire,* edited by L. Brisson, with English translation by J. M. Dillon. 2 vols. Paris: Vrin, 2005.

PROCLUS: *Commentary on Plato's Timaeus*, edited and translated by H. Tarrant and D. Baltzly. 5 vols. (Vol. 2 edited with M. Share and D. T. Runia). Cambridge: Cambridge University Press: 2007–2013.

———: *De Sacrificio et Magia*, edited by J. Bidez. Catalogue des manuscrits alchimiques grecs. 6 vols. Brussels: Lamertin, 1928.

———: *Commentary on Plato's Parmenides*, translated by G. R. Morrow and J. M. Dillon. Princeton: Princeton University Press: 1987.

———: *Parmenides usque ad finem primae hypothesis nec non Procli Commentarium in Parmenidem, pars ultima adhuc inedita interprete G. de Moerbeka*, edited by R. Klibansky and C. Labowsky. London: Warburg Institute, 1953. Reprint, Nendelm/Liechtenstein: Kraus, 1962.

PSEUDO-IAMBLICHUS: *Theologoumena Arithmeticae*, edited by V. de Falco. Leipzig, 1922.

———: *In Nicomachi Arithmeticam Introductionem*, edited by H. Pistelli and U. Klein. Leipzig: Teubner, 1894. Reprint, Stuttgart: Teubner, 1975.

SEXTUS EMPIRICUS: *Sextus Empiricus*, edited by R. G. Bury. Loeb Classical Library. 4 vols. Cambridge, MA: Harvard University Press, 1933–1949.

———: *Sexti Empirici Opera*, edited by H. Sextus and M. Mutschmann. 3 vols. Leipzig: Teubner, 1954–1962.

SPEUSIPPUS: *Fragmenta*, edited by L. Tarán. Leiden: Brill, 1981.

STOBAEUS: *Anthologium*, edited by C. Wachsmuth and O. Hense. 5 vols. Berlin, 1884–1923.

HELLENISTIC PHILOSOPHERS: Anthony A. Long and David N. Sedley. *The Hellenistic Philosophers*. Vol. 1: *Translation of the Principal Sources, with Philosophical Commentary*. Cambridge: Cambridge University Press, 1987 [LS].

STOIC PHILOSOPHERS: *Stoicorum Veterum Fragmenta*, edited by J. von Arnim. 4 vols. Leipzig: Teubner, 1903–1924 [*SVF*].

II. Editions and Translations of the *Enneads*

Plotini Opera, edited by Paul Henry and Hans-Rudolph Schwyzer. *Editio Maior*. 3 vols. Paris/Brussels: Musaeum Lessianum, 1951–1973 [HS_1].

Plotini Opera, edited by Paul Henry and Hans-Rudolph Schwyzer. *Edition Minor.* 3 vols. Oxford: Clarendon Press, 1964–1982 [HS_2].

Plotins Schriften, übersetzt von Richard Harder. Anmerkungen von Rudolph Beutler und Willy Theiler. Hamburg: Meiner Verlag, 1956–1967 [BHT].

Plotinus, with an English translation, edited by A. H. Armstrong. 7 vols. Loeb Classical Library. Cambridge, MA: Harvard University Press, 1966–1988.

Plotin, Ennéades, Texte établi et traduit par É. Bréhier. 7 vols. Paris: Les Belles Lettres, 1924–1938.

Plotin, Traité sur la liberté et la volonté de l'Un [Ennéade VI, 8 (39)], translated with commentary by G. Leroux. Paris: Vrin, 1990 [Leroux].

Plotin, Traités, edited by L. Brisson and J. F. Pradeau. 9 vols. Paris: Flammarion, 2002–2010.

Plotin, Traités 38–41, edited by L. Brisson and J. F. Pradeau. Paris: Flammarion, 2007 [Lavaud].

Plotino, Ennéadas, J. Igal. Madrid: Gredos, 1982, 1985.

Plotino: Enneadi, V. Cilento. 3 vols. Bari: Laterza, 1947–1949.

Plotinus, The Enneads, Stephen MacKenna. 2nd edition. Revised translation. London: Faber, 1956.

Neoplatonic Philosophy: Introductory Readings, J. M. Dillon and L. Gerson. Indianapolis: Hackett, 2004.

III. Studies on *Ennead* VI.8 and Related Works

Beierwaltes, W. 2001a. "*Causa sui*. Plotins Begriff des Einen als Ursprung des Gedankens der Selbstursächlichkeit." In *Das wahre Selbst. Studien zu Plotins Begriff des Geistes und des Einen*, 123–159. Frankfurt am Main: Klostermann.

Benz, E. 1932. *Marius Victorinus und die Entwicklung der Abendländischen Willensmetaphysik*. Stuttgart: W. Kohlhammer.

Bussanich, J. R. 1988. *The One and its Relation to Intellect in Plotinus* (201–220, commentary on VI.8.16). Leiden: Brill.

———. 1996. "Plotinus' metaphysics of the One." In *The Cambridge Companion to Plotinus*, edited by Lloyd P. Gerson, 38–65. Cambridge: Cambridge University Press.

Charrue, J. M. 2013. "Plotin et la Liberté Humaine." A paper presented to the Congrès de Cardiff de l'ISNS, 12–15 June, 2013 [a copy of which was kindly given to us by the author].

Cilento, V. 1973a. "Liberta divina e discorso temerario." In *Saggi su Plotino*, 97–122. Milan: U. Mursia.

Collette-Dučić, B. 2014. "Plotinus on Founding Freedom in *Ennead* VI.8 [39]." In *The Routledge Handbook of Neoplatonism,* edited by Pauliina Remes and Svetla Slaveva-Griffin, 421–436. London/ New York: Routledge.

Copenhaver, B. 1988. "Hermes Trismegistus, Proclus and a Philosophy of Magic." In *Hermeticism and the Renaissance: Intellectual History and the Occult in Early Modern Europe,* edited by I. Merkel and A. G. Debus. Washington, DC: Folger Books.

Corrigan, K. 2015. "Divine and Human Freedom: Plotinus' New Understanding of Creative Agency." In *Causation and Creation in Late Antiquity,* edited by Anna Marmodoro and Brian D. Prince, 131–149. Cambridge: Cambridge University Press.

———. 2017. "The Sources and Structures of Power and Activity in Plotinus." In *Divine Powers in Late Antiquity,* edited by A. Marmadoro and I. F. Viltanioti, 17–37. Oxford: Oxford University Press.

Crocker, J. B. 1956. "The Freedom of man in Plotinus." *Modern Schoolman* 34 (1): 23–35.

Dihle, A. 1982: *The Theory of Will in Classical Antiquity.* Berkeley: University of California Press.

Eliasson, E. 2008. *The Notion of* That Which Depends on Us *in Plotinus and Its Background.* Leiden/New York: Brill.

Frede, M. 2007. "The *Eφ' HMIN* in Ancient Philosophy." *Philosophia* 37: 110–123.

Gleede, B. 2012. "Endorsing a Cliché. On Liberty and Necessity in the Christian and Neoplatonist Account of Creation." In *Religion and Philosophy in the Platonic and Neoplatonic Traditions: from Antiquity to the Early Medieval Period,* edited by Kevin Corrigan, John D. Turner, and Peter Wakefield, 277–294. Sankt Augustin: Akademie Verlag.

Hadot, P. 1971. "Causa sui." *Historisches Wörterbuch der Philosophie* I, 976–977. Basel-Stuttgart: Schwabe Verlag.

Harl, M. 1960. "Problèmes posées par l'histoire du mot autexousion: liberté stoïcienne et liberté chrétienne." *Revue des études grecques* 73: xxvii–xxviii.

Henry, P. 1931. "Le problême de la liberté chez Plotin." *Revue néoscolastique* 33: 50–79, 180–215, 318–339.

Horn, C. 2007. "The Concept of Will in Plotinus." In *Reading Ancient Texts: Essays in Honour of D. O'Brien.* Vol. 2, edited by S. Stern-Gillet and K. Corrigan, 153–178. Leiden/Boston: Brill.

Kahn, Charles. 1988. "Discovery of the Will: From Aristotle to Augustine." In *The Question of Eclecticism*, edited by J. M. Dillon and A. A. Long, 234–259. Berkeley: University of California Press.

Lavaud, L. 2007. *Traité 39 (VI.8).* Présentation, traduction et notes. In *Plotin. Traités 38–41*, edited by L. Brisson and J. F. Pradeau. Paris: Flammarion.

———. 2012. "La métaphore de la liberté, liberté humaine et liberté divine chez Plotin." *Archives de Philosophie* 75 (1): 11–25.

Leroux, G. 1996. "Human Freedom in the thought of Plotinus." In *The Cambridge Companion to Plotinus*, edited by Lloyd P. Gerson, 292–314. Cambridge: Cambridge University Press.

Linguiti, A. 2009. "Plotino e Platonici Sull' autodeterminazione e la possibilita di Scelta." In *Anima e Liberta in Plotino. Atti del Convegno nazionale (29–30 gennaio 2009)*, edited by Maria Di Pasquale Barbanti and Daniele Iozzia, 213–226. Catania: Edizioni CUECM.

Narbonne, J. M. 1993. "Plotin, Descartes et la notion de *Causa Sui*." *Archives de Philosophie* 56 (2): 177–195.

———. 2007. "Divine Freedom in Plotinus and Iamblichus (*Tractate VI.8* [39] and *De Mysteriis* III, 17–20)." In *Reading Ancient Texts: Essays In Honour of D. O'Brien.*

Vol. 2, edited by S. Stern-Gillet and K. Corrigan, 179–197. Leiden/Boston: Brill.

———. 2011. *Plotinus in Dialogue with the Gnostics.* Leiden/Boston: Brill.

O'Meara, D. 1992. "The Freedom of the One. Review of *Plotin: Traité sur la liberté et la volonté de l'Un* by Georges Leroux." *Phronesis* 37 (3): 343–349.

Rist, J. M. 1975. "*Prohairesis,* Plotinus, Philo and Origen." *De Jamblique à Proclus (Entretiens Fondation Hardt XXI),* 103–122. Vandoeuvres-Génève: Fondation Hardt.

Romano, F. 1999. "Azione morale e libero arbitrio in Plotino—La virtu non ha padrone (arête adespoton)." In *La Republica di Platone nella tradizione antica,* edited by M. Vegetti and M. Abbate, 151–191. Florence: Bibliopolis.

Spataro, L. 1994. "Il linguaggio della Liberta in *Enneadi VI, 8." Verifiche: Rivista Trimestrale di Scienze Umane* 23 (3–4): 329–373.

Trouillard, J. 1949. "La liberté selon Plotin." *Actes du IVè congrès de philosophie de langue française,* 353–357. Neuchatel: LaBaconnière.

Weismann, F. J. 1997. "Plotino e il tema de la libertad." *Revista agustiniana* 38: 1163–1197.

Westra, L. 1990. *Plotinus on Freedom, a meditation on* Ennead *VI, 8*. Lewiston: Edwin Mellen Press.

IV. General Publications

Armstrong, A. H. 1966–1988. *Plotinus*. 7 vols. Loeb Classical Library. Cambridge, MA/London: Harvard University Press.

———, ed. 1967. *The Cambridge History of Later Greek and Early Medieval Philosophy*. Cambridge: Cambridge University Press.

———. 1971. "Eternity, Life and Movement in Plotinus' accounts of Nous." *Le Néoplatonisme*, edited by P. M. Schul and P. Hadot, 67–74. Royaumont: CNRS.

Atkinson, M. 1983. *Plotinus: "Ennead" V.1: A Commentary with Translation*. Oxford: Oxford University Press.

Barry, C., W.-P. Funk, P.-H. Poirier, and J. D. Turner. 2000. *Zostrien (NH VIII, 1)*. Bibliothque copte de Nag Hammadi, section "Textes" 24. Québec/Louvain-Paris: Presses de l'Université Laval/Éditions Éditions Peeters.

Beierwaltes, W. 1965. *Proklos. Grundzüge seiner Metaphysik*. Frankfurt am Main: Klostermann.

———. 1972. *Platonismus und Idealismus*. Frankfurt am Main: Klostermann.

———. 1985. *Denken des Einen*. Frankfurt am Main: Klostermann.

———. 1991. *Selbsterkenntnis und Erfahrung der Einheit.* Frankfurt am Main: Klostermann.

———. 2001b. "Das wahre Selbst." In *Das Wahre Selbst,* 84–122. Frankfurt am Main: Klostermann.

———. 2002. "Le vrai soi." In *Le conaissance de soi. Études sur le traité 49 de Plotin,* edited by M. Dixsaut, with Pierre-Marie Morel and Karine Tordo-Rombaut, 11–40. Paris: Vrin.

Blumenthal, H. J. 1971. *Plotinus' Psychology.* The Hague: Nijhoff.

Bouillet, M.-N. 1859. *Les Ennéades de Plotin.* Hachette: Paris.

Bussanich, J. R. 1988. *The One and its Relation to Intellect in Plotinus.* Leiden: Brill.

———. 1996. "Plotinus' metaphysics of the One." In *The Cambridge Companion to Plotinus,* edited by Lloyd P. Gerson. Cambridge: Cambridge University Press.

Chiaradona, R. 2002. *Sostanza movimento analogia: Plotino critico di Aristotele.* Naples: Bibliopolis.

———. 2014. "Substance." In *The Routledge Handbook of Neoplatonism,* edited by Pauliina Remes and Svetla Slaveva-Griffin, 216–230. London/New York: Routledge.

Cilento, V. 1971. *Paideia antignostica. Ricostruzione d'un unico scritto da Enneadi III 8, V 8, V 5, II 9*. Florence: Monnier.

———. 1973b. "Contemplatzione." In *Saggi su Plotino*, 5–27. Milan: U. Mursia.

Clarke, E. C, J. M. Dillon, and J. P. Hershbell. 2003. *Iamblichus, De Mysteriis*. Atlanta: Society of Biblical Literature.

Corrigan, K. 1986. "Plotinus, 'Enneads' 5, 4 [7], 2 and Related Passages: A New Interpretation of the Status of the Intelligible Object." *Hermes* 114 (2): 195–203.

———. 1987. "Amelius, Plotinus and Porphyry on being, intellect, and the One: A reappraisal." *Aufstieg und Niedergang der römischen Welt* 36 (2): 974–973.

———. 1996a. *Plotinus' Theory of Matter-Evil and the Question of Substance: Plato, Aristotle, and Alexander of Aphrodiasias*. Leuven: Peeters.

———. 1996b. "Solitary Mysticism in Plotinus, Proclus, Gregory of Nyssa, and Pseudo-Dionysius." *Journal of Religion* 76 (1): 28–42.

———. 1996c. "Essence and Existence in the *Enneads*." *The Cambridge Companion to Plotinus*, edited by Lloyd P. Gerson, 105–129. Cambridge: Cambridge University Press.

———. 2004a. *Reading Plotinus: A Practical Introduction to Neoplatonism*. West Lafayette, IN: Purdue University Press.

———. 2008. "*Ousia* and *Hypostasis* in the Trinitarian theology of the Cappadocian Fathers: Basil and Gregory of Nyssa." *Zeitschrift für Antikes Christentum* 12: 113–34.

———. 2014. "How did the Unmoved Mover Come to Love Everything by the End of the Ancient Pagan Tradition?" *Dionysius* 32: 82–115.

Corrigan, K. and E. Glazov-Corrigan. 2004b. *Plato's Dialectic at Play: Argument, Structure and Myth in the Symposium*. University Park, PA: University of Pennsylvania Press.

Corrigan K. and J. D. Turner. 2016. "Plotinus and the Gnostics: the Peculiar Impact of the Tripartite Tractate and Later Works." In *Estratégias anti-gnósticas nos escritos de Plotino. Atas do colóquio internacional realizado em São Paulo em 18–19 de março 2012*, edited by M. Marsilio, 91–124. Serie Classica. São Paulo: Rosari et Paulus.

Daniélou, J. 1944. *Platonisme et Théologie mystique*, Paris/Aubier: Éditions Montaigne.

Deck, J. 1967. *Nature, Contemplation and the One: A Study in the Philosophy of Plotinus*. Toronto: Toronto University Press.

Des Places, E. 1973. *Numénius. Fragments*. Paris: Les Belles Lettres.

Dillon, J. M. 1996. *The Middle Platonists 80 B.C. to A. D. 220*. Revised edition. Ithaca: Cornell University Press.

———. 1993. *Alcinous. The Handbook of Platonism*. Oxford: Clarendon Press.

Dillon, J. M. and H. J. Blumenthal. 2015. *Ennead IV.3—4.29: Problems Concerning the Soul*. Las Vegas: Parmenides Publishing.

Dillon, J. M., E. C. Clarke, and J. P. Hershbell. 2003. *Iamblichus, De Mysteriis*. Atlanta: Society of Biblical Literature.

Dillon, J. M. and J. F. Finamore. 2002. *Iamblichus De Anima*. Text, translation, and commentary. Leiden/Boston/Köln: Brill.

Dillon, J. M., and A. A. Long, eds. 1988. *The Question of Eclecticism*. Berkeley: University of California Press.

Dörrie, H. 1970. "Der König. Ein platonisches Schlüsselwort von Plotin mit neuem Sinn erfüllt." *Revue international de philosophie* 24: 217–235.

———. 1976. "*Hypostasis*, Wort und Bedeutungsgeschichte." In *Platonica Minora*, 35–92. Munich: W. Fink.

Emerson, Ralph Waldo. 1979. *The Collected Works of Ralph Waldo Emerson*. Vol. 2, edited by Alfred Riggs Ferguson, Joseph Slater, and Jean Ferguson Carr. Cambridge, MA: The Belknap Press of Harvard University Press.

Emilsson, E. K. 1988. *Plotinus on Sense Perception: A Philosophical Study*. Cambridge: Cambridge University Press.

———. 2007. *Plotinus on Intellect*. Oxford: Clarendon Press.

———. 2009. "Plotinus on Act and Power." In *The World as Active Power: Studies in the History of European Reason*, edited by J. V. , 71–88. Leiden/Boston: Brill.

Fattal, M. 2001. *Logos, pensée et vérité dans la philosophie grecque*. Paris: L'Harmattan.

———, ed. 2003. *Logos et langage chez Plotin et avant Plotin*. Paris: L'Harmattan.

———. 2015. *Existence et Identité. Logos et technê chez Plotin*. Paris: L'Harmattan.

Ferwerda, R. 1965. *La signification des images et des métaphores dans la pensée de Plotin*. Diss. Free University of Amsterdam. Groningen: Wolters.

Finamore, J. F. and J. M. Dillon. 2002. *Iamblichus De Anima: text, translation, and commentary*. Leiden/Boston/Köln: Brill.

Frede, M. 2012. *A Free Will: Origins of the Notion in Ancient Thought*. Berkeley: University of California Press.

Fronterotta, F. 2006. *Traité 37. Présentation, traduction et notes*, edited by L. Brisson, and J. F. Pradeau. Paris: Flammarion.

Funk, W.-P., M. Scopello, P.-H. Poirier, and J. D. Turner. 2004. *L'Allogène (XI,3)*. Bibliothèque copte de Nag Hammadi. Section "Textes" 30. Québec: Presses de l'Université Laval / Louvain-Paris: Éditions Peeters.

Gerson, L. P. 1994. *Plotinus*. London and New York: Routledge.

———. 1996. *The Cambridge Companion to Plotinus*. Cambridge: Cambridge University Press.

———, ed. 2010. *The Cambridge History of Philosophy in Late Antiquity*. 2 vols. Cambridge: Cambridge University Press.

———. 2013a. *From Plato to Platonism*. Ithaca and London: Cornell University Press.

———. 2013. *Ennead V.5: That the Intelligibles are not External to Intellect, and on the Good*. Las Vegas: Parmenides Publishing.

Gerson, L. P. and J. M. Dillon. 2004. *Neoplatonic Philosophy: Introductory Readings*. Indianapolis: Hackett.

Graeser, A. 1972. *Plotinus and the Stoics. A Preliminary Study*. Leiden: Brill.

Hadot, P. 1960. "Être, vie et pensée chez Plotin et avant Plotin." *Entretien sur l'Antiquité classique*. Vol. 5. Vandoeuvres-Génève: Fondation Hardt.

———. 1963. *Plotin ou la simplicité du regard*. Paris: Plon.

———. 1968. *Porphyre et Victorinus*. 2 vols. Paris: Études augustiniènnes.

———. 1988. Plotin, *Traité 38*. Paris: du Cerf.

Irwin, T. H. 1988. *Aristotle's First Principles*. Oxford: Oxford University Press.

———. 1992. "Who Discovered the Will?" *Philosophical Perspectives* 6: Ethics, 453–473.

Joachim, H. H. 1970. *Aristotle. The Nicomachean Ethics*. Oxford: Oxford University Press.

Krämer, H. J. 1964. *Der Ursprung der Geistmetaphysik. Untersuchungen zur Geschichte des Platonismus zwischen Platon und Plotin*. Amsterdam: Schippers.

Kremer, K. 1987. "*Bonum est diffusivum sui.* Ein Beitrag zum Verhältnis von Neuplatonismus und Christentum." *Aufstieg und Niedergang der römischen Welt* 36 (2): 994–1032.

Lampe, G. W. H. 1961. *A Patristic Greek Lexicon*. Oxford: Oxford University Press.

Lear, J. 1988. *Aristotle. The Desire to Understand*. Cambridge: Cambridge University Press.

Lloyd, A. C. 1990. *The Anatomy of Neoplatonism*. Oxford: Oxford University Press.

Mahé, J. P. and P. H. Poirier. 2007. Écrits *gnostique, La bibliothèque de Nag Hammadi*. Gallimard: Bibliothèque de la Pléiade.

Mansfeld, J. 1991. "The Idea of the Will in Chrysippus, Posidonius, and Galen." *The Boston Area Colloquium in Ancient Philosophy* VII, 107–145.

Majercik, R. 1989. *The Chaldean Oracles*. Leiden/New York/København/Köln: Brill.

Marmadoro, A. and B. Prince, eds. 2015. *Causation and Creation in Late Antiquity*. Cambridge: Cambridge University Press.

Meyer, M. 2007. *The Nag Hammadi Scriptures*. HarperCollins, New York.

Morrow, G. R. and J. M. Dillon. 1993. *Proclus' Commentary on Plato's Parmenides*. Princeton: Princeton University Press.

Mortley, R. 2013. *Plotinus, Self and the World*. Cambridge: Cambridge University Press.

Narbonne, J.-M. 1999. "L' *ou ti* de Plotin." In *Cahiers philosophiques de Strasbourg.* Vol. 8, 25–51.

———. 2011. *Plotinus in Dialogue with the Gnostics.* Leiden/Boston: Brill.

———. 2012. *Plotin. Oeuvres Complètes. Introduction. Traité1 (I 6), Sur le Beau.* Avec la collaboration de Martin Achard, texte établi par Lorenzo Ferroni, introduit, traduit et annoté par Martin Achard et Jean-Marc Narbonne. Paris: Les Belles Lettres.

O'Brien, D. 1977. "Le volontaire et la necessité: reflexions sur la descente de l'Ame dans la philosophie de Plotin." *Revue philosophique de la France et de l'etranger* 167 (4): 401–422.

———. 1993. *Theodicée plotinienne, theodicée gnostique.* Leiden: Brill.

———. 2012. "Plotinus on the Making of Matter. Part III: The Essential Background." *International Journal of the Platonic Tradition* 6: 27–80.

O'Daly, G. J. P. 1973. *Plotinus' Philosophy of the Self.* Shannon: Irish University Press.

Ousager, A. 2004. *Plotinus on Selfhood, Freedom, and Politics.* Aarhus: Aarhus University Press.

Peterson, E. 1933. "Herkunft und Bedeutung des Monos pros Monon-formel bei Plotin." *Philologus* 88: 30–41.

Petty, R. 2012. *Fragments of Numenius of Apamea*. Westbury, Wiltshire: Prometheus Trust.

Rasimus, T. 2010. "Porphyry and the Gnostics: Reassessing Pierre Hadot's Thesis in Light of the Second and Third Century Sethian Treatises." In *Plato's Parmenides and its Heritage*. Vol. 2: *Its Reception in Neoplatonic, Jewish, and Christian Texts*, edited by J. D. Turner and K. Corrigan. Supplements to Writings from the Ancient World 3. Atlanta: Society of Biblical Literature / Leiden: Brill.

Remes P. 2007. *Plotinus on Self, the Philosophy of the We*. Cambridge: Cambridge University Press.

———. 2014. "Action, Reason and the Highest Good." In *The Routledge Handbook of Neoplatonism*, 453–470. London and New York: Routledge.

Remes, P. and S. Slaveva-Griffin, eds. 2014. *The Routledge Handbook of Neoplatonism*. London and New York: Routledge.

Rist, J. M. 1964. *Eros and Psyche: Studies in Plato, Plotinus and Origen*. Toronto: Toronto University Press.

———. 1967. *Plotinus. The Road to Reality*. Cambridge: Cambridge University Press.

Rutten, C. 1956. "La Doctrine des Deux Actes dans la Philosophie de Plotin." *Revue Philosophique* 146: 100–106.

Sharples, R. W. 1982. "Alexander of Aphrodisias on Divine Providence: Two Problems." *The Classical Quarterly* 32 (1): 198–211.

Schniewind A. 2003. *L'Ethique du Sage chez Plotin. Le paradigm du spoudaios*. Paris: Vrin.

Schroeder, F. M. 1986. "Conversion and Consciousness in Plotinus, 'Enneads' 5, 1 [10], 7." *Hermes* 114 (2): 186–195.

Schroeder, F. M. and R. B. Todd. 1990. *Two Greek Aristotelian Commentators on the Intellect*. Toronto: Pontifical Institute of Medieval Studies.

Sells, M. 1994. *Mystical Languages of Unsaying*. Chicago: University of Chicago Press.

Slaveva-Griffin, S. and P. Remes. 2014. *The Routledge Handbook of Neoplatonism*. London and New York: Routldege.

Stern-Gillet, S. 2014. "Plotinus on metaphysics and morality." In *The Routledge Handbook of Neoplatonism*, edited by S. Slaveva-Griffin and P. Remes, 396–420. London and New York: Routledge.

Theiler, W. 1930. *Die Vorbereitung des Neuplatonismus*. Leipzig: Akademie Verlag.

Thomassen, E. and L. Painchaud. 1989. *Le Traité Tripartite (NH I, 5)*. Quebec: Presses de L'Université Laval.

Tracy, T. T. 1994. *The God Who Acts: Philosophical and Theological Explorations*. Philadelphia: Pennsylvania University Press.

Trouillard, J. 1955. *La procession plotinienne*. Paris: Presses Universitaires de France.

Turner, J. D. 2001. *Sethian Gnosticism and the Platonic Tradition*. Quebec: Presses de L'Université Laval / Paris: Peeters.

———. 2009. "Sethian Gnosticism and the Platonic Tradition." In *Gnose et Philosophie. Études en hommage à Pierre Hadot*, edited by J.-M Narbonne and P.-H. Poirier, 147–221. Collection "Zêtêsis." Québec: Presses de l'Université Laval / Paris: Vrin.

Turner, J. D. and Edward Moore. 2010. *Gnosticism*. In *The Cambridge History of Philosophy in Late Antiquity*, edited by Lloyd P. Gerson, 174–196.

Turner, J. D. and K. Corrigan. 2010. *Plato's Parmenides and its Heritage*. Vol. 1: *History and Interpretation from the Old Academy to Later Platonism and Gnosticism*. Vol. 2: *Its Reception in Neoplatonic, Jewish, and Christian Texts*. Supplements to Writings from the Ancient World 2. Atlanta: Society of Biblical Literature / Leiden: Brill.

———. 2017. "Plotinus and the Gnostics: the Peculiar Impact of the Tripartite Tractate and Later Works." In

Estratégias anti-gnósticas nos escritos de Plotino. Atas do colóquio internacional realizado em *São Paulo* em 18–19 de março 2012, edited by M. Marsilio, 91–124. Serie Classica. São Paulo: Rosari et Paulus.

Vaggione, R. P., ed. 1987. *Eunomius, The Extant Works.* Oxford: Oxford University Press.

Wallis, R. T. 1995. *Neoplatonism.* 2nd edition. Foreword and Bibliography by Lloyd P. Gerson. Indianapolis: Hackett.

Whittaker J. 1975. "The Historical Background of Proclus' Doctrine of the ΑΥΘΥΠΟΣΤΑΤΑ." In *De Jamblique à Proclus,* 193–237. Geneva: Fondation Hardt.

———. 1989. "Self-generating Principles in Second-Century Gnostic Systems." In *The Rediscovery of Gnosticism.* Vol. 1: *The School of Valentinus,* edited by Bentley Layton, 176–193. Studies in the History of Religions 41. Leiden: Brill.

Wilberding, J. 2006. *Plotinus' Cosmology. A Study of* Ennead *II.1 (40). Text, Translation, and Commentary.* Oxford/New York: Oxford University Press.

Willms, L. 2011/2012. *Epiktets Diatribe "Über die Freiheit" (4.1),* Vol. 1: Einleitung, Übersetzung und Kommentar (§§1–102), and Vol. 2: Kommentar (§§103–177), Übersetzung, Register und Literaturverzeichnis. (Wissenschaftliche Kommentare zu griechischen und lateinischen Klassikern.) Heidelberg: Universitätsverlag Winter.

Wurm, Klaus. 1973. *Substanz und Qualität: Ein Beitrag zur Interpretation der plotinischen Traktate VI 1, 2, und 3*. Berlin/New York: De Gruyter.

Zandee, J. 1961. *The Terminology of Plotinus and of Some Gnostic Writings. Mainly the Fourth Treatise of the Jung Codex*. Istanbul: Nederlands Historisch-Archaeologisch Insituut in Het Nabije Oosten.

Zimmerman, B. 2013. "Does Plotinus Present a Philosophical Account of Creation?" *Review of Metaphysics* 67 (1): 55–105.

Index of Ancient Authors

Index of Names and Subjects

• ALSO AVAILABLE FROM PARMENIDES PUBLISHING •

PRE-SOCRATICS

By Being, It Is: *The Thesis of Parmenides* by Néstor-Luis Cordero

The Fragments of Parmenides: *A Critical Text with Introduction and Translation, the Ancient Testimonia and a Commentary by A. H. Coxon. Revised and Expanded Edition edited with new Translations by Richard McKirahan and a new Preface* by Malcolm Schofield

The Legacy of Parmenides: *Eleatic Monism and Later Presocratic Thought* by Patricia Curd

Parmenides and the History of Dialectic: *Three Essays* by Scott Austin

Parmenides, Venerable and Awesome: *Proceedings of the International Symposium* edited by Néstor-Luis Cordero

Presocratics and Plato: *A Festschrift in Honor of Charles Kahn* edited by Richard Patterson, Vassilis Karasmanis, and Arnold Hermann

The Route of Parmenides: *Revised and Expanded Edition, With a New Introduction, Three Supplemental Essays, and an Essay* by Gregory Vlastos by Alexander P. D. Mourelatos

To Think Like God: *Pythagoras and Parmenides. The Origins of Philosophy. Scholarly and fully annotated edition* by Arnold Hermann

The Illustrated To Think Like God: *Pythagoras and Parmenides. The Origins of Philosophy* by Arnold Hermann (with over 200 full color illustrations)

PLATO

A Stranger's Knowledge: *Statesmanship, Philosophy, and Law in Plato's* Statesman by Xavier Márquez

God and Forms in Plato by Richard D. Mohr

Image and Paradigm in Plato's *Sophist* by David Ambuel

Imperial Plato: Albinus, Maximus, Apuleius by Ryan Fowler

Interpreting Plato's Dialogues by J. Angelo Corlett

One Book, the Whole Universe: *Plato's Timaeus Today* edited by Richard D. Mohr and Barbara M. Sattler

Platonic Patterns: *A Collection of Studies* by Holger Thesleff

Plato's Late Ontology: *A Riddle Resolved* by Kenneth M. Sayre

Plato's *Parmenides*: *Text, Translation & Introductory Essay* by Arnold Hermann. Translation in collaboration with Sylvana Chrysakopoulou, with a Foreword by Douglas Hedley

Plato's Universe by Gregory Vlastos

The Philosopher in Plato's *Statesman* by Mitchell Miller

ARISTOTLE

Aristotle's Empiricism: Experience and Mechanics in the Fourth Century B.C. by Jean De Groot

One and Many in Aristotle's Metaphysics—*Volume I: Books Alpha-Delta* by Edward C. Halper

One and Many in Aristotle's Metaphysics—*Volume 2: The Central Books* by Edward C. Halper

Reading Aristotle: Physics VII.3 "What is Alteration?" *Proceedings of the International ESAP-HYELE Conference* edited by Stefano Maso, Carlo Natali, and Gerhard Seel

HELLENISTIC PHILOSOPHY

A Life Worthy of the Gods: *The Materialist Psychology of Epicurus* by David Konstan

THE *ENNEADS* OF PLOTINUS

Translations with Introductions & Philosophical Commentaries
Series edited by John M. Dillon and Andrew Smith

Ennead **I.6:** ***On Beauty*** by Andrew Smith

Ennead **II.5:** ***On What Is Potentially and What Actually*** by Cinzia Arruzza

Ennead **II.9:** ***Against the Gnostics*** by Sebastian Ramon Philipp Gertz

Ennead **IV.3–IV.4.29:** ***Problems concerning the Soul*** by John M. Dillon and H. J. Blumenthal

Ennead **IV.4.30–45 & IV.5:** ***Problems concerning the Soul*** by Gary M. Gurtler

Ennead IV.7: ***On the Immortality of the Soul*** by Barrie Fleet

Ennead **IV.8:** ***On the Descent of the Soul into Bodies*** by Barrie Fleet

Ennead **V.1:** ***On the Three Primary Levels of Reality*** by Eric D. Perl

Ennead **V.5:** ***That the Intelligibles are not External to the Intellect, and on the Good*** by Lloyd P. Gerson

Ennead **VI.4 & VI.5:** ***On the Presence of Being, One and the Same, Everywhere as a Whole*** by Eyjólfur Emilsson and Steven Strange

ETHICS

Sentience and Sensibility: *A Conversation about Moral Philosophy* by Matthew R. Silliman

PHILOSOPHICAL FICTION

Pythagorean Crimes by Tefcros Michaelides

The Aristotle Quest: A Dana McCarter Trilogy. Book 1: Black Market Truth by Sharon M. Kaye

AUDIOBOOKS

The Iliad (unabridged) by Stanley Lombardo

The Odyssey (unabridged) by Stanley Lombardo

The Essential Homer by Stanley Lombardo

The Essential Iliad by Stanley Lombardo

FORTHCOMING

Ennead **I.1:** ***What Is the Living Thing? What Is Man?*** by Gerard O'Daly

Ennead **I.2:** ***On Virtues*** by Suzanne Stern-Gillet

Ennead **I.3:** ***On Dialectic*** by Pauliina Remes

Ennead **I.4:** ***On Well-Being*** by Kieran McGroarty

Ennead **I.5:** ***On Whether Well Being Increases With Time*** by Danielle A. Layne

Ennead **I.8:** ***On the Nature and Source of Evil*** by Anne Sheppard

Ennead **II.4:** ***On Matter*** by Anthony A. Long

Ennead **II.7:** ***On Complete Blending*** by Robert Goulding

Ennead **II.8:** ***On Sight*** by Robert Goulding

Ennead **III.4:** ***On Our Allotted Guardian Spirit*** by Wiebke-Marie Stock

Ennead **III.5:** ***On Love*** by Sara Magrin

Ennead **III.6:** ***On Impassibility*** by Eleni Perdikouri

Ennead **III.7:** ***On Eternity and Time*** by László Bene

Ennead **III.8:** ***On Nature and Contemplation*** by George Karamanolis

Ennead **IV.6:** ***On Sense-Perception and Memory*** by Peter Lautner

Ennead **V.2, V.4, and V.6:** ***On the One and Intellect*** by Eleni Perdikouri

Ennead **V.3:** ***On the Knowing Hypostases*** by Marie-Élise Zovko

Ennead **V.8:** ***On Intelligible Beauty*** by Andrew Smith

Ennead **V.9:** ***On Intellect, Ideas, and Being*** by Matthias Vorwerk

Ennead **VI.1-2:** ***On the Genera of Being (I+II)*** by Damien Caluori and Regina Füchslin

Ennead **VI.3:** ***On the Genera of Being (III)*** by Riccardo Chiaradonna

Ennead **VI.7:** ***The Forms and the Good*** by Nicholas Banner

Ennead **VI.9:** ***On the Good or the One*** by Stephen R. L. Clark